Drink
and
Disorder

Drink and Disorder

Temperance Reform in Cincinnati from the Washingtonian Revival to the WCTU

Jed Dannenbaum

University of Illinois Press
Urbana and Chicago

Portions of this study appeared in earlier versions in the
Cincinnati Historical Society Bulletin, *Ohio History*, and the
Journal of Social History, and are reprinted with permission.

Publication of this work was supported in part by
a grant from the Andrew W. Mellon Foundation.

This book is printed on acid-free paper.

Library of Congress Cataloging in Publication Data

Dannenbaum, Jed, 1947–
   Drink and disorder.

   Includes bibliographical references and index.
      1. Temperance—Ohio—Cincinnati—History—19th
century.   2. Washingtonian Revival (Association)—His-
tory—19th century.   3. Women's Christian Temperance
Union—History—19th century.   I. Title.
HV5298.C5D36   1983   363.4′1′0977132   83-3671
ISBN 0-252-01055-8

For My Parents,
Jinny and George Dannenbaum

Contents

Preface

For most Americans, the phrase "temperance movement" brings to mind an array of negative images. Temperance reformers have been stereotyped as humorless, censorious, arch-conservative Puritans; as overbearing fanatical women armed with hatchets; and as narrow-minded, hypocritical farmers with an intense hatred for cities and their inhabitants. Whereas other reform movements led to "noble" results—abolitionism culminated in the emancipation of the slaves, and the women's rights movement brought the enfranchisement of women— the temperance movement resulted in what has been widely viewed as a historical embarrassment, national prohibition. In the public mind, prohibition was a disastrous attempt to legislate morality, one that inevitably backfired to produce widespread disrespect for the law, a crime wave, and increased rather than decreased drinking. In this view, national prohibition and the decades of temperance reform that preceded it were at best an aberration, at worst an example of some of the least attractive characteristics of American society.

Until very recently most historians shared this popular view, dismissing temperance reform as either a minor historical curiosity or as an unfortunate manifestation of a peculiarly American tendency toward puritannical moralizing and meddling. In the last decade, however, social historians examining the lives of Americans in the nineteenth and early twentieth centuries have discovered a pervasive concern about alcohol: studies pointed to the vast grass-roots popularity and influence of temperance organizations, the political salience and divisiveness of drink issues, the support for temperance principles among large segments of the laboring population, and the profound opposition of many women to drinking culture and saloon life. Although the study of temperance reform itself has not yet caught up with this new realization of its importance, research recently published or currently underway will do much to rescue temperance reform from the historical obscurity to which it has been confined.

But these studies are only a beginning. We are dealing with a social movement that was far more broadly based, diverse, and long-lived than, for example, the abolitionist movement. When we consider how much complexity and controversy historians have encountered in the study of abolitionism, we should anticipate similar difficulties in developing an overall view of the temperance movement. The drink conflict touched on most major issues in American life: social mobility, economic development, family structure, gender roles, political organization, religious experience, immigration, social order and welfare, the relationship between the individual and society, and the role of the state in effecting social change. Even to speak of a single "temperance movement" can be misleading: as this study will attempt to demonstrate, there were many different phases in the history of the reform, some entirely distinct from others in their concerns, tactics, goals, and demographic characteristics. I hope that this book will help to clarify this complexity, and to reveal the underlying relationship between the development of temperance agitation and the development of the society in which it flourished.

At the outset, I would like to clear away some misconceptions regarding alcohol use and temperance reform. If we fail to look beyond the benign and pleasant role alcohol has in most of our lives, and beyond the humorous images of drunkenness presented to us through movies, television, comic strips, and the like, we will probably fail to comprehend fully why drinking has been such a powerful social issue in our history. Alcohol is a drug, sometimes a dangerous and for some an addictive drug, and it inflicts heavy damage on any society where its use is widespread. Even today, when far less alcohol is drunk than in the early nineteenth century, 10 to 12 million Americans are alcoholics. Drunkenness is implicated in roughly half of all traffic deaths (which numbered 51,000 in 1981), and over half of other violent deaths by means such as homicide, fire, and drowning. Excessive drinking causes major medical problems, including neurological syndromes (such as delirium tremens) and liver disease. Other social damage, such as family instability, domestic violence including spouse and child abuse, and poor work performance, is harder to measure accurately, but the seriousness of these problems is evident. Of course, acknowledging the social costs of alcohol use does not in itself explain the timing, structure, specific concerns, or development of the temperance movement, any more than acknowledging the human damage caused by slavery explains the abolitionist movement. But recognition of the potential dangers of drink forms a context in which this study must be set.

We should also bear in mind that advocates of prohibition were not necessarily fools to think that laws against the sale of alcohol could actually prevent drinking. Contrary to the popular belief that national prohibition encouraged alcohol use, during the early years of prohibition the total per capita consumption of alcohol dropped to one-third the pre–World War I level; during the later years of prohibition, when enforcement was most lax, consumption remained at only two-thirds the prewar level; and deaths from liver cirrhosis, the best statistical index of the prevalence of alcoholism, were fewer during all the years of prohibition than before or since. However we may judge prohibition efforts historically, we cannot simply dismiss them as ridiculous attempts to change unalterable drinking habits.

For many years I have looked forward to thanking publicly the many people who helped me complete this study. The greatest contribution came from Susan Dannenbaum, whose ideas, advice, and encouragement were invaluable. Paul Goodman and Roland Marchand skillfully and patiently guided the project as it developed. Nora Faires's astute, extensive suggestions for rewriting improved the final manuscript immensely. Many colleagues working on related topics—Jack Blocker, Ruth Bordin, Bob Hampel, Nancy Hewitt, Susan Dye Lee, Mark Lender, Bill Rorabaugh, and Ian Tyrrell—freely shared with me their own research findings and offered their responses to mine. Several people read the entire manuscript at some stage in its preparation and supplied valuable suggestions and criticisms, including Geoffrey Blodgett, Dave Brody, Jinny Dannenbaum, Frederic Jaher, and Zane Miller. Many others read or heard parts of the study or conversed or corresponded with me about the topic, and I profited from their responses; Jim Barrett, Clyde Binfield, Dan Calhoun, Peter Cline, Kathleen Dowdey, Gail Filion, Irwin Flack, Bill Gienapp, Sam Hays, Charles Isetts, Randall Jimerson, Hugh Kearney, Cliff Kuhn, Dottie Lewis, Frank Lortie, Bob McMath, Stephen Nissenbaum, Jan Rieff, Allen Russell, Don Swain, and Vic Walsh all made contributions to the final manuscript. I also received generous assistance from Ted Appel, Laura Chace, Mrs. Elmer S. Forman, Allen Hastings, Sue Oines, Judy Rogers, Susan Staggs, and Jane Wilson.

At the institutional level, many libraries were helpful well beyond the call of duty, including those of Cambridge University, the Ohio Historical Society, St. Olaf College, the Ohio and the national WCTUs, and, most of all, the Cincinnati Historical Society. I also gratefully acknowledge the financial support I have received, from a University of California graduate fellowship, a Fulbright-Hays graduate fellowship, a University of Pittsburgh Mellon postdoctoral fellowship, and grants from the University of California Patent Fund and the American Philosophical Society.

Finally, I would like to express my gratitude to the late Bob Starobin, who gave me encouragement and support at a critical moment in my training as a historian.

Introduction

In 1823 several families made a seventeen-day overland trip to Indianapolis. Each family consisted of husband, wife, and several children, the eldest of whom were fifteen to seventeen years old; the party also included four teamsters and a young man looking for work. One of the husbands, recounting the trip, described the supplies of whiskey used: "At this tavern we fell in with two Contuckiens that had come to see the country and had a two horse wagon and a barrel of whiskey to sell out to pay their expenses. In our crowd each family had a keg and had laid in a supply but some thought that their stock was running low so they bought several gallons. Our cag which held eight gallons was filled on the Miami [river] at eight cents a gallon."[1] From this description it seems likely that each family was consuming something like a half-gallon of whiskey every day. Nor is such a figure surprising for the times. Americans in the early nineteenth century drank nearly three times as much alcohol per capita as they do today.[2]

Drinking in the colonial and early national periods of American history was an established, often ritualized part of nearly every aspect of life. No festival, holiday, christening, wedding, funeral, building dedication, or ordination was considered complete without plentiful toasts. When entertaining guests at home, an invitation to the sideboard was an obligatory part of hospitality. As a temperance reformer recalled in later years, drinking was thought "necessary to good fellowship, the flashes of wit, the flow of humor, or the outpouring of the soul in genial, brilliant and eloquent conversation."[3]

Men at work considered alcoholic beverages an essential,

indispensable part of their workday; drink, they believed, increased one's longevity and imparted strength, vigor, and stamina. In artisan shops, the masters and journeymen stopped several times a day to drink liquor that apprentices had brought from a nearby tavern. Taverns served alcohol to refresh weary travelers and to fortify them against the elements. Local taverns also often served as community centers, providing heat, public toilets, lodging, and meeting space for local societies, town councils, and church vestries. Business deals were sealed with a drink. It was not uncommon for a bottle to be passed around at a trial, even to the judge and jury. Voters expected politicians to treat them to drinks at election time. When neighbors gathered in rural areas for house raisings, huskings, land clearings, and reaping, they had on hand plenty of alcoholic refreshment. Considered even by doctors to be an all-purpose medical treatment, liquor was taken for nearly every complaint, particularly for digestive ills and infection, and as a pain killer. Parents sweetened alcohol with sugar to make it palatable for sick children.[4]

Many Americans drank only alcoholic beverages. Coffee and tea were expensive luxuries before 1830. Milk might be spoiled or come from diseased cows. Water was considered valueless, since it lacked nutritional properties and did not aid digestion. It was also likely to be bad tasting, if not contaminated, especially in urban areas. Cincinnati physician Daniel Drake described in 1815 the "often impure" water most people drew in barrels from the muddy Ohio River. Wealthier citizens had wells that supplied an unpalatable water "slightly impregnated with iron, and . . . salts."[5] As late as 1845 the *Cincinnati Commercial* noted the deplorable conditions of the city reservoir: dead animal carcasses floated on the surface, dirty water ran in, surrounded by dead and dying vegetation, and twenty feet from the reservoir a chemical establishment chimney poured out "poison gas."[6] Generally, Americans thought of alcoholic drinks as the safest and healthiest beverages available.

There were few formal strictures against alcohol use. In Boston public drunkenness was not a crime until 1835; before then only habitual drunkenness was punishable, and that law went unenforced. Even the Methodist church made no attempt to regulate its members' use of liquor. John Wesley's original ban on drunkenness and on the buying, selling, and consumption of hard liquors had never been enforced in America, and the Methodist General Conference in 1790 specifically rescinded the ban on trafficking in hard liquor. Even ministers of the church sometimes supplemented their incomes by distilling or retailing liquor. With alcohol so integral and universally accepted a part of everyday life, nondrinkers in the early 1800s were extremely rare.[7]

Between 1810 and 1830 the annual per capita consumption of absolute (pure) alcohol for the population aged fifteen and older amounted to 7.0 gallons. Since females drank relatively little, the figure for males must have been considerably higher. In 1975 the comparable figure was 2.7 gallons. Hard cider accounts for about half of the early nineteenth-century total; it was a rural drink, about 10 percent alcohol, and its use was declining. Wine, although savored by the wealthy, was too expensive for most people; in terms of the total consumption of absolute alcohol, its importance was negligible. Beer also was too expensive to be a popular drink. The remaining half of the total intake of alcohol came from hard liquors such as rum, gin, and whiskey. By 1830 the average American of drinking age was consuming 9.5 gallons of hard liquor per year, mostly in the form of whiskey. Again, considering the less even distribution of consumption according to sex then, it is safe to conclude that most males drank well in excess of four times as much hard liquor in the early nineteenth century as they do today.[8]

This high level of alcoholic consumption is not enough in itself, however, to explain the emergence of the temperance movement. Consumption had been nearly as high during the eighteenth century, but few Americans expressed concern. Historian Redmond Barnett, discussing Massachusetts in the 1780s, has concluded that drinking "seemed a minor problem, controllable by existing communal institutions."[9] By the 1830s drinking seemed a major problem; by the 1850s the communal institutions Barnett refers to—the family, the congregation, the town—seemed inadequate to deal with the problem, and many turned to the centralized power of state government to regulate behavior that had once been controlled within the confines of the community.

Why did a level of consumption appropriate in the eighteenth century become inappropriate in the nineteenth? The answer is not simple. It lies in the myriad changes related to the rapid commercialization and urbanization that occurred in American society after 1815. Those changes—the multiplication of urban areas, the integration of local economies into regional and national markets, the replacement of agrarian seasonal work with regimented commercial production—and related developments such as the spread of evangelical religion, the extension of the voting franchise, and the decline of family-centered work environments all form a familiar litany for readers of American history. Rather than recounting these developments in detail once again, the following discussion will concentrate on how they affected the social context of drinking in the United States.[10]

Between 1800 and 1860 the number of cities in America with more than 10,000 inhabitants grew from 6 to 93; the number of communities with populations greater than 2,500 increased from 33 to 392. Before the years of massive immigration from Ireland and Germany in the late 1840s and early 1850s, most of this urban growth resulted from men and women migrating from farms and villages to towns and cities. In the agrarian society they left behind, drinking usually took place in controlled settings. As much as four-fifths of all alcohol was consumed at home, usually in small amounts taken throughout the day so that inebriation did not result. Very little drinking occurred in public establishments. The two principal types of establishments that retailed alcoholic beverages were taverns (or inns), which sold by the glass and also served meals and housed travelers, and groceries and drug stores, which sold by the bottle or in larger quantity but not for consumption on the premises. Because taverns required substantial capital, were licensed by local governing councils, and were few in number, they were usually reputable, orderly, and integrated into the community. Drunkenness was generally confined to seasonal festivals and holidays; even then, community expectations about acceptable and unacceptable drunken behavior shaped, to a large extent, what that behavior would be.[11]

As society became more urban and commercial, the drinking environment became less controlled. Drinking was predominantly a feature of male culture, and as young men poured into the towns and cities, they found themselves cut off from clearly defined domestic and community restraints on their behavior. Unmarried men often lived in boarding houses that were dreary and congested, and offered little in the way of warm social contact. Many sought the recreation, amusement, and companionship provided by the public saloons that sprang up in growing communities. They were joined by married men who increasingly worked outside the home as wage earners, and who formed bonds with other males at their workplaces. Commercialization imposed a discipline on the workplace that began to eliminate on-the-job drinking, so men were more likely to stop by saloons after work to quench their thirst and relax with friends.[12]

Saloons, at first called grog-shops, dram-shops, tippling houses, and later coffee houses, sold liquor by the glass as their primary function. Unlike taverns, they did not take in guests, served little or no food, and therefore required little capital to open. Sometimes they provided a form of entertainment such as nine- or ten-pin alleys or, later, billiard tables, but often they consisted of no more than a plank on boxes and a few glasses in the retailer's front room off the street. Because they could be such small operations, saloons were hard to control through licensing laws; because in increasingly class-divided communities they served a working-class clientele, they were resistant to public pressure from wealthier segments of the community.[13]

Whereas in agrarian society, months of nearly continuous labor might precede a harvest-time drinking spree, wage-earning economy encouraged weekly payday binges. For the first time inebriation outside the context of communal celebrations and festivals became common. Drunkenness in public saloons frequently spilled out onto the adjoining streets creating public nuisance and danger for others. The most notorious drinkers were the transient workers. Boatmen, stage drivers, agricultural laborers in commercial farming areas, canal and railroad workers moved through commercial communities with few effective restraints on their behavior. But even workers in other segments of the economy moved frequently, seeking employment and opportunity. Cut off from the more established residents, they felt less stake in the community. The loneliness, culture shock, and economic anxiety experienced by many of these men may have added elements of compulsiveness and destructiveness to their drinking.[14]

Uncontrolled drinking threatened social order, and that threat was intensified by a growing association in the public mind between alcohol and crime. The philosophy and theology of the nineteenth century taught that humans were born innocents, not sinners; the moral character of the child was then developed through parental example and training, education, religious guidance, and healthy social surroundings. Crime indicated some fault in this nurturing environment, the presence of corruptive, depraving elements. Drinking and saloon life seemed likely to be such corruptive influences. The rough-and-tumble world of a dockside saloon could produce disorderly conduct, brawling, and sometimes serious violence. It might also serve as a center for gambling and prostitution. Whereas the Americans of an earlier age might have seen such a rowdy establishment as a haven for those naturally drawn to sin, by the nineteenth century they were more likely to view the saloon as a nursery for sin, a school of bad example, a training ground for vice and crime.[15]

In addition to these direct problems of public order and safety, concerns of a more abstract nature related to drunkenness emerged as well. Political theory held that democracy, if left uncontrolled, could easily degenerate into anarchy. One of the bulwarks against such degeneracy was a rational, enlightened electorate. In the first third of the nineteenth century suffrage spread to nearly all white males, competitive political parties developed, and campaigns became more intense and extended. As one result, the tradition of politicians "treating" voters to alcoholic beverages before elections grew dramatically. By the 1830s voters could drink free liquor for several weeks before an election, and political contests became times of widespread drunkenness. For example, in 1831 a Moravian minister in Indiana described a meeting at which "a number of candidates for Congress, State Governor and Assembly at the impending elections made speeches to the people and great excesses were committed. . . . I have rarely seen so many people drunk and nowhere so many brawls and rows, for the populace of Indiana develops a fearful rudeness on such occasions." [16]

Drunkenness in the electorate seemed to endanger the political welfare of the young republic; similarly, intoxication could be seen as inimical to its spiritual welfare. As the revivals of the Second Great Awakening spread across the nation in the early nineteenth century, evangelicalism focused increasingly on the concept of personal salvation; grace was not preordained for a select few but available to all who would open themselves to God. Inebriates, however, seemed so befuddled in mind and degraded in spirit that they were unlikely to be receptive to God's message. Evangelists began to preach sobriety as a requisite step to conversion, and revivals sometimes focused as much on alcohol as on theology. During a protracted 1842 religious revival in Hillsboro, Maryland, Caroline Meeker Nichols wrote to her husband of an event "long to be remembered in the Annals of Hillsboro: upwards of 100 gallons of spirits were poured not down people's throats but on the sand and I believe there is now none in the place. Dean and Knotts [liquor sellers] have become members of the Temperance Society and are now earnestly seeking religion. The two causes seem to be moving on simultaneously." [17] As in the political sphere, drunkenness in the context of nineteenth-century evangelical religion appeared to threaten not only the individual but the welfare of the nation.

Intemperance could also have harsh economic repercussions for the drinker and, by apparently leading to poverty, could create a burden on the society's welfare institutions. In the boom and bust cycle of a commercial economy, prosperity was uncertain and a supply of surplus capital became desirable; the money spent on alcohol might better be put into a savings bank. The machinery and the production demands of large shops, manufactories, factories, and construction sites made punctuality and safety important factors in the booming economy. Employers seeking reliable employees for their skilled jobs began to avoid hiring workers known as immoderate drinkers. At the same time, for young entrepreneurs upward social mobility might hinge on being granted financial credit, and banks and credit bureaus found drinking habits a convenient, concrete index of industriousness and seriousness of purpose. For artisans, small shopkeepers, and budding entrepreneurs a propensity for drink could mean economic peril through loss of reputation even if their work performance was not affected.

These economic ramifications of drink are implicit in David Mann's 1835 letter to his daughter in Greenville, Ohio. Mann expressed his "deep mortification and regret" on learning that his son-in-law had sunk "from the elevated situation he held, as a man of honor, to that of the ale house tippler— He has a good trade, is a good workman, possesses sufficient intellect not only to be respected, but to become popular and highly respectable, if he used half the industry to become so, that he uses to debase and degrade himself . . . how changed his conduct from the sober industrious mechanic."[18] If drinking sometimes led to poverty, the taxpayers of the community who paid the bills for poor relief suffered as a result. "Of all causes of pauperism," an 1821 report concluded, "intemperance, in the use of spirituous liquors, is the most powerful and universal."[19]

Drinking could also seem inconsistent with proper family life. Wages squandered on liquor undermined the male role of provider, saloon culture took men out of the home, and men returning home drunk could spark domestic quarrels and violence. Praising the spread of temperance societies, the West Bradford (Massachusetts) Female Temperance Society in 1832 asserted that "millions have felt their happy influence—wives have found lost husbands, and *more* than orphan children their fathers."[20]

The claim that temperance reform influenced millions was not exaggerated. Between 1830 and 1840, the adult per capita consumption of absolute alcohol dropped from 7.1 gallons to 3.1 gallons; by 1845 the figure was 1.8 gallons. The drinking habits of a nation had changed dramatically in a remarkably short time. The temperance movement certainly shaped and propelled this transformation, but in part the temperance movement itself was a reflection of the fact that heavy drinking no longer seemed appropriate in a changed American society. People gave up alcohol because it worked for them; they thought themselves better off without it. When Griffen Smith of Georgetown, Illinois, became an abstainer in 1841, he wrote to a friend: "I am doing a better business than I have ever done before, I find home dearer to me than it ever was, my health is better than it has ever been in the Western Country. Although I have more to call my attention—yet I read a great deal more; in fact life itself is dearer. . . ."[21]

This study examines the grass-roots appeal of the temperance movement, the organized agitation against drinking and the drink trade that emerged in the nineteenth century. As such, it is not directly concerned with either drinking or non-drinking. Millions of Americans changed their drinking habits without ever joining the ranks of temperance activists. The preceding discussion of problems related to alcoholic consumption forms a necessary background for a study of the temperance movement, but the movement both drew upon and influenced a broader spectrum of social behavior than that specifically concerned with drinking. To explore the broad appeal, the adaptability, and the power of the temperance issue, the following chapters examine at the community level the changing structure, tactics, goals, membership, and public impact of organized temperance activism.

Specifically, three phases of the temperance movement are considered in depth: social temperance, epitomized by the fraternal temperance orders established in the 1840s; political temperance, which culminated in the state prohibition campaigns of the 1850s; and female-dominated confrontational temperance, which grew from isolated incidents of saloon destruction in the 1850s to the Woman's Crusade of 1873–74. Cincinnati serves as a case study for the development of temperance reform, although for the third phase, in which the experience of Cincinnati was less typical, a broader framework is used.

Chapter One surveys the history of temperance reform nationally before 1841, and the development of Cincinnati during those same years. Chapter Two focuses on the Washingtonian movement in Cincinnati, and the fraternal organizations that developed from it. The third chapter explores the transition from moral suasion to prohibitionism, and therefore serves as a link between the social and political phases. Chapter Four looks in depth at the political context and consequences of the Ohio campaign for prohibition in 1853. Chapters Five and Six link the political phase with the female-dominated confrontational phase: the fifth considers the alliance between political temperance reform and organized nativism, and their subsequent decline, while the sixth centers on the development after 1850 of a distinctly female approach to temperance reform. Chapter Seven discusses the phenomenon that emerged from that approach, the Woman's Crusade, and also treats the Crusade's transformation into the Woman's Christian Temperance Union (WCTU). An Afterword briefly evaluates the overall character of the temperance movement.

The temperance movement developed in distinct phases, and each phase had its different concerns, structures, tactics, and ranks of activist supporters; each reflected different issues and influenced different areas of American society. But the thread running through the various phases of the temperance crusade was that of order and control—the control of the behavior of others and the control of oneself. Alcohol changes human behavior, and in commercializing, urbanizing America, inebriation seemed to many to be synonymous with qualities of behavior they wished to eradicate in themselves and in their rapidly changing society: irrationality, instability, self-indulgence, dependency, disorderliness, bestiality, and loss of self-control. By taking away rationality and self-control, alcohol deprived its users of free will, of freedom. Even before the rise of the abolitionist movement, temperance reformers were referring to drink as "enslaving," and that remained a constant theme as the movement developed. The West Bradford Female Temperance Society wrote of intemperance in 1830: "Let us not call her [America] a land of freedom, while held in thraldom by one of the most despotic tyrants [intemperance]."[22]

If alcohol represented the disorder and loss of control experienced by people in a rapidly transforming society, temperance became its mirror image: rejection of alcohol stood for order, discipline, stability, humaneness, self-denial, rationality, free will, and control over one's own destiny.

Temperance reform was not the only manifestation of a reordering of society in antebellum America. It was one of an array of reforms and religious revivals, all centered in rapidly growing and commercializing areas and all responding to the transformation of society engendered by that expansion and development.[23]

On the surface these reforms appear to have been interlocking and sometimes nearly coextensive. Historians have often highlighted the common concerns of these reform movements, and the many ways in which they interconnected and mutually reinforced one another. Such an approach has obvious value, but it can also be misleading. At the rank-and-file level, it is likely that most people who shared the reformist outlook only had the time or inclination to support actively one, or perhaps two, reform causes. Reform organizations sometimes seemed more like competitors for supporters than cooperative allies. New York reformer and editor Virginia Allen in 1846 attacked abolitionists for agitating the slavery issue while doing nothing about the "thousands of black and white in this city [who are] slaves of intemperance," or about the underpaid female seamstresses, "slaves of the most brutal and degraded task-masters the world can show. . . ."[24] The Plymouth, Illinois, Sons of Temperance in 1850 planned a session to consider "which is the greatest Moral & Political Evil, Negro Slavery or Intemperance."[25] Reformers often had to choose which of the many social problems calling for their attention would receive their personal time and effort.

Moreover, many of these reform movements had quite different social configurations and developed along diverse paths. An issue such as prison reform attracted widespread sympathy, but active support came from only a handful of reformers. Abolitionists never constituted more than a tiny minority of the population even in the North, and were the subject of intense hostility. Conversely, temperance organizations drew hundreds of thousands of dues-paying members to weekly meetings, and few Americans by mid-century were willing to speak against the abstract principle of "temperance." Indeed, because temperance organizations had such a broad base of support, they feared that association with more controversial groups would alienate supporters, and often struggled to appear neutral in regard to other reforms.

Even within individual reform movements there was sometimes more dissension than harmony. Groups splintered over issues, tactics, and goals, and their divisions often reflected divisions in the membership along the lines of class, occupation, gender, age, religion, and ethnic and regional background.

This book examines points of convergence and interaction between temperance and other reforms where such points significantly influenced the development of one or the other cause. It is more concerned with the temperance movement's specific, unique configurations, those that enabled the crusade against drink to surpass all other reforms in popularity, longevity, and cumulative influence. The ability of the drink question to speak to the concerns of so many people over so long a period of time makes it one of the most vital and revealing issues of recent history.

Notes

1. J. T. Campbell Papers, Indiana State Library, "Andrew Ten Brooks Autobiography," 19.

2. W. J. Rorabaugh, "Estimated U.S. Alcoholic Beverage Consumption, 1790–1860," *Journal of Studies on Alcohol*, 37 (1976): 360–61, and *The Alcoholic Republic: An American Tradition* (New York, 1979), 225–36; Norman Clark, *Deliver Us from Evil: An Interpretation of American Prohibition* (New York, 1976), 20.

3. *Cincinnati Commercial*, July 30, 1853; *Ohio Organ of the Temperance Reform*, Dec. 30, 1853; John A. Krout, *The Origins of Prohibition* (New York, 1925), 38–39.

4. *Ohio Organ of the Temperance Reform*, June 24, Aug. 5, 1853; *Crusader*, June, 1858, 29; Oct., 1858, 147; *Templar's Magazine*, Dec., 1859, 381; Krout, *Origins*, 39–40; Rorabaugh, *Alcoholic*, 19–20; Susan E. Hirsch, *Roots of the American Working Class: The Industrialization of Crafts in Newark, 1800–1860* (Philadelphia, 1978), 9.

5. Daniel Drake, *Natural and Statistical View* (Cincinnati, 1815), 139,

quoted in Rorabaugh, *Alcoholic*, 96; see also 97–107. Paul W. Gates, in *The Farmer's Age: Agriculture, 1815–1860* (vol. 3 of *The Economic History of the United States,* New York, 1960), has written that "the charge that eight or nine thousand children died annually in New York [in the mid-nineteenth century] from drinking contaminated milk is believable" (238).

6. *Cincinnati Commercial,* Feb. 18, 1845.

7. Roger Lane, *Policing the City: Boston, 1822–1885* (Cambridge, Mass., 1967), 49; Lora Britton Pine, "The Attitudes of the Methodist Episcopal Church toward Temperance and Prohibition" (M.A. thesis, University of Pittsburgh, 1931), 6, 12–13, 22.

8. Rorabaugh, *Alcoholic,* 232–33.

9. Redmond J. Barnett, "From Philanthropy to Reform: Poverty, Drunkenness, and the Social Order in Massachusetts, 1780–1825" (Ph.D. thesis, Harvard University, 1973), 102, 126; Rorabaugh, *Alcoholic,* 232–33; Mark Edward Lender, "Drunkenness as an Offense in Early New England· A Study of 'Puritan' Attitudes," *Quarterly Journal of Studies on Alcohol,* 34 (1973): 353–66.

10. The following studies have particularly influenced my understanding of American society in the first half of the nineteenth century: Mary P. Ryan, *Cradle of the Middle Class: The Family in Oneida County, New York, 1790–1865* (Cambridge, Mass., 1981); Don H. Doyle, *The Social Order of a Frontier Community: Jacksonville, Illinois, 1825–70* (Urbana, Ill., 1978); Douglas T. Miller, *The Birth of Modern America, 1820–1850* (New York, 1970); Ronald G. Walters, *American Reformers, 1815–1860* (New York, 1978); Thomas Bender, *Community and Social Change in America* (New Brunswick, N.J., 1978); Zane Miller, *The Urbanization of Modern America: A Brief History* (New York, 1973); David Montgomery, "The Shuttle and the Cross: Weavers and Artisans in the Kensington Riots of 1844," *Journal of Social History,* 5 (1972): 411–46; Stuart Blumin, *The Urban Threshold: Growth and Change in a Nineteenth Century American Community* (Chicago, 1976); Paul Faler, "Working Men, Mechanics, and Social Change: Lynn, Massachusetts, 1800–1860" (Ph.D. thesis, University of Wisconsin, 1971); Paul Johnson, *A Shopkeeper's Millennium: Society and Revivals in Rochester, New York, 1815–1837* (New York, 1978); Rorabaugh, *Alcoholic*; Rowland Berthoff, *An Unsettled People: Social Order and Disorder in American History* (New York, 1971).

11. *Historical Statistics of the United States, Colonial Times to 1957* (Washington, D.C., 1960), 14; Rorabaugh, *Alcoholic,* 16, 35, 149–83; Richard Stivers, *A Hair of the Dog: Irish Drinking and American Stereotype* (University Park, Pa., 1976), 101–6, 164–68. A recent sociological study has shown that the conduct of drunken persons is in large part regulated by social expectations; that is, the behavior of people while inebriated varies greatly from culture to culture, and is determined by what a particular culture "teaches" about how one is supposed to comport oneself while drunk (Craig MacAndrew and Robert B. Edgerton, *Drunken Comportment: A Social Explanation* (London, 1969), 172 and *passim*).

12. Herbert G. Gutman, "Work, Culture, and Society in Industrializing America, 1815–1919," *American Historical Review*, 78 (1973): 544–45, 582; Montgomery, "Shuttle," 421–22; Faler, "Working Men," 267–70; Rorabaugh, *Alcoholic*, 35–36; Paul R. Meyer, Jr., "The Transformation of American Temperance: The Popularization and Radicalization of a Reform Movement, 1813–1860" (Ph.D. thesis, University of Iowa, 1976), 25–26, 39; Bruce Laurie, "'Nothing on Compulsion': Life Styles of Philadelphia Artisans, 1820–1850," *Labor History*, 15 (1974): 344–52; Johnson, *Shopkeeper's*, 46, 59; Ryan, *Cradle*, 129, and "The Power of Women's Networks: A Case Study of Female Moral Reform in Antebellum America," *Feminist Studies*, 5 (1979): 70–79.

13. *Cincinnati Commercial*, June 27, 1845, July 12, 1851, May 10, 1982; *Cincinnati Gazette*, Apr. 16, 1853; George E. Stevens, *The Queen City in 1869: The City of Cincinnati* . . . (Cincinnati, Ohio, 1869), 129–33, 175; Charles Cist, *Cincinnati in 1841: Its Early Annals and Future Prospects* (Cincinnati, Ohio, 1841), 33; Eugene H. Roseboom, *The Civil War Era, 1850–1873* (vol. 4 of *The History of the State of Ohio*, ed. Carl Wittke, Columbus, 1944), 22; Rorabaugh, *Alcoholic*, 35. For a discussion of saloon culture in a later period, see Perry Ray Duis, "The Saloon and the Public City: Chicago and Boston, 1880–1920" (Ph.D. thesis, University of Chicago, 1975).

14. Miller, *Urban*, 35–37; Paul Boyer, *Urban Masses and Moral Order in America, 1820–1920* (Cambridge, Mass., 1978), 37; Peter R. Knights, *The Plain People of Boston, 1830–1860: A Study in City Growth* (New York, 1971); Doyle, *Social Order*, 112–15; Richard C. Wade, *The Urban Frontier: The Rise of Western Cities, 1790–1830* (Cambridge, Mass., 1959), 120–21; William Graham Davis, "Attacking 'the Matchless Evil': Temperance and Prohibition in Mississippi, 1817–1908" (Ph.D. thesis, Mississippi State University, 1975), 3–4; Rorabaugh, *Alcoholic*, 140. Robert Louis Hampel has concluded that "transience was the most striking characteristic" of those arrested for drunkenness, in his analysis of arrest records for Taunton, Mass., 1834–45, and Salem, Mass., 1827–38 ("Influence and Respectability: Temperance and Prohibition in Massachusetts, 1813–1852" (Ph.D. thesis, Cornell University, 1980), 90–91).

15. David J. Rothman, *The Discovery of the Asylum: Social Order and Disorder in the New Republic* (Boston, 1971), 64–67, 76–77.

16. Ludwig David von Schweinitz, "Report on a Journey Undertaken by Br. Ludwig David von Schweinitz . . . to visit the congregations gathering in Goshen, Bartholemew County, Ind. . . . from May 13th to July 21st, 1831," English version, Indiana State Library, 20; Mark Edward Lender and James Kirby Martin, *Drinking in America: A Social-Historical Interpretation, 1620–1980* (forthcoming), ch. 2.

17. William Blake Dean and Family Papers, Minnesota Historical Society, Caroline Meeker Nichols to John Nichols, Jan. 17, 1842; see also West Bradford (Mass.) Female Temperance Society, Records, 1829–34, Essex In-

stitute, Secretary's Report for 1831 (Apr. 10, 1832); Johnson, *Shopkeeper's*, 113–14.

18. M. C. Severin Papers, Indiana State Library, David Mann to Rachel Wiley, Greenville, Ohio, Feb. 2, 1835; Don H. Doyle, "The Social Functions of Voluntary Associations in a Nineteenth-Century American Town," *Social Science History*, 1 (1977): 345; Ryan, *Cradle*, 141–42.

19. Rothman, *Discovery*, 163.

20. West Bradford Female Temperance Society, Secretary's Report for 1831.

21. Schuyler Colfax Papers, Indiana State Library, Griffen Smith, Georgetown, Ill., to Colfax, New Carlisle, Ind., Mar. 10, 1841.

22. West Bradford Female Temperance Society, Secretary's Report for 1830 (Nov. 26, 1830).

23. Walters, *American Reformers*, 3–9; William McLoughlin, Jr., *Modern Revivalism* (New York, 1959).

24. *The Pearl: A Ladies' Weekly Literary Gazette Devoted to the Advocacy of the Various Ladies' Total Abstinence Associations*, Nov. 7, 1846; Walters, *American Reformers*; Alice Felt Tyler, *Freedom's Ferment: Phases of American Social History from the Colonial Period to the Outbreak of the Civil War* (Minneapolis, 1944); Whitney R. Cross, *The Burned-over District: The Social and Intellectual History of Enthusiastic Religion in Western New York, 1800–1850* (Ithaca, N.Y., 1950).

25. Sons of Temperance, Plymouth (Ill.) Division, Minutes, 1850–55, Illinois Historical Society, Dec. 15, 1850.

1

Temperance Reform prior to the Washingtonian Revival

Between the founding of the first national temperance organization in 1826 and the phenomenal outburst of temperance enthusiasm in 1841 known as the Washingtonian Revival, changes within temperance organizations transformed the character of American temperance reform. In that decade and a half the characteristic profile of the temperance reformer shifted from that of a wealthy member of an established family who encouraged the use of wine, ale, and cider as substitutes for whiskey and rum, to that of a journeyman artisan who pledged never to drink, traffic in, or serve to others any alcoholic beverage whatsoever. This change came from the grass-roots level, and total abstinence from all alcohol was not so much the catalyst as it was the symbol, the rallying cry, of a new membership that held a new social perspective. Temperance reform in the 1830s became a mass movement, one infused with the aspirations of upwardly mobile Americans and the zeal of religious perfectionists.

In 1813 a group of elite Massachusetts men founded the first reform society that focused specifically on the issue of temperance, the Massachusetts Society for the Suppression of Intemperance. The organization's 117 members were nearly all prominent members of society: half were clergymen, nearly one-quarter were merchants and other businessmen, and most of the rest were lawyers, physicians, and public officials. They condemned immoderate drinking but otherwise approved the use of alcohol.[1]

Local auxiliaries of the MSSI formed throughout the state. In the town of Sandy Bay the first sign of heightened concern about drinking occurred in 1814, when five citizens filed a complaint against sixteen others who were "in the constant habit of selling liquors mixed and drank in their shops in open violation of the statute laws of this Commonwealth."[2] The saloon had come to Sandy Bay. Seven months later twenty-seven men formed the town's first temperance society. As at the state level, the membership of the local branches came from the wealthier, more established segments of the town's population. Among Concord's taxpayers, members of the temperance society paid, on average, twice the property tax of nonmembers; they were also more likely to hold town office and to be active in other associational groups such as the Library Society and the Social Circle.[3]

The principal activities of these societies were annual meetings; they attempted little in the way of specific action against excessive drinking. The members hoped that merely the example of a concentration of the better classes in such an organization would have a beneficial effect. As one of them noted, "the influence of the higher classes of society upon the lower . . . is immense. Their habits of living and thinking . . . always descend in some form, and have their counterpart, among their inferiors."[4] This passive strategy produced little perceptible effect upon the drinking habits of other classes, and the members' interest waned until by the mid-1820s the organization had practically disbanded.

Upper-class enthusiasm for temperance reform revived in 1826 largely through the efforts of Massachusetts Congregational minister Justin Edwards. He advocated a more active attack on the growing problem of intoxication and was instrumental in the organization of the American Temperance Society. Although at first largely centered in Massachusetts, the ATS considered itself to be addressing drink as a national problem. It had an aggressive plan of action, modeled after that of the American Tract Society, which published material promoting evangelical religion. The memberships of the two organizations overlapped considerably, and the temperance advocates adopted the Tract Society technique of publicizing their position through widely disseminated pamphlets. In addition to making use of newly available printing technology, the ATS also took advantage of improved transportation facilities, and incorporated into their organizational structure the revivalistic technique of sending traveling agents from town to town to speak on temperance reform from the pulpits of evangelical churches.[5]

Such innovations produced a significant change in the potential impact of reform efforts. Activists at the time recognized how vital the printing press was to their success. Reformer Gerritt Smith wrote in 1832 to Mathew Carey of their mutual interest in the antislavery Colonization Society: "We must *print more*—a hundred fold more than we have been . . . our New York State Temperance Society has in the last 15 months printed more than has been printed by the Coln. Society in the 16 years of its existence—and the consequence is that there is a blaze of Temperance light all over the State. . . ."[6]

The use of itinerant speakers may have had an even greater impact. Some orators became immensely popular attractions, their appeal a mixture of public social concern and desire for entertainment. One of the nineteenth century's most famous speakers was temperance advocate John Gough. When he came to Cincinnati in 1851, the hoopla and excitement rivaled that accompanying the visit of the famous singer Jenny Lind. The *Cincinnati Commercial* wrote that Gough was "creating a tremendous sensation. He is undoubtedly a great man. He is comic, tragic, melo-dramatic, statesmanlike, and everything that is rare, in his manner and speech."[7] But Gough's speeches were more than entertainment; he thrilled his listeners with forceful arguments and stirred them to action. Susan B. Anthony, later a leading national reformer herself, heard Gough in 1849 while she was still a school teacher in Canajoharie, New York, and wrote her mother: "What a lecture, what arguments, how can a man or woman remain neutral or be a moderate drinker."[8] Unfortunately, the verbal delivery of arguments, so important in the nineteenth century, is largely lost to the historian. It is useful to keep in mind the potential emotional impact and nuance of what today on paper may seem a dry, lengthy, repetitive speech. The 1859 diary entry of Adelia J. Haughton, a young woman in Ohio, gives us a glimpse of what verbal delivery could convey. She described the lecture of a well-known temperance advocate: "While speaking of the sad wrecks of families and individuals his voice would falter and he seemed ready to weep with those desolate ones while on the other hand when his attention turned upon the dealers in the beverage the causers as he claimed of all this misery his whole soul seemed stirred with disgust, contempt and hatred, from his manner as much as his words one would judge that he would hardly deign to trample them under his feet. . . ."⁹

In addition to its adoption of innovative technologies and techniques to spread the message of temperance, the ATS incorporated a change in the meaning of the word "temperance." Acting on Lyman Beecher's pronouncement in his 1826 tract *Six Sermons* that "the daily use of ardent spirits [i.e. distilled liquor], in any form, or in any degree, is intemperance," the society forbade the use of hard liquor while still allowing (and often encouraging) the moderate use of wines, ales, and ciders.¹⁰

Since the founders of the American Temperance Society drank mostly fine wines themselves, this shift to an "anti-spirits" doctrine was not in itself a sharp break with their own cultural traditions. At first, in fact, the social composition of the American Temperance Society closely resembled that of the earlier Massachusetts Society for the Suppression of Intemperance, despite the organization's tactical changes. In its first annual report the society noted that it carefully selected as members men "of known and expansive benevolence, who are blessed with property," and who "could be relied on . . . as to correctness of sentiment, integrity and zeal. . . ." There were at first only 119 members: fifty clergymen, twenty-one merchants and other businessmen, fifteen public officials, seven attorneys, six physicians, three gentlemen, one benevolence worker, one editor of a religious journal, and fifteen others of unknown occupation.¹¹ Two-thirds of the initial subscriptions came from thirty-two men who donated over $100 each. The members assumed that their influence would "extend to those only, who have a regard to their reputation in respectable and virtuous society, and who feel the force of moral obligation."[12] Not aiming at or anticipating a mass membership, the society set as its goal the removal of respectable society's sanction of either trading in or imbibing hard liquor.

At first, local branches of the ATS echoed the social composition and elitist viewpoint of the national leadership. Patriarchs of old families gathered at annual meetings and spoke harshly of lower-class drunkards who filled poorhouses, prisons, and asylums and raised the taxes of responsible citizens. Wealth and established status seem to have been the most salient characteristics of these early temperance advocates.[13]

Within a few years, however, a dramatic change began to take place as other social groups heard the temperance message, adapted it to their own ends, and began to organize new sorts of temperance associations beyond the control of the elite founders of the movement. Agents of the American Temperance Society in the late 1820s began to find, upon arriving in communities, that auxiliaries had already been formed "without waiting for approval or direction from the national executive or society agents."[14] Temperance organizing began to spread with amazing rapidity, and many communities and states formed independent societies with no links to the ATS. This new surge of temperance enthusiasm transcended the class, gender, and regional configurations of the earlier groups, and frequently appeared in tandem with evangelical revivalism. This wave of temperance activity had an immediate and profound effect upon a broad segment of the populace. E. F. Peabody, an Indiana state legislator, wrote to his wife at the beginning of the 1829–30 legislative session:

> There has been a public meeting to organize, or reorganize, a Bible, Tract, Sunday School, or Temperance Society almost every evening since I arrived [in Indianapolis]. The effect of the Temperance Society is the most manifest. Judging from the present appearance there will not be one-fourth as much spirits used by the members of the legislature this session as there was at the last session. The Bottle is no longer considered as a necessary part of the furniture of our rooms, and indeed so great is

the change of public sentiment on the subject that few persons will keep a Bottle in public view.[15]

Soon the majority of temperance societies lay outside the jurisdiction of the ATS, and that organization began to serve mostly as a clearing house for information about the reform. By 1831 it listed approximately 2,200 distinct temperance societies with a total membership of 170,000, and by 1833 the figures had climbed to 6,000 societies and a million members. When it became evident that some new sort of central organizational structure was needed, the executive committee of the ATS called for a national meeting of representatives from all county and state societies. Four hundred representatives of organizations from twenty-one states attended the May, 1833, meeting and formed the United States Temperance Union, a federation of all temperance societies that wished to join under the banner of the anti-spirits pledge.[16]

This vast popular response to the temperance issue came primarily from the middle ranks of society. Many of the new temperance groups were self-styled "Workingmen's," "Mechanics'," "Young Men's," and "Female" organizations, and most were located in commercial areas. Although higher-status members continued to hold most of the leadership positions, skilled laborers, small business proprietors, and women accounted for increasing portions of these societies' rank-and-file memberships in the early 1830s. Spontaneously, local societies began to adopt a new pledge, the total abstinence or teetotal pledge, that forswore using any alcoholic beverages whatsoever, participating in any aspect of the drink trade, or offering alcoholic beverages to anyone, including guests. Given the traditional and pervasive use of alcohol throughout American culture at the time, teetotalism was a shockingly extreme doctrine, so antitraditional that it alienated most of the conservative elements of society. This push for teetotalism within the movement, according to contemporary temperance leaders, came from "the common man," while elites formed the core of resistance to it.[17]

Teetotalers saw moderate drinking as the first step in a process of degradation and downward mobility. "Who cannot point to some poor, despised, ruined individual" who began as a moderate drinker in the highest social circles, asked the Young Men's and Ladies Total Abstinence Society of Harrisburg, Pennsylvania, in 1841, "but having there acquired the habit & taste for liquor, finished his career, in the lowest rumshop . . . or perhaps in the Poor-house!" [18] Any drinking might create an unnatural craving for alcohol, or at least draw the moderate drinker into the corruptive environment of the public saloon. Even drinking at home set a bad example for the members of the "rising generation" who in their youth might not be able to resist the temptations of the saloon. Mothers in temperance societies often viewed total abstinence as the only safe road for their children.

Teetotalism was also part of the "self-help" movement among artisans and small businessmen. They saw in it a way to demonstrate their sobriety, industriousness, will power, thriftiness, and high character. Sometimes their societies included provisions for mutual benefits or for savings funds, and they emphasized the money that members would save by giving up drink entirely. At a time when young, rootless, single, male, urban workers were becoming notorious for drunken rowdiness, the temperance societies attracted a different sort of worker: the more geographically stable, upwardly mobile, churchgoing family man. [19]

Yet another line of development fed into the growth of total abstinence sentiment. Some evangelicals had begun to focus on the eradication of all social imperfections as a prelude to the arrival of the millennium. They embraced both the total and immediate abolition of slavery and the total abstinence pledge. At Oberlin College, a center for radical evangelicalism, the temperance society was teetotal from its inception in 1834. [20] Total abstinence not only fit well with evangelical theology but it also enabled new converts to make an immediate, tangible change in their lives that could serve as evidence of their spiritual rebirth. Teetotalism proved, to one's minister, to fellow converts, and to oneself, a willingness to embrace the discipline and self-denial necessary in the quest for God's grace. [21]

Teetotalism was facilitated by the increasing group identity and solidarity among temperance society members. Whereas earlier temperance groups had generally scheduled meetings only once a year, the newer associations usually met monthly. More frequent contact renewed the members' commitment, gave them the opportunity to engage in more active reform efforts, provided a social circle of like-minded men and women, and served as a milieu in which to indoctrinate young people with temperance principles.

Total abstinence societies grew far more rapidly than anti-spirits societies in the early 1830s, and by mid-decade tee-totalers had enough power to begin forcing county and state organizations to change their pledges. At an 1836 national meeting of the United States Temperance Union (thereafter the American Temperance Union), the total-abstinence delegates were in the majority, and passed resolutions that endorsed their position although they avoided for the moment requiring the new pledge of all member societies. Within the next few years, however, the teetotalers at the state and local levels pressed their advantage and forced out of the movement individuals or groups that would not adopt the principle of total abstinence.[22]

As acceptance of the teetotal pledge became obligatory, state societies lost many of their wealthy and prestigious members. Elites, who had long championed wine as a replacement for hard liquor, generally refused to endorse the extreme position of total abstinence from all alcoholic beverages. Clergymen were offended by the implication that the sacramental use of wine might be improper, and many church hierarchies withdrew their earlier endorsement of the movement.[23]

The economic depression that began in 1837 accelerated this trend. Wealthy supporters of temperance organizations were hard hit with financial losses and cut off much of their funding for the reform. On the other hand, hard times made struggling artisans and small businessmen more concerned with self-help philosophy and mutual benefit associations.[24]

The growth of broadly based temperance organizations was not the only response to drink during the 1830s. Throughout the decade communities made sporadic attempts to control the spread of saloons, primarily through the enforcement of licensing laws dating back to colonial times. There is little reason to consider such efforts as part of the organized temperance movement. License enforcement, since it attacked working-class drinking without interfering with elite drinking, appealed to those wealthy members who had founded the early temperance organizations, but sometimes drew the wrath of the new champions of teetotalism. In general, the licensing issue had a life of its own outside the sphere of organized temperance reform. By and large the new temperance associations of the 1830s avoided coercive legal measures and relied instead on the methods of persuasion and education that came to be known as "moral suasion." Their goal, in the words of the York (Maine) Young Men's Temperance Society in 1833, was to "use no compulsive or undue measures, to effect your object but act upon the principle of candour and reason."[25]

Early temperance societies in Cincinnati developed along the national pattern. In 1829 there were three different organizations: the "Cincinnati Temperance Society, No. 1, Auxiliary to the American Temperance Society," a separate "Cincinnati Temperance Society," and a newly formed "Young Men's Temperance Society." By 1834 the "Young Men's" society had 370 members; Theodore Dwight Weld, young evangelist and radical reformer at Lane Seminary, was one of the officers. The only other group in existence that year was the "Hamilton County Temperance Society, Auxiliary to the Ohio State Temperance Society." The "Cincinnati Total Abstinence Temperance Society," probably the outgrowth of the "Young Men's" group, was the only remaining organization in 1841 when the "Cincinnati Washingtonian Temperance Society" formed.[26]

Cincinnati's first municipal corporation charter, granted by the state legislature in 1827, gave the city authority to "grant licenses to tavern keepers, inn holders, retailers of spirituous liquors; keepers of ale and porter houses and shops, and all other houses of public entertainment. . . ."[27] Cincinnati supported approximately 223 saloons and taverns in 1834, or roughly one for every thirty-eight males in the city aged fifteen and older.[28] Liquor licenses had to be renewed annually, and the license fees brought a significant amount of income into the city treasury: $9,682 in 1834, for example, 18 percent of all city revenues. Thus the city government had an important financial stake in the local liquor trade.

Moreover, the regional commerce in whiskey became an increasingly significant part of the local economy in the 1830s. Farmers in southwestern Ohio liked to market their corn either as hogs or as whiskey. Both were lower in bulk and cheaper to transport than corn. Fifteen bushels of corn could generally produce either one 200-pound hog or one and a half barrels (about forty-seven gallons) of whiskey. The profits for the two products were about equal, but whiskey had the advantage of storing easily and increasing in value with age; it also could better sustain improper handling and bad weather. Improvements in distilling technology had made the process inexpensive and feasible on a small local scale, so that rural areas were dotted with stills. Whiskey warehousing, wholesaling, and shipping became a major segment of Cincinnati's commercial trade. By 1840 over 43,000 barrels arrived in the city through the Miami Canal, and more than twice that came overland or down the Ohio River.[29]

By 1841 Cincinnati was the regional focus of the drink trade. From the lowly saloons that dotted the landscape to the opulent houses of rich whiskey merchants, Cincinnati encompassed all that the temperance movement challenged. The city had also become the West's pre-eminent urban and commercial center; its spectacular growth and economic expansion were striking examples of the processes of change that engendered temperance reform throughout the country. Cincinnati was about to become the center of temperance activism in the West.

Historians have discovered little about the development of the temperance movement at the local level; outside of the Northeast even less is known. Because the interconnections between changes in American society and the development of the temperance movement are writ large in Cincinnati, it serves well as a case study of that development. In addition, as an organizational and publishing center, the city produced an array of historical sources that are not available for most western towns and cities of the period. All communities are unique, but available evidence suggests that the dynamics of temperance reform in Cincinnati exemplify the experience of many communities, both large and small, in mid-nineteenth-century America.

Cincinnati was founded on the Ohio River at the mouth of the Little Miami River and opposite the mouth of the Licking. Its early economy was based almost entirely on river trade. In about 1817 steamboats began to stop regularly at Cincinnati, bringing with them the promise of greatly increased growth and prosperity. "Cincinnati is growing very fast," wrote a visitor to the city in 1819. "The river is lined with Steam boats, flatt Bottoms &c."[30] The depression of 1819–23 brought a period of economic stagnation, but the city was expanding rapidly again by the mid-1820s. In 1825 workers began construction on Ohio's Miami Canal, which linked Cincinnati to Middletown by 1827, to Dayton by 1829, and to Toledo by 1840, thereby creating the first line of transport to join the Great Lakes and the Ohio River. Cincinnati real estate values rose 20 to 25 percent in the three years following the opening of the canal, and export trade increased from $1 million to $4 million between 1826 and 1832. Fortunes were made, not only in commerce but in real estate. Nicholas Longworth, for example, had come to Cincinnati in 1810 as a lawyer; the fee for his first case was a copper still which he traded for thirty acres of land then on the town's outskirts. By 1830 his lot was in the heart of the business district, and Longworth was one of the richest men in America.[31]

The Miami Canal served primarily to bring agricultural goods into Cincinnati for re-export. The three principal exports, flour, pork, and whiskey, generally moved southward to the cotton plantation regions of the Southwest, or to New Orleans and from there to the Atlantic Coast and foreign markets. Pork packing became a major Cincinnati industry, earning the city the nickname "Porkopolis." Altogether in 1840 the Cincinnati manufacturing establishment produced goods valued at $17 million, compared to about $2.6 million in 1818–19.[32]

As its economy expanded, the city attracted a heterogeneous influx of migrants from other areas of the country and

Table 1. Birthplaces of white adult males in Cincinnati,
1819 and 1840.

	1819	1840
New England	18%	9%
Mid-Atlantic	40	22
South Atlantic	14	11
East North Central	2	10
East South Central	2	3
Great Britain	10	10
Ireland	7	6
Germany	3	28
Other European	2	2
Unknown	2	0

immigrants from abroad (see Table 1). Between 1810 and
1840 the population grew from 2,500 to 46,000, primarily as
a result of in-migration.

The religious character of the city was also diverse. In
1829 the city directory listed twenty-three religious institutions: six Methodist (including three Methodist Episcopal,
and one each African Methodist, Associated Methodist, and
Methodist Society); four Baptist; four Presbyterian; two Episcopal; and one each Friends, Jewish, Lutheran, Roman Catholic, Swedenborgian, Unitarian, and Universalist. A local Presbyterian minister (New School) wrote to revivalist Charles
Grandison Finney two years later recommending Cincinnati as
a city badly in need of religious revival. He estimated that out
of the 28,000 residents there were 3,000 Presbyterians, 3,000
other "evangelicals," and 3,000–4,000 others (Catholics, Jews,
Swedenborgians, Unitarians, Universalists, Campbellite Bap-
tists, and members of the Christian Society and the New Light
Society). That left 18,000 nonchurchgoers, including "Infidels,
Owenites, Atheists, and Fanny Wright men. . . ."[33]

The overall picture of Cincinnati in its early years is that
of a city growing and commercializing rapidly, but without
strikingly anomalous economic, demographic, or religious influences to strongly color its character.

The city's temperance movement, like the national movement, had rejected the patronizing attitudes of the founders of
temperance reform. Between 1826 and 1841 organized temperance reform had moved from elite to mass membership,
from endorsement of light alcoholic beverages to insistence on
total abstinence. Yet the movement lacked a clearly defined
goal. Once one had taken the pledge, and had convinced as
many of one's acquaintances as possible to do the same, the
next step was not at all clear. Most people assumed that confirmed drunkards could not be reclaimed, and that the best
hope was to prevent others from following the same path, so
that the next generation might be free from the curse of drink.
This passive attitude went against the grain of evangelical per-
fectionism, but no alternative seemed apparent. For a brief period around 1840 the temperance movement appeared to be
floundering. But then in 1841 a spontaneous and spectacular
eruption of temperance activity occurred that both revivified
the movement and once again altered some of its basic percep-
tions about drink and society. Temperance reform entered that
phase of its history known as the Washingtonian period.

Notes

1. Paul R. Meyer, "The Transformation of American Temperance: The
Popularization and Radicalization of a Reform Movement, 1813–1860"
(Ph.D. thesis, University of Iowa, 1976), 15–62.

2. Marshall W. S. Swan, *Town on Sandy Bay: A History of Rockport,
Massachusetts* (Canaan, N.H., 1980), 108–9.

3. Robert Louis Hampel, "Influence and Respectability: Temperance
and Prohibition in Massachusetts, 1813–1852" (Ph.D. thesis, Cornell University, 1980), 36–45.

4. John Ware, *An Address Delivered before the Massachusetts Society
for the Suppression of Intemperance at Their Annual Meeting, May, 1825*
(Boston, 1825), quoted in Meyer, "Transformation," 55.

5. John A. Krout, *The Origins of Prohibition* (New York, 1925), 85,
96, 101; Meyer, "Transformation," 63–80; Ian R. Tyrrell, "Drink and the
Process of Social Reform: From Temperance to Prohibition in Ante-Bellum
America, 1813–1860" (Ph.D. thesis, Duke University, 1974), 36–57, and
*Sobering Up: From Temperance to Prohibition in Antebellum America,
1800–1860* (Westport, Conn., 1979), 54–86.

6. Mathew Carey Papers, Historical Society of Pennsylvania, Gerritt Smith, Peterboro, N.Y., to Carey, Philadelphia, July 13, 1832; Nancy Hewitt, "Religious Benevolence or Social Control: A Critique and a Reinterpretation" (unpublished manuscript, University of Pennsylvania), 21.

7. *Cincinnati Commercial*, Feb. 25, 1851.

8. Susan Brownell Anthony Papers, Schlesinger Library, Harvard University, Anthony, Canajoharie, N.Y., to her mother, Mar. 7, 1849.

9. Margaret Best Papers, Toledo–Lucas County Public Library, Ohio, Diary of Adelia J. Haughton (Best), Dec. 23, 1859.

10. Lyman Beecher, *Six Sermons*, quoted in Krout, *Origins*, 106.

11. Meyer, "Transformation," 75, 63–65.

12. American Temperance Society, *First Annual Report*, quoted in Tyrrell, "Drink," 42; see also 61, 67; Krout, *Origins*, 116, 134–36; Paul Faler, "Cultural Aspects of the Industrial Revolution: Lynn, Massachusetts, Shoemakers and Industrial Morality, 1826–1860," *Labor History*, 15 (1974): 368–69.

13. Mary P. Ryan, *Cradle of the Middle Class: The Family in Oneida County, New York, 1790–1865* (Cambridge, Mass., 1981), 111; Bruce Laurie, *Working People of Philadelphia, 1800–1850* (Philadelphia, 1980), 40; Paul E. Johnson, *A Shopkeeper's Millennium: Society and Revivals in Rochester, New York, 1815–1837* (New York, 1978), 79.

14. Tyrrell, "Drink," 66; Meyer, "Transformation," 81.

15. E. B. Newcomb Collection, Indiana State Library, E. F. Peabody, Indianapolis, Dec. 14, 1829.

16. Krout, *Origins*, 127–33; Tyrrell, "Drink," 66.

17. Meyer, "Transformation," 111, 88–92; Krout, *Origins*, 141; Asa E. Martin, "The Temperance Movement in Pennsylvania prior to the Civil War," *Pennsylvania Magazine of History and Biography*, 49 (1925): 202–3; Tyrrell, "Drink," 119, 123; Hampel, "Influence," 118–19; Johnson, *Shopkeeper's*, 5–6; Ryan, *Cradle*, 12–13.

18. McCreath Family Papers, Pennsylvania State Archives, Young Men's and Young Ladies' Total Abstinence Society of Harrisburg (Pa.), 4th Annual Report of the Board of Managers, 1841.

19. Jill Siegel Dodd, "The Working Class and the Temperance Movement in Ante-Bellum Boston," *Labor History*, 19 (1978): 512–29; Laurie, *Working People*, 120–21, and "'Nothing on Compulsion': Life Styles of Philadelphia Artisans, 1820–1850," *Labor History*, 15 (1974): 344–52; Don H. Doyle, *The Social Order of a Frontier Community: Jacksonville, Illinois, 1825–70* (Urbana, Ill., 1978), 190.

20. John L. Thomas, "Romantic Reform in America, 1815–1865," *American Quarterly*, 17 (1965): 656–57; Robert S. Fletcher, *A History of Oberlin College from Its Foundation through the Civil War* (Oberlin, Ohio, 1943), 1:336.

21. W. J. Rorabaugh, "From Drinking to Abstinence: A Revolution in Social Behavior" (paper presented at Annual Meeting of Organization of

American Historians, San Francisco, Apr. 11, 1980), 9; Johnson, *Shopkeeper's*, 113–14; Hewitt, "Religious Benevolence," 19.

22. Krout, *Origins*, 155–61.

23. Ibid.; Tyrrell, "Drink," 129; *Ohio Organ of the Temperance Reform*, May 13, 1853; Meyer, "Transformation," 119.

24. Tyrrell, *Sobering Up*, 150–51; Laurie, *Working People*, 120–21.

25. Mark Dennett Papers, New York Public Library, Young Men's Temperance Society, York, Me., Dec., 1833, Report; Roger Lane, *Policing the City: Boston, 1822–1885* (Cambridge, Mass., 1967), 41–43; Johnson, *Shopkeeper's*, 130–33.

26. *City Directory*, Cincinnati, 1829, 1834; Crafts J. Wright, *Report Read by Crafts J. Wright, Esq., at the Anniversary Meeting of the Young Men's Temperance Society, February 26th, 1835* (Cincinnati, Ohio, 1835), 12.

27. Quoted in Alan I. Marcus, "In Sickness and in Health: The Marriage of the Municipal Corporation to the Public Interest and the Problem of Public Health, 1820–1870. The Case of Cincinnati" (Ph.D. thesis, University of Cincinnati, 1979), 33–34.

28. A rough calculation of the ratio of drinking establishments per capita of the total population suggests that the ratio was declining throughout the period covered by this study: 1829: 1/279; 1834: 1/166; 1841: 1/119; 1850: 1/96; 1853: 1/86; 1873: 1/76. This declining ratio indicates that although consumption itself may have dropped over these years, the public saloon steadily proliferated. See Wright, *Report*, 12; *Western Temperance Journal*, June 1, 1841; *New York Organ*, Jan. 26, 1850, quoted in Tyrrell, "Drink," 230; *Ohio Organ of the Temperance Reform*, Jan. 21, 1853; National WCTU, *Minutes of the Second Convention of the National Woman's Christian Temperance Union Held in Cincinnati, Ohio, Nov. 17, 18, and 19, 1875* (Chicago, 1889), 44.

29. *City Directory*, Cincinnati, 1834, 225–26; *City Directory*, Cincinnati, 1840; Edward H. Rastatter, "Nineteenth Century Public Land Policy: The Case for the Speculator," in *Essays in Nineteenth Century Economic History: The Old Northwest*, ed. David C. Klingaman and Richard K. Vedder (Athens, Ohio, 1975), 123–26; Harry N. Scheiber, *The Ohio Canal Era: A Case Study of Government and the Economy, 1820–1861* (Athens, Ohio, 1969), 225; W. J. Rorabaugh, *The Alcoholic Republic: An American Tradition* (New York, 1979), 64, 69, 85–87.

30. Calvin Fletcher, *The Diary of Calvin Fletcher*, ed. Gayle Thornbrough and Dorothy L. Riker (Indianapolis, 1973), 1:14, Fletcher, London, Ohio, to his father, Ludlow, Vt., June 18, 1819.

31. Carl W. Condit, *The Railroad and the City: A Technological and Urbanistic History of Cincinnati* (Columbus, Ohio, 1977), 3–6; Scheiber, *Canal*, 205; Richard C. Wade, *The Urban Frontier: The Rise of Western Cities, 1790–1830* (Cambridge, Mass., 1959), 53–58, 109, 171–72, 189–90; Constance McLaughlin Green, *American Cities in the Growth of the Nation* (New York, 1965), 45–50.

32. Irwin F. Flack, "Who Governed Cincinnati? A Comparative Analysis of Government and Social Structure in a Nineteenth Century River City: 1819–1860" (Ph.D. thesis, University of Pittsburgh, 1978), 35; Rastatter, "Public Land," 123, 126; Scheiber, *Canal*, 206, 221, 225.

33. Amos Blanchard to Charles Grandison Finney, Jan. 1, 1831, quoted in Fletcher, *Oberlin*, 1:47; *City Directory*, Cincinnati, 1829.

2

Social
Temperance

By 1840, being a temperance adherent also meant being a teetotaler. Unlike many forms of benevolent work, religious mission work, or reforms such as antislavery or prison reform, temperance advocacy mandated an observable change in one's daily, personal life. In a society in which custom, habit, and tradition continually placed males in situations where they were expected to drink, where they would be ridiculed or even ostracized if they did not drink, abstainers of necessity created new, alternative social groups that facilitated the restructuring of their private lives. By forming a circle of friends with other nondrinkers, teetotalers could remove themselves from ridicule, abuse, and temptation to drink, and could reinforce one another's resolve and sense of virtue.

The need for this sort of combined reform organization/social group arose in the 1830s with the shift to total abstinence. Temperance groups responded by holding meetings more frequently than the annual interval that had been customary with anti-spirits groups, and by planning temperance picnics, entertainments, and other outings. But changes both in the direction of temperance reform and in the underlying fabric of American society in the 1840s greatly intensified the need for temperance organizations to provide a separate social context for their members. In 1841 a wave of temperance enthusiasm known as the Washingtonian movement swept across the country. Generated by economic concerns, evangelical millenarianism, and sharpened awareness of the destructive potential of alcohol, and dominated by artisans steeped in the philosophy of self-help, Washingtonianism sought to convert habitual drinkers and even confirmed inebriates to total abstinence. Suddenly the need to provide social support for problem drinkers became paramount.

The foundering of Washingtonianism within a few years of its inception, compounded with the heightened level of social dislocation in growing, commercializing communities in the 1840s, created the need for stable, well-organized, socially oriented temperance organizations. The Sons of Temperance and similar fraternal lodges filled this need and became immensely popular. Fraternal temperance institutionalized teetotalism, brought hundreds of thousands of people to a public advocacy of temperance reform, and made possible the prohibition campaigns of the 1850s.

Six drinkers in Baltimore, Maryland, organized a temperance society in April, 1840, and named it the "Washington Temperance Society" in patriotic honor of George Washington. The organization might have developed like thousands of others, had not the founders made three novel decisions. They styled themselves "reformed drunkards" (although they were no more than heavy regular drinkers); they decided that their meetings would consist solely of members describing the benefits total abstinence had brought to their lives; and they made these gatherings entirely open to the public. The drama of the meetings, and the promise of redemption from poverty and shame, attracted large crowds. Destitute alcoholics were especially welcomed and treated with respect and sympathy. Many swore off alcohol and, with the support and encouragement of their fellow Washingtonians, were able to resume a more respectable and productive life. These converts, in turn, told of their transformation at subsequent meetings and implored others to follow their path.

The Baltimore society met immediate success and attracted widespread attention first in the city and then throughout the country. In the spring of 1841 the Baltimore group began to send out delegations to implant Washingtonianism in other communities. Soon nearly every city in the East had its own Washingtonian societies. Everywhere the meetings drew large crowds. Tens of thousands—drunkards, moderate drinkers, and nondrinkers—came forward to sign the pledge of total abstinence.[1]

Although only men spoke publicly at the meetings, women added their names to the pledge lists, and thereby committed themselves not only to abstain but also to refuse to serve alcoholic beverages or countenance their use. In addition, women organized separate "Martha Washington" societies which undertook to provide food and used clothing for reformed inebriates and their families, both for relief and to give the head of the household a respectable appearance so that he might "seek employment with any hope of success."[2]

Cincinnati's *Western Temperance Journal* (hereafter referred to as the *Journal*) first reported on Baltimore's Washingtonian excitement in January, 1841. The *Journal* observed the good work being done in the East, and wondered "when shall we have a Cincinnati Washingtonian Temperance Society formed? We ask—when?"[3] The city's temperance activists felt that they could not start Washingtonian meetings on their own, but had to wait to be visited by an initiate who would, in a manner that echoed the pattern of religious revivalism, bring them "the word." (Once Cincinnati's Washingtonian society was established, it was besieged by requests to send delegations to surrounding communities.) Representatives from Baltimore finally arrived in late July, and the Cincinnati Washingtonian Temperance Society met for the first time on July 26, 1841. Almost immediately the city's meetings were filled to overflowing; at least one, and sometimes two or three, were held every night, and even by late November there was no sign of lessening interest. Thousands signed the pledge; many came back night after night to hear the tales of shame, sin, and degradation that ended with a joyful affirmation of redemption through the Washingtonian movement.[4] By the end of 1841 the city's Washingtonians estimated that 8,000 had pledged. Cincinnati had become the western center of the temperance revival.[5]

Artisans and the wives of artisans dominated the movement. For them, Washingtonianism represented the culmination of the trends that in the 1830s had made temperance reform increasingly attractive to skilled workers. The movement derived its striking intensity and enormous popularity from the economic impact of changes in occupational patterns; from the millenarian mindset created by the Second Great Awakening; from the increased problems generated by alcoholic beverages in the wake of the massive political campaigns of 1840; and from the accentuation of all these factors by the severe economic depression that followed the Panic of 1837.[6]

Between 1819 and 1840 the proportion of the Cincinnati work force engaged in commerce dropped from 21 to 15 percent. This change suggests that as the city's economy matured, individuals may have had fewer opportunities to move upward through the occupational ranks. Hard times in the late 1830s accelerated this trend and painfully brought home to workers their insecurity and their defenselessness against an economic structure that increasingly responded to regional and national forces beyond local control.[7]

By 1841 Cincinnati was languishing in its fourth year of severe economic depression. Local trade unions had disintegrated beyond hope of recovery. Building practically ceased, and what little was done usually had to be carried out under a barter arrangement because of the scarcity of money. In these circumstances the economic arguments for total abstinence took on greater weight than ever before. Temperance publications pointed out the substantial savings a nondrinker could accumulate by putting aside the amount that would otherwise be spent on alcohol. Employers seeking a reliable work force increasingly favored the hiring of abstinent workers. Budding entrepreneurs found they had additional economic incentive to abandon drink: records from that time for the R. G. Dunn Company, a national credit agency, show that a reputation for "intemperate habits" in regard to alcohol practically guaranteed a bad credit rating. By the Washingtonian outbreak, temperance had become a crucial attribute for economic advancement and even, in some cases, for economic survival.[8] One Indiana temperance reformer cheerily noted that as a result of the Washingtonian crusade, "nearly half of the Drunkards in the state have reformed. If these be the results of *hard times* let them come."[9]

The depression years also brought a new wave of religious revivalism. Even before 1837 evangelicalism seems to have been attracting increasing numbers of wage earners. With the onset of the depression, some interpreted their economic plight as divine punishment for "the extravagance of living . . . which a few years since pervaded the United States,"[10] and turned to God for solace and salvation. But the severity of the economic collapse limited the effectiveness of this revival, as people became preoccupied with the day-to-day problems of physical well-being and survival. They longed not only for the reassurance and the catharsis of revivalism but also for a promise of immediate earthly salvation from poverty and suffering.[11] The Washingtonian movement appealed to those who sought such worldly redemption. It was at heart a secularized revival and was often called the "Washingtonian Revival." It promised financial security and social respectability to habitual drinkers and even to confirmed inebriates, if only they would adopt the principle of total abstinence.

At the same time Washingtonianism attracted those evangelicals who sought to perfect society in preparation for the millennium. Up until then, as a Pennsylvania temperance society noted, there existed "a vast field of devastation and ruin, yet remaining unfurrowed by a single impression from the great moral ploughshare of Total Abstinence."[12] But the Washingtonian crusade reached out to save all. If even confirmed inebriates could be rescued from spiritual degradation, that seemed surely to be a sign that God's grace was close at hand for all. Samuel Fenton Cary, an active Cincinnati Washingtonian and soon to be the pre-eminent temperance reformer in Ohio, later recalled these millennial expectations: "The 'Washingtonian' movement had swept over our land like a moral tornado, giving sight to the blind, healing to the broken-hearted, deliverance to the captives, a year of Jubilee. Miracles of healing had been wrought, and many hoped that the millennium had dawned!"[13] The vivid religious imagery of Cary's account underscores the close relationship between the Washingtonian phenomenon and the revival tradition of the Second Great Awakening.

Many Americans in the spring of 1841 were particularly aware of the ravages wrought by an uncontrolled drinking habit. Since colonial times it had been customary for politicians to "treat" citizens, voters and nonvoters, to alcoholic beverages before an election. With the growth of the second-party system, the efforts to outtreat the opposition intensified and extended throughout the campaign period. The presidential contest of 1840 between Harrison and Van Buren, the "hard cider" campaign, raised the practice of treating to a new level, and free liquor flowed in saloons throughout the country. "The past year has been one of peculiar trial and danger to the Cause of Temperance," a Pennsylvania temperance society wrote after the election, "and full many a drunkard has been manufactured during that memorable excitement [the political campaign]. . . . Deluges of Brandy, gin, whiskey, and hard cider were poured down the throats of the [politically] wavering. . . ."[14] The social pressure not only to drink but to drink beyond one's capacity must have been tremendous. The campaigns of 1842 and 1844 gave renewed evidence of the dangers of treating; both were periods of severe "backsliding," the term used to describe the breaking of Washingtonian pledges by reformed drinkers.[15]

The social origins of Washingtonianism differed from those that had produced earlier temperance agitation. But the difference did not stop there. The movement represented more than just a momentary outburst of temperance enthusiasm, a new tactic, a broadened goal. Its philosophy differed profoundly from the earlier temperance movement, and its membership reflected that difference. For the first time the temperance movement reached out to help those who actually suffered from the use of drink, and it therefore became much more explicitly a humanitarian reform.

Prior to 1841 the temperance movement had addressed itself only to persuading moderate drinkers to abandon the use of alcohol before they became habitual inebriates. Reformers assumed that once the line was crossed, and a drinker became a drunkard, the downward path to ruin was inevitable. The Reverend Justin Edwards, one of the founders of the American Temperance Society, voiced this belief when he wrote to a friend in 1825 about plans for the ATS: "We are at present fast hold of a project for making all people in this country, and in all other countries, temperate; or rather, a plan to induce those who are now temperate to continue so. Then, as all who are intemperate will soon be dead, the earth will be eased of an amazing evil." [16]

The Washingtonians rejected this viewpoint absolutely. The drunkard not only could but should be saved. Samuel Cary, later the leader of the Ohio temperance movement, began his involvement in the reform during the Washingtonian period while a young Cincinnati lawyer. A ragged drunkard wandered in off the street during one meeting. "What had rendered him an alien and an outcast?" Cary recalled asking the inebriate. "Was he not charmed by a serpent whose sting was death . . . ? I bid him resolve, tendered him the right hand of fellowship, and the sympathies of the good and virtuous; assured him that others had broken the tyrant's chain—that he was a man and a brother, and had only 'fallen in the way we had in weakness trod. . . .'" Cary's solicitous attention so overwhelmed the drunkard that he cast down his bottle and signed the pledge.[17] John Hawkins, a former hatmaker, a reformed drunkard, and one of the best-known national leaders, said of the Washingtonians: "We don't slight the drunkard; we love him, we nurse him, as a mother does her infant learning to walk." The inebriate, he concluded, "needs our sympathy and is worthy of it. Poor and miserable as he is, he did not design to become a drunkard. . . ."[18]

Washingtonianism was not reserved exclusively for former inebriates. Indeed, the focus of the movement was on creating a support network that would link drunkards and moderate drinkers with long-standing abstainers, drawing those who wished to give up alcohol into a social milieu that would reinforce rather than denigrate those intentions. The typical proportion of problem drinkers in Washingtonian societies appears to have been about 10 percent or less of the total membership. In Cincinnati one source estimated that there were 900 inebriates among the 8,000 who had signed the pledge.[19]

By offering the drunkard sympathy and aid, the temperance movement allied itself unmistakably with the host of humanitarian reforms that sprang up in America between 1830 and 1850. Indeed, practically every prominent reformer of the period, whether best known for advocating slavery abolition, women's rights, or other reform, was also an abstainer and a supporter of the temperance movement. Susan B. Anthony, Amelia Bloomer, Frederick Douglass, William Lloyd Garrison, Horace Greeley, Wendell Phillips, Elizabeth Cady Stanton, and Lucy Stone, to cite just a few examples, were all advocates of total-abstinence temperance reform.

At the same time that the Washingtonian phase broadened the appeal of the temperance cause among humanitarian reformers, it served to alienate nearly all remaining official church support for the movement. Most clergymen believed that the first step in saving degraded drunkards' souls was to ensure that they devoutly sought God's guidance and support. The Washingtonian reformers, although most of them were quite religious, believed just the reverse: it was pointless to try to turn a faithless drunkard toward God; first he must be shown the path to sobriety and then, once physically redeemed, he might be more receptive to religious conversion. The temperance movement in the past had consisted almost entirely of church members, but Washingtonianism attracted many who did not attend church. The movement's leaders did not wish to repel these potential converts with excessive religious trappings, so they severely curtailed or even eliminated the prayers, hymns, and sermons that had been standard at earlier temperance meetings. "Now anyone who knows anything about drunkenness," wrote one Washingtonian, "knows that most drunkards are strongly averse to religion, if not infidel at heart. They want to hear nothing about '*moral reform*' and 'church societies.'"[20]

To the clergy, Washingtonians seemed to be turning their backs on God and promising an earthly, secular salvation that did not rely at all upon divine intervention. Cincinnati's Methodist journal, for example, believed that temperance had been "divorced from religion." "Washingtonianism," it charged, "has been called Christianity, and said to be Gospel enough for men."[21] Temperance activists admitted that some reformed drunkards "place the temperance cause above religion, or make it religion itself," but asked, "Is it strange that [they] should regard the cause as a savior?"[22] Samuel Cary believed that clerical hostility to the reform was mere jealousy directed against a movement beyond "the pale of their influence and ecclesiastical jurisdiction. . . ."[23] Bitter about the opposition of the churches, he wrote later that "eternity will reveal the measure of guilt which those ministers and professors of religion incurred, who folded their arms and did nothing as the battle was waging."[24] For more than a decade after the Washingtonian period, the clergy generally withheld their endorsement of organized temperance reform, although most continued to support the principle of total abstinence for church members.

Washingtonianism drove others besides clergymen out of the temperance movement. Already the numbers of elites who were willing to support organized temperance reform had been reduced by the shift to total abstinence in the 1830s. Members of society's upper ranks were far more repelled by Washingtonianism, so that very few remained active in the reform after 1841. "[M]en in the higher circles of life," noted a Washingtonian, "would revolt at the idea of taking a drunkard by the arm in the street. . . ."[25] They were also offended by the impropriety of placing at the podium unpracticed and uneducated men "who but yesterday were rolling in the gutters. . . ,"[26] and who sometimes used crude language or made embarrassing attempts to give a "set speech" rather than just relating their experience. Elites, moreover, were accustomed to exercising leadership and to commanding the respectful deference of their social inferiors, yet they frequently found themselves rudely displaced by less affluent Washingtonians, their advice and experience ignored. This feeling of rejection was aggravated by the fact that the immense popularity of Washingtonianism undermined the support for and the financing of older societies and their journals. In Cincinnati, the Total Abstinence Temperance Society disbanded in the face of the new

Cincinnati, c. 1830. (courtesy Cincinnati Historical Society)

Cincinnati, c. 1845. (courtesy Cincinnati Historical Society)

"Samuel F. Cary, Installed Most Worthy Patriarch of the Order of the Sons of Temperance of the United States, June 20, 1848, at Baltimore, Md." (from Cary, *The National Temperance Offering and Sons and Daughters of Temperance Gift*, 1850)

"The Story of the Bottle"—Samuel Cary persuades a drunkard to cast down his bottle during Washingtonian meeting. (from Cary, *National Temperance Offering*)

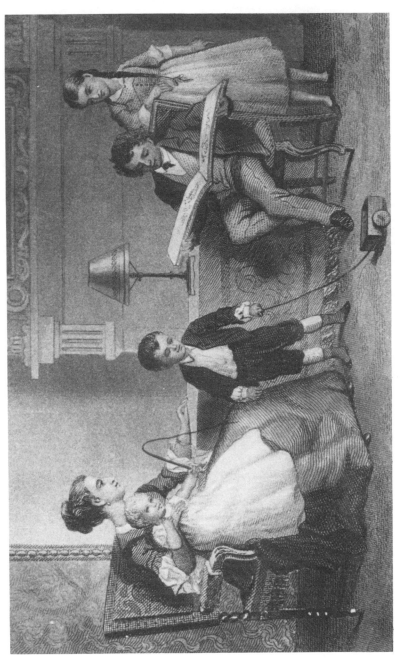

"Home of the Temperate." (from J. E. Stebbins and T. A. H. Brown, *Fifty Years History of the Temperance Cause,* 1876)

"Home of the Intemperate." (from Stebbins and Brown, *Fifty Years History*)

Ohio Washingtonian Organ and Sons of Temperance Record, front-page banner, Sept. 19, 1846.

Washingtonian Temperance Society, and the *Western Temperance Journal* was forced to merge with the Washingtonian *Morning Star.*[27]

More than just a shift in the tactical methods of the temperance movement, Washingtonianism was a distinctly new and different phase of temperance reform, with a changed philosophy, a revised set of objectives, and a different set of members. Thus by 1841 a clear pattern of discontinuity was already evident in the development of temperance reform. The elite founders of the American Temperance Society in the 1820s had little in common with the heterogeneous, popular movement for total abstinence in the 1830s and even less in common with the Washingtonians of the 1840s.

Washingtonianism, however, was short-lived. By the winter of 1842–43 the movement was rapidly declining throughout the country. A traveler outside of Cincinnati in 1843, sharing a public coach with a group of young men from the city who drank whiskey at every stop, noted in his diary: "One or 2 years ago the Washingtonion [*sic*] reform prevented drinking but now I think it will return again upon the community. . . ."[28] Samuel Cary, recounting in 1851 the history of the Washingtonian revival, analyzed the reasons for its rapid demise: "There was no *organized* effort, either to reform or keep the reformed inebriate. All seemed to act from one benevolent impulse, without system, without concert, without, in short, any of the elements of permanence or stability. The *pledge was all*; there were no regular meetings, no discipline, no systematic way of securing contributions to sustain the reformed, or keep up the interest. The consequences were, that in less than two years from the origin of the movement at Baltimore, there was a general, a universal apathy. . . ."[29] Cary's emphasis on organization, although colored by his later experience in the Sons of Temperance, does single out one of the underlying weaknesses of Washingtonianism. Structurally it was a hodgepodge, with little or no coordination or consistency between localities. At the same time, conflict and hostility between Washingtonians and the older temperance reformers they had replaced undermined organizational efforts.[30]

There were other serious problems as well. The "experience" stories told by former drunkards at meetings at first fascinated and entertained audiences; these accounts seemed like real-life versions of theatrical melodrama. But as Lyman Beecher wrote from Cincinnati in January, 1845, "The novelty of the commonplace narrative is used up, and we cannot raise an interest. . . ."[31] Washingtonian society memberships leveled off, and as they did, there were fewer new converts to tell fresh stories of degradation and salvation. Old members began to recount their experiences again and again, so that many "tired of the dull monotony" of the meetings.[32]

As had been the case with religious revivals, the Washingtonian wave crested and then subsided, its leaders unable to sustain the emotional fervor that had characterized the initial stages of the movement. Moreover, when many supposedly reformed drunkards returned to their former drinking habits, they undermined the credibility of the Washingtonian promise of redemption. Finally, returning prosperity blunted the financial desperation and guilt that had originally been the cutting edge of the revival. Since at the peak of its popularity Washingtonianism had replaced all earlier temperance organizations, when it collapsed it left nothing in its place. For a brief period the temperance movement languished, represented by nothing more than skeletal Washingtonian groups.

Soon a new organization, the Order of the Sons of Temperance, spread throughout the country. The brotherhood was designed to remedy the faults of Washingtonianism by establishing an orderly, disciplined temperance organization with weekly meetings, regular dues, standardized procedures, and a centralized, hierarchical authority structure. At the same time the Sons, modeled on the increasingly popular Independent Order of Odd Fellows, was designed to attract members through mutual benefit provisions and the use of regalia, secret rituals, and passwords.

The Order of the Sons of Temperance originated in New York City. Sixteen founders met in September, 1842, and soon adopted a constitution, an initiation rite, and official regalia. They then sent out circulars to all temperance newspapers calling for the formation of a nationwide organization. Within two years Grand Divisions appeared in New York, New Jersey, Maryland, Pennsylvania, Connecticut, and Massachusetts. Membership was not open to all. Each subordinate division voted on applications for admission. A prospective member was required to be male, white, in good health, have gainful employment, display good character, and adhere to total abstinence. Five blackballs excluded an applicant. Once admitted, and having paid a $2 fee, each new brother underwent initiation in a secret ritual. He thereafter paid dues of 6¼¢ per week, and was entitled to $4 per week during sickness, $30 for his family or friends upon his death, and $15 if his wife should die. Divisions often established supplementary trust funds for the widows and orphans of members. Each brother purchased his own regalia, which usually cost $5 for the standard white collar, white tassels, and red, white, and blue rosette, but which could run to $25 or more for the uniform of a high officer.[33]

The structure of the Sons of Temperance was hierarchical yet democratic. Members in the subordinate divisions annually elected the officers, whose positions carried elegant titles such as Worthy Patriarch, Recording Scribe, Conductor, and Outside Sentinel. Each subordinate division sent representatives to the Grand (state) Division, and the Grand Divisions elected the members of the National Division. At each level constitutions and sets of rules ordered the organization. The total abstinence pledge and the motto "Love, Purity, and Fidelity" declared the brotherhood's guiding principles.

Samuel Cary learned of the new organization in 1844 while co-editing the Cincinnati-based *Ohio Temperance Organ*. Cary, who within a few years would emerge as the unquestioned leader of Ohio's temperance movement, had already at age thirty established himself as a dedicated and effective laborer for the cause. A son of one of the area's early settlers, he had studied at Miami University in Oxford, Ohio, graduating in 1835 with first honors. In 1837 he received his degree from the Cincinnati Law School and within a very short time had established a large and lucrative legal practice in the city. While at Miami University, Cary had been a member of the student antislavery society, but in Cincinnati his attention turned to temperance reform. A close friend later wrote that

Cary's work as a criminal lawyer had given him "daily opportunities of knowing that intemperance was the great central vice, the radiating point of all crime."[34]

During the Washingtonian Revival Cary began to spend more and more time as a temperance organizer, writer, and speaker. His talents in all three areas were outstanding, but it was as a public speaker that he was most impressive. His addresses were dynamic and rousing yet always erudite, lucid, and logical. He spoke "like a Greek," according to one journalist, "with the simplicity, the cultivated naturalness, the pungency and the unembarrassed force of the ancient orators."[35] Another listener remarked after a particularly masterful speech: "Never have we seen those black eyes of his sparkle so vividly, or heard his voice give utterance to words and bursts of eloquence of such magnitude and beauty as upon this occasion."[36] He could speak for "3 or 4 hours in open air for successive days or weeks" without tiring, and always without notes or manuscripts.[37] His appearance inspired confidence and admiration. Tall, handsome, and robust, he dramatically contradicted the popular belief that a man could not be strong or healthy without drinking alcoholic beverages.[38]

The appeal of temperance reform to a young man like Cary lay partly in the moral and humanitarian context it provided for personal achievement. Cary undoubtedly could have won success in law, politics, or other professional careers. But, like many young Americans in the reforming atmosphere of the 1830s and 1840s he felt the need to do something more spiritually fulfilling, something that would aid others and help to create a better, more humane society. In one New Year's Day editorial Cary asked his readers to reflect on the way they had passed the previous year. "Has our time been occupied in maturing plans in amassing wealth to curse our children, or to win the applause to the fickle multitude? If so, we have been poorly employed, and our labors perish with us. . . . Have we been toiling for the good of man? . . . [If we were to die now] would a solitary pilgrim seek the spot where our ashes repose, and with a tearful eye and grateful heart bless God that we had lived?"[39] Cary felt that he could answer this last question affirmatively. Four years after the Washingtonian crusade, a woman approached him and blessed him for saving her husband from drink. "The reader cannot imagine my emotions at that moment. I would not have exchanged them for those of Wellington after the Battle of Waterloo. . . . All the gold of California laid at my feet would not have afforded equal gratification. . . . To have a home in the heart of an obscure woman . . . —to be assured that God has made us the instrument of delivering a soul from death, . . . rebuilding a broken-down family altar—these are stars in the crown of rejoicing that never grow dim—laurels that never fade—riches that never perish." [40]

Cary's humanitarian zeal and his quest for a more meaningful and less materialistic personal existence typified the reformist concerns of many members of his generation. But in one important respect he was atypical: he chose to dedicate his entire life to the temperance movement. The vast majority of the millions of Americans who became involved in temperance reform or other reforms during the nineteenth century did so in their spare time, spending at most a few hours a week on their cause. But Cary stunned his friends in 1845 by announcing that he was giving up law to devote himself to temperance work. At the time, wrote a friend, "no man of his age in the State of Ohio had a larger practice or more enviable reputation as an advocate." [41] Cary's decision was made possible by the fact that he had become moderately wealthy through inheritance: in 1850 he paid over $600 in property taxes, among the 200 highest totals in Cincinnati. He was therefore able to retire comfortably and donate his time and skills to the temperance cause, often paying his own expenses on speaking tours. A friend claimed in 1853 that Cary had spent $20,000 of his own money in the crusade against drink. [42] His full-time, independently financed reform efforts, combined with his natural talents, assured that he would become a prominent leader in the movement. His rise to the position of Ohio's pre-eminent temperance advocate, however, was aided and accelerated by his championing of the Order of the Sons of Temperance just at the moment that fraternalism emerged as the new dominant mode of temperance organization.

Through Cary's initiative and under his guidance, eight

other Cincinnatians joined him to form Ohio Division No. 1 of the Sons of Temperance in August, 1844, and thereby established the first chapter in the West. Within six months Ohio Division No. 1 grew to over 100 members (see Table 2). It reached nearly 400 in October, 1845, by which time six other divisions had sprung up in the city as well. By May, 1846, there were about 2,400 members in thirteen divisions in Cincinnati. Each week forty to fifty new brothers entered the order. In August the Cincinnati Sons started a journal, the *Western Washingtonian and Sons of Temperance Record* (hereafter referred to as the *Record*). Cincinnati had become the brotherhood's principal stronghold in the West, and thus the focal point of all temperance activity in that section of the country.[43]

The order quickly began to spread beyond Cincinnati, at first primarily to towns in its immediate environs, and to those stretching northward along the Miami Canal and the Little Miami River. The brotherhood enjoyed its greatest success in the rapidly growing cities and trading towns along Ohio's major transportation routes. Of the seventy-four divisions (in sixty-five communities) located outside Hamilton County by January, 1847, fifty-seven (77.0 percent) were on major canals, rivers, railroads, or on the National Road. Another thirteen (17.6 percent) were within seventy-five miles of Cincinnati, close enough to have direct wagon trade with the city. Twenty-seven communities with Sons of Temperance lodges had their populations listed in both the 1840 and the 1850 censuses; their average growth rate was 78.6 percent during the 1840s, compared to 30.3 percent for all of Ohio in that decade. Only two towns with Sons of Temperance divisions failed to surpass this state average.[44] Clearly the Ohio Sons of Temperance in the 1840s found their most fertile ground in rapidly growing trading regions, not in rural backwaters or economically stagnant communities. Other historians have reached similar conclusions about the dominance of commercial growth centers as sources of mid-nineteenth-century temperance activism for areas as disparate as Massachusetts, New York, Vermont, Virginia, Mississippi, Ontario, Ireland, and England. Even in predominantly rural areas of Georgia and North Carolina,

Table 2. Cincinnati divisions and membership, Order of the Sons of Temperance.

		Jan., 1845	Oct., 1845	May, 1846
Division No.	1	103	396	567
	2		281	316
	3		163	246
	4		168	287
	5		115	175
	9		42	234
	10		40	133
	17			165
	18			111
	24			56
	28			49
	30			47
Total		103	1,205	2,386

SOURCE: P. Peirce, *A History of the Introduction and Progress of the Order of the Sons of Temperance in the State of Ohio* (Cincinnati, Ohio, 1849).

Sons of Temperance members were disproportionately town-dwelling artisans, merchants, and professionals.[45]

Temperance fraternal orders flourished in Ohio in the mid- and late 1840s. It was in those same years, following Ohio's recovery from the depression of 1839–43, that new canals brought a period of unprecedented growth and economic expansion to most areas of the state. In Cincinnati during the 1840s both the population and the industrial output of the city nearly tripled. Real estate values, $5 million in 1838, soared to nearly $33 million by mid-century. Whereas only nine taxpayers had owned property worth more than $30,000 in 1838, twelve years later more than 200 surpassed that figure. This growth and prosperity brought economic opportunity, but it also weakened the traditional roles that the family, neighborhood, work group, and church had played in ordering life in smaller, more stable communities.[46] As migrants from rural areas poured into towns and cities, the brotherhoods helped recreate for them the sense of community that had been lost in the transition from rural to urban life. Historians and sociologists have recently recognized that in urbanizing communities, such voluntary associations helped to replace older neighborhood and kinship ties with new methods of assigning status, providing mutual protection, and setting standards of conduct. The use of secret rituals, elaborate titles, and mutual aid benefits in these groups conveyed to the members a sense of belonging, of clearly established order and position, and of neighborly concern and economic security, all qualities lacking in the mobile and impersonal environment of a newly urbanized community. When members moved to a different community, their transfer card gave them immediate entry into that town's social network.[47] In addition, lodge membership allowed aspiring young professionals and entrepreneurs to meet older, more established men who could be important economic contacts.[48]

Cincinnati's Sons of Temperance lodges served this integrative function for many newcomers to the city. Data on members active between 1844 and 1850 suggest that they were a geographically mobile group (see Table 3). Of the 164 men who were identified as Sons for those years, 140 (85.4 percent) were located by residential address in at least one city directory, and 126 (76.8 percent) appeared in two or more. Of those who were listed at least once, fewer than half appeared in the 1840 directory, and only a little better than half had listings in 1853. Some may have been in the city in 1840 but have been too young to have their own directory listings, and some may have been dead by 1853. Even allowing for these factors and others such as name changes, it seems likely that members of the order were moving in and out of the city rapidly.

Even while these Sons of Temperance lived in Cincinnati, they had little residential stability. For the period just before and during the time they were active in the order, listings in the Cincinnati city directories show that their residential addresses changed with remarkable frequency (see Table 4). For the 122 members listed in at least two of the directories published in 1840, 1843, 1846, 1850, and 1853, only twelve (9.8 percent) had the same address for all their listings. Of the

Table 3. Listings in Cincinnati city directories for Sons of Temperance members active between 1844 and 1850.

Year of Directory	Number of Sons listed	Percentage of Total Number (140)
1819	3	2.1%
1825	12	8.6
1829	16	11.4
1834	23	16.4
1840	61	43.6
1843	87	62.1
1846	114	81.4
1850	93	66.4
1853	72	51.4
1856	60	42.9
1860	49	35.0

Note: An additional 24 members either were not listed in any directory, or were listed but with no address given.

eighty-six found in three or more directories, a mere three (3.5 percent) stayed at the same address. Fifty-nine of these eighty-six (68.6 percent) changed addresses three or more times. Moving from place to place within the city, while not as disorienting as moving to an entirely new community, must nevertheless have undermined neighborhood ties and friendships.

Moreover, many of the Sons were boarders. Nearly one-fourth (23.6 percent) of the 140 Sons whose addresses were found in the directories resided in a boarding house at some point in the 1840s, usually in their first directory listing. It is likely that these were young men, new to the city and new to living away from their families. It is easy to see why the temperance lodge room, providing as it did an immediate circle of "brothers" pledged to befriend and support one another, held an appeal for these newcomers.

The Daughters of Temperance, a sororal organization modeled on but independent from the Sons of Temperance, provided for women, as the fraternal meetings did for men,

Table 4. Total number of residential addresses in the Cincinnati city directories of 1840, 1843, 1846, 1850, and 1853 for Sons of Temperance active between 1844 and 1850, and listed in at least two directories (N = 122; cross-tabulated by total number of listings).

		1	2	3	4	5
Number of	2	9	27			
Directory	3	1	13	24		
Listings	4	1	5	10	11	
	5	1	6	6	4	4

Number of Different Addresses

Note: Because addresses were given in approximate terms in the city directories for this period, the ruling assumption in calculating these figures was that similar addresses were in fact the same address (e.g. "Front between Vine and Race" was considered the same as "Race and Front").

much-needed social contact in the mobile and impersonal environment of urbanizing communities. Like their male counterparts, many of the Daughters of Temperance were doubtless newcomers to the city. The organization afforded both regular occasions for friendly meetings and the opportunity to engage in meaningful reform activities. As long as moral suasion remained the primary focus of temperance agitation, the Daughters of Temperance continued to play a vital role in the movement, even though the all-male Sons of Temperance dominated the public sphere of temperance reform.

Although the Daughters, unlike the Sons, could not march in parades or speak before public meetings without violating standards of propriety, they could discuss at their meetings the all-important question of how best to promote total abstinence in the home. Some divisions, including those in Cincinnati, also undertook ambitious charitable programs, attempting to provide employment for destitute women and making visitations to the needy during the winter. Established in Cincinnati in February, 1846, the local order grew to over 200 members by 1848. Nationally, the Daughters of Temperance reached a peak membership of about 30,000 in 1848, thereby constituting what was, up to that time, one of the largest organizations for women in American history.[49]

The growth of both the Sons and the Daughters of Temperance was itself a part of the overall burgeoning of fraternal organizations that accompanied Ohio's urban and economic expansion in the mid- and late 1840s. One of the most popular of the new organizations was the Independent Order of Odd Fellows. The expansion of the Odd Fellows, which closely paralleled that of the Sons, illustrates the salience of the Sons' fraternal structure for its success.

The Odd Fellow order had been brought to the United States from England in 1819, and a national Grand Lodge had formed in 1825. An official history of the order, written in 1895, noted that "American Odd Fellowship is composed of the great middle, industrial classes almost exclusively. . . . The main objects of Odd Fellowship are, to afford mutual relief and protection . . . , to cultivate social relations among its members, teach them to be industrious and frugal, inculcate correct moral principles and increase, by the practice of charity, their love for their fellow men."[50] The Odd Fellows order embodied the artisan self-help philosophy but took no position on abstinence for its members.

The first Ohio Odd Fellow lodge had formed in Cincinnati in 1830, but the brotherhood's development in the following decade was slow (see Table 5). By 1839 there were only about 1,200 members and nine lodges in the state (four in Cincinnati and one each in Dayton, Steubenville, Lancaster, Piqua, and Columbus). Then the size of the order began to increase at a much faster rate, particularly in the late 1840s, so that by 1852 over 200 chapters claimed a total membership of more than 14,000. In Cincinnati the number of Odd Fellow lodges leapt from four to seventeen in the 1840s.[51]

Fraternal organizations like the Odd Fellows and the Sons of Temperance served as small-scale communities which temporarily eased the anxieties and dislocations that accompanied

Table 5. Lodges and membership, Cincinnati and Ohio Independent Order of Odd Fellows.

	Cincinnati Lodges	Ohio Lodges	Ohio Members	National Members
1830	1	1		3,036
1836				6,819
1839				9,381
1840	4	9	1,241	
1841	4	10	1,311	
1842		16	1,563	
1843		26	1,869	
1844		35	2,554	40,238
1845				61,853
1846				90,753
1847				118,961
1852	17	202	14,320	
1854		255	18,214	204,000

SOURCES: *City Directories*, Cincinnati, 1834, 1840, 1851–52; *Cincinnati Commercial*, Mar. 19, 1845, Aug. 26, Dec. 25, 1852, Jan. 21, 1853, Aug. 22, 1854; W. T. Coggeshall Papers, MS, Cincinnati Historical Society; Henry A. Ford and Kate B. Ford, *History of Hamilton County, Ohio, with Illustrations and Biographical Sketches* (Cleveland, Ohio, 1881), 214.

rapid change, growth, and economic development. Yet even as the fraternal structure of the Sons drew adherents to the temperance cause, at the same time it undermined the organization's focus on temperance reform. One of the Cincinnati founders later recalled that "despite the scrutiny which was, or should have been used to keep out unworthy members, hundreds crept into the Order for the mere novelty of the thing, hundreds for the benefits to be had during sickness, and hundreds from no particular object, except perhaps, a desire to please the friends who proposed them."[52] As a result, some brothers violated the total abstinence pledge, neglected "prompt payment of dues," and took up much time "in discussion and settling claims upon [the] funds" of the division, which were frequently "found to be insufficient to meet the demands upon the treasuries."[53] Many members gradually left, through disinterest or disgust with monetary quibbling, and some had to be expelled.

Those who actually violated the pledge were a small minority; most Sons were sincerely dedicated to the principle of total abstinence. But for many, perhaps most, the order was not so much an organization for reform activism as it was a social support group for teetotalers. Although the founders had intended the brotherhood to be a disciplined temperance army that would systematically save the drunkard and destroy the power of the purveyors of drink, in practice the members began to place less and less emphasis on seeking converts through street meetings, public speeches by well-known temperance orators, or pamphleteering. Such "outdoor work" became subordinate to the quiet and comfort of the weekly division meeting, and to the picnics, celebrations, and holiday festivities where teetotalers could enjoy recreation and social contact without the presence of alcohol. As early as the Quarterly Session of the Ohio Grand Division in July, 1847, some members warned that one of the original purposes of the order was being lost. Cincinnati delegates Samuel Cary, Caleb Clark, and P. R. L. Peirce proposed to assess each member 2¢ a week for an "agitation fund," noting that since the Sons "had obtained possession of the Washingtonian ground, [they] must perform the Washingtonian labor."[54] The *Record*, under Cary's editorial lead, joined the campaign, urging the order to collect statistics, send out lecturers, and distribute pamphlets and tracts. It warned: "Too much has the out door labor given place to indoor Division duties—too much has been expected from the latter—too little from the former."[55]

Samuel Cary, while serving as Most Worthy Patriarch of the National Division of the Sons during 1848 and 1849, struggled to overcome the same trend in the national organization. Addressing delegates from throughout the United States and Canada who were meeting in Cincinnati in 1849, Cary bemoaned the lack of work outside the division rooms. He argued that if "three hundred thousand dollars of last year's receipts could have been appropriated to the prosecution of our mission, how much good might have been accomplished. That

sum would have kept in the field one hundred and fifty lecturers at a salary of $1,000 each, and printed and circulated
one hundred million pages of temperance tracts."[56] Cary's enthusiastic plans to make use of the order's potential for efficient, heavily financed, and centrally controlled agitation campaigns made little headway at either the state or the national
level. The Sons of Temperance continued to grow more isolated from the day-to-day battle against the liquor evil.

Much of this reluctance to undertake an active reform
program stemmed from the widespread belief in the mid-
1840s that the temperance movement was already inexorably
winning the battle against drink. Temperance advocates saw
the history of the reform, despite temporary setbacks, as one
of steady progress. "If intemperance did not vanish before . . .
[the temperance movement] like a meteor," wrote the *Cincinnati Commercial*, "it receded like mist before the rising sun."[57]
Moreover, modern estimates of alcoholic consumption in
the mid-nineteenth century strongly support the temperance
movement's claims of success. The annual adult per capita consumption of absolute alcohol declined by a startling 75 percent
in fifteen years of national temperance activity, from 7.1 gallons in 1830 to 1.8 gallons in 1845. Total abstinence from all
alcoholic beverages, the far-fetched and radical idea of a few
firebrands in the early 1830s, had become the standard respectable behavior of those in the middle ranks of American
society by the late 1840s.[58]

Looking back reflectively after the collapse of organized
temperance activity in the late 1850s, the *Templar's Magazine*
noted that many people considered "the temperance enterprise
. . . a failure . . . [because] more liquor is drank now, and more
intoxicated persons are seen now, than ever before." But the
journal argued that in

> deciding whether the cause is advancing, we should compare
> the present number of teetotalers, as well as tipplers, with the
> number thirty years ago . . . [At that time, alcohol] was in very
> common use as a . . . [medicine], even among young chil-
> dren. . . . Now it is very seldom used that way. Thirty years ago,
> it was thought a birth, christening or wedding, could not be got
> along with, without ardent spirits; now its use on such occa-

sions is very generally dispensed with. In 1825, almost every minister of the Gospel used spirits daily; now but few use it even "for the stomach's sake." Thousands of families that make no pretensions to temperance or religion, swayed by the general custom, have abandoned its use.[59]

Fraternal temperance institutionalized this change in customs and helped make abstaining from drink an easy, comfortable, and unremarkable practice. By grouping together and by proclaiming their beliefs openly, teetotalers could decline drink and could refuse it to others without feeling awkward, defensive, or extreme. They were so successful that by the 1850s it was the drinkers within the middle class, rather than the teetotalers, who had been placed on the defensive.

With so much already accomplished by the mid-1840s, the Sons understandably believed that simply by proclaiming themselves teetotalers, and regularly demonstrating their collective strength and social respectability, they would inevitably overwhelm the remaining opposition. The temperance army did not have to engage in battle; it only had to display its potential power. One 1846 march by the Cincinnati divisions included 1,500 Sons who stretched six city blocks: "At the appointed hour," the *Commercial* reported, "the procession moved off to the stirring notes of the Bands; banners floated high in the breeze, while in admirable order the 'Sons of Temperance' followed keeping regular step—their regalia giving them a uniform appearance, producing an effect that elicited the general attention of the city."[60] In a sense, fraternal temperance was a middle-class version of the early American Temperance Society: an effort to create an abstaining nation through example and indirect social pressure rather than through direct action.

Although teetotalism met with overwhelming acceptance within the middle ranks of American society, it continued to be repudiated by elites and by non-skilled workers. As one of the city's temperance spokesmen noted at mid-century, he occasionally met "some *would be aristocrats*, who look *down* upon the temperance movement with contempt. . . . Another exception may also be properly made. The *dregs* of society are, like the mud and sediment of the river, left behind . . . all, except the two classes mentioned, are convinced of the truth of temperance principles. . . ."[61] The wealthy considered total abstinence boorish, uncultured, and excessive. To link together the savoring of a fine wine by a gentleman and the guzzling of whiskey by an inebriate seemed to them absurd. They believed that their temperate enjoyment of alcohol served as an admirable model of self-control and moderation. Moreover, they resented the way they had been pushed out of the temperance movement in the 1830s and early 1840s, and were offended by the frequent abuse they received from teetotalers. Laborers, on the other hand, not only continued to find alcohol relaxing and pleasurable but also depended on saloons as one of the very few sources of amusement and recreation available to them. The influx of heavy-drinking German and Irish immigrant workers in the 1840s strongly reinforced this class division over drinking.

The membership of the Sons of Temperance reflected the broad acceptance of teetotalism among artisans and the middle class, and its rejection by laborers and wealthy elites. Of 164 Cincinnati Sons of Temperance active between the years 1844 and 1850, the occupations of 144 can be identified from the city directories. Of these 43 percent were skilled workers. More than half of this group were from the city's prosperous and upwardly mobile building trades.[62] Only 2 percent of the Sons were nonskilled workers, although 32 percent of the Cincinnati labor force held nonskilled positions.[63] Professionals, most of whom were lawyers, made up a strikingly high 24 percent of the temperance brotherhood. Another 19 percent were commercial proprietors, but few of these were wealthy. Nearly all ran businesses requiring relatively little initial capital—grocers, dry goods storekeepers, cigar manufacturers. Many had recently been artisans: for example, a tinner had turned stove manufacturer, and a cabinet maker had become a furniture manufacturer. Of more than 200 Cincinnatians paying property taxes of over $500 in 1850, only two appear in the Sons' membership lists: Samuel Cary, wealthy through inheritance, and an English-born Quaker hardware merchant. Temperance reform by the mid-1840s clearly no longer attracted the participation of the local elites.[64]

The brotherhood, in short, brought together the middle ranks of the city. Included within this broad range of membership were those who saw in total abstinence the route to the millennium, to humanitarian reform, or to upward social mobility, as well as those who saw teetotalism not as primarily a means but rather as an end in itself, a sign of proper behavior and respectable character. For this last group the temperance movement was less a proselytizing instrument than it was a source of social activity. Rutherford B. Hayes, a young Cincinnati lawyer in 1850, exemplified this kind of commitment to the reform when he noted in his diary that he had set aside Wednesday evenings to be "devoted to my Odd Fellow brethren; Thursdays to 'Sons of Temperance' ditto . . . and Saturdays, the best of all, to the [Literary] Club." He added a resolve to speak as often as possible at the Literary Club, and "'to show my hand' oftener in the [Sons of Temperance] 'Division Room' and the [Odd Fellows] 'Lodge.'" A few weeks later he wrote that he had "opened up a temperance meeting in Reverend [James] Prestley's church (Associate Reformed Presbyterian). . . . The remarks were extempore, being the first speech of the kind I ever made to a mixed audience. . . . In time, I fancy, I can make a decent temperance speech."[65] Although Hayes was a firm abstainer, his dedication to the public sphere of the movement did not match his personal adherence to teetotalism. Temperance was only one of numerous reforms he supported and the Sons of Temperance order but one of several sources of social contact. As total abstinence became not only accepted but expected behavior, the sense of personal sacrifice and commitment among teetotalers like Hayes declined. As one result, the temperance movement in the 1850s, although it won great numbers of supporters, found it could not command the unwavering dedication of these supporters.

Despite its rather bland, all-encompassing nature, fraternal temperance had aroused heated controversy when it first appeared. For some evangelicals, the secrecy of the Sons smacked of Masonry, and the elaborate rituals were reminiscent of Catholicism. The Cincinnati Presbytery (New School), for example, passed a resolution in the spring of 1847, aimed expressly at the Sons, that officially condemned participation in secret societies. The city's clergy became more hostile than ever toward the reform; only one of Cincinnati's ninety-seven ministers participated in a huge temperance parade in 1846, although a place of honor at the head of the procession had been reserved for them.[66]

Fraternalism also alienated some former Washington supporters. As had happened with the shifts to total abstinence and to Washingtonianism, past leaders felt they were being rudely displaced. Sons attacked the Washingtonian movement as lazy, listless, and unimaginative. Washingtonian leaders replied that the new order was unnecessary. Efforts to promote reconciliation and cooperation failed, as much because the Sons "saw no need for it"[67] as from an uncompromising stance among the older leaders. The Sons confidently believed they had discovered the key to winning the temperance battle, and they declined to defer to elders whose tactics had proven faulty. The *Record* remarked: "It is painful for us to differ with the old veterans in the ranks of Total Abstinence. There are many who toiled in days of yore, who are suspicious of any new movement, especially if it is likely to overshadow their favorite scheme. . . . This is an age of improvement, and it is not surprising the gray-headed should cling to the objects of their youthful affections, and look with suspicion upon every new scheme."[68] Available evidence suggests that most Sons had not been active in the Washingtonian period. Thus, at the leadership level and probably at the rank-and-file level as well, fraternalism once again displayed the temperance movement's tendency to break with the past and to experience rapid turnovers of active supporters.

Although the Order of the Sons of Temperance dominated the temperance movement in the late 1840s, there were two other fraternal temperance organizations in the field. The Independent Order of Rechabites, founded in England in 1835, had 14,253 members in the United States and Canada by 1848 (compared to 149,372 for the Sons).[69] No Rechabite "tents" formed in Cincinnati during these years, but the city did prove to be fertile ground for the other temperance brotherhood, the Templars of Honor. Originally conceived as an order within an order, the Templars at first recruited exclusively from the Sons of Temperance. The initiation fee was $5 (compared with $2 for the Sons), and the annual dues of $4 were also higher; the Templars offered three elaborate and ornate degrees which required initiation fees, and also established secret signs and handshakes. With greater income from the initiation fees, the Templars were able to offer members much more generous benefits in case of sickness or death. For this reason the order appealed particularly to artisans; nearly two-thirds of Cincinnati's Templars active between 1846 and 1850 were employed at skilled labor. Moreover, the progressive awarding of degrees and the greater ornateness of their rituals would, the Templars claimed, create more interest and variety at the weekly meetings.

Six of the first ten temple charters in Ohio went to Cincinnati, the first in 1846. By 1848, twenty-seven temples reported a total Ohio membership of 972, compared to 360 divisions with over 15,000 members in the state's Sons of Temperance. The Templars proposed to unite officially with the Sons in 1847 and again in 1848, but were rebuffed both times, primarily because the Sons feared the more elaborate rituals of the Templars would further antagonize evangelical leaders. The 1849 meeting of the National Temple, held in Cincinnati, voted overwhelmingly to end the requirement of joint membership, so that Templars no longer had first to be Sons. The Templars established their own national journal in 1850, edited and published in Cincinnati by physician Joshua Wadsworth.[70]

When the Templars severed their link with the Sons, Alexander Van Hamm, Cincinnati lawyer and head of the National Temple, pledged that the members of the new order did not harbor "any spirit of opposition to the Sons of Temperance," but only meant to act "as co-workers with them in the same enterprise, only aiming in a different way, in induce all . . . to join with us in advancing the common cause."[71] But instead of cooperation, competition, hostility, and recrimination marked the relationship between the two organizations. The division and conflict between the two orders simply added to the discord that marred fraternal temperance.

The Sons of Temperance reached a height of popularity in Ohio in 1848, with 543 state divisions and 21,566 paid members (see Table 6). Then suddenly the order began to decline as

Table 6. Divisions and membership, Cincinnati, Ohio, and
national Orders of the Sons of Temperance.

	Cincinnati Divisions	Ohio Divisions	Ohio Members	National Members
1845	8	30	1,000	17,000
1846	12	96	3,000	40,000
1847	16	360	5,000	100,000
1848	16	543	15,000	149,372
1849	13	450	21,566	221,478
1850				232,233
1851	4			238,903
1852	2			221,056
1853	3	153	9,591	198,985
1854	3		7,584	152,090
1855				134,176
1856				99,172
1857		24	1,499	71,233
1858		43	2,459	64,508

SOURCES: Sons of Temperance of North America, Grand Division of
Ohio, *Proceedings . . . 1847 . . . 1848* (Cincinnati, Ohio, 1847–48);
P. Peirce, *A History of the Introduction and Progress of the Order of the
Sons of Temperance in the State of Ohio* (Cincinnati, Ohio, 1849), 35, 41,
76, 108, 115; *Ohio Organ of the Temperance Reform*, Sept. 2, 1853,
Jan. 6, 1854; *City Directory*, Cincinnati, 1850, 1851–52; *Western Wash-
ingtonian and Sons of Temperance Record*, Oct. 25, 1845; *Ohio Wash-
ingtonian Organ and Sons of Temperance Record*, May 9, 1846; *Spirit of
Temperance Reform* (Chicago), Aug. 26, 1845; Cary, *Historical Sketch*,
4–9.

rapidly as it had grown. By 1851 Cincinnati had only four divisions compared to sixteen in 1848. Statewide, the organization had lost nearly three-quarters of its strength by 1853. The
reasons for the abrupt decline lay partly in structural and tactical deficiencies within the brotherhood itself, and partly, as
discussed in the following chapter, in the rapidly changing social context of drinking and intemperance in the late 1840s.

The order had hampered its effectiveness as a teetotal social gathering by ruling that all "discussions of a nature foreign
to the subject of temperance are inadmissible in a Division
Room. . . ." As the same group of men met week after week,
year after year, to talk of nothing but temperance, the meetings

gradually became, in the words of a Cincinnati member, "dry and unprofitable."[72] And, as noted above, the divisions spent more and more time haggling over claims on the order's beneficial funds.

Moreover, the effectiveness of the order as a tool for reform came to be openly questioned in the late 1840s as people perceived an increase in drinking and public intoxication. The *Commercial* observed in 1847 that at "all hours of the day and night, inebriated men can be seen in our streets in far greater numbers than a few years since; nor is this the case in Cincinnati alone. . . ." It asked if the Order of the Sons of Temperance was "doing as much good as it was one year ago?"[73] Even the brotherhood's staunchest defenders had to admit that something was wrong. "That [the order] has not, as yet, fulfilled the high expectations of its most devoted friends and warm advocates . . . cannot be denied," wrote a Cincinnati leader in 1849.[74]

Rapidly increasing social disorder at mid-century caused temperance advocates to believe, incorrectly, that alcoholic consumption was also rising and that they were therefore losing ground in the battle against drink. Rather than rolling back the tide of intemperance, as early advocates of the Sons had predicted, the order appeared to have dallied in the division room while the drink trade gathered strength and once again gained the upper hand. A member of the Sons reflected the order's growing sense of purposelessness when he wrote in 1853 that those remaining in his division "all love the Order; but there is no *life* in us, no energy, no enthusiasm."[75] The brotherhood's membership continued to decline throughout the early and mid-1850s, even while public interest in and support for the temperance movement reached its highest level yet.

The primary significance of fraternal temperance lies not so much in what it did, or failed to do, but rather in the very fact of its immense popularity. At its peak the Order of the Sons of Temperance had sixteen separate divisions meeting weekly in Cincinnati, over 21,000 members in Ohio, and nearly 225,000 members nationally. These figures reflect unmistakably the marked change in American drinking patterns that fraternal temperance institutionalized. The rigorous and often successful prohibition campaigns of the 1850s would have been inconceivable without this pronounced shift in the social habits of millions of Americans. In 1830 drinking permeated American social custom; by mid-century the nation was divided sharply into two camps: drinkers and abstainers. The disruptive potential of this division was made greater by the fact that the two groups also tended to separate along ethnic, religious, and class lines. The debate over the use of alcohol was about to become a powerfully disturbing force within American society and particularly within American politics.

Notes

1. Ian R. Tyrrell, *Sobering Up: From Temperance to Prohibition in Antebellum America, 1800–1860* (Westport, Conn., 1979), 159–60.

2. Milton A. Maxwell, "The Washingtonian Movement," *Quarterly Journal of Studies on Alcohol*, 11 (1950): 430; Lorenzo D. Johnson, *Martha Washingtonianism, or a History of the Ladies Temperance Benevolent Societies* (New York, 1843), 11–12 and *passim*; *Western Temperance Journal*, Aug. 19, Sept. 1, 1841; *Morning Star*, Feb. 12, 1842; Tyrrell, *Sobering Up*, 180; Leonard U. Blumberg, "The Significance of the Alcohol Prohibitionists for the Washington Temperance Societies, with Special Reference to Paterson and Newark, New Jersey," *Journal of Studies on Alcohol*, 41 (1980): 46–47, 60.

3. *Western Temperance Journal*, June 1, Jan. 15, 1841.

4. Ibid., Aug. 1, Sept. 1, Oct. 15, Nov. 25, 1841.

5. Maxwell, "Washingtonian Movement," 421, 427.

6. For the predominance of artisans in the Washingtonian movement, see Blumberg, "Significance," 62, 64; Maxwell, "Washingtonian Movement," 412, 416; Tyrrell, *Sobering Up*, 165; C. C. Pearson and J. Edwin Hendricks, *Liquor and Anti-Liquor in Virginia, 1619–1919* (Durham, N.C., 1967), 94.

7. Irwin F. Flack, "Who Governed Cincinnati? A Comparative Analysis of Government and Social Structure in a Nineteenth Century River City: 1819–1860" (Ph.D. thesis, University of Pittsburgh, 1978), 54–57.

8. Don H. Doyle, "The Social Functions of Voluntary Association in a Nineteenth-Century American Town," *Social Science History*, 1 (1977): 345; Mary P. Ryan, *Cradle of the Middle Class: The Family in Oneida County, New York, 1790–1865* (Cambridge, Mass., 1981), ch. 3.

9. Merrill Family Papers, Indiana Historical Society Library, Samuel Merrill to his brother, Rev. David Merrill, Apr. 1, 1842, quoted in Calvin Fletcher, *The Diary of Calvin Fletcher*, ed. Gayle Thornbrough and Dorothy L. Riker (Indianapolis, 1973), 2: 393, fn. 24.

10. *City Directory*, Cincinnati, 1843, 3; *Templar's Magazine*, Apr., 1858, 130; Paul E. Johnson, *A Shopkeeper's Millennium: Society and Revivals in Rochester, New York, 1815–1837* (New York, 1978), 119.

11. Whitney R. Cross, *The Burned-over District: The Social and Intellectual History of Enthusiastic Religion in Western New York, 1800–1850* (Ithaca, N.Y., 1950), 12, 269; *Western Temperance Journal*, Aug. 1, 1841.

12. McCreath Family Papers, Pennsylvania State Archives, Young Men's and Young Ladies' Total Abstinence Society of Harrisburg (Pa.), *Fourth Annual Report of the Board of Managers*, 1841, 1.

13. Samuel F. Cary, *Historical Sketch of the Order of the Sons of Temperance: An Address Delivered at the Fortieth Annual Session of the National Division . . .* (Halifax, Nova Scotia, 1884), 3; Francis Lauricella, Jr., "The Devil in Drink: Swedenborgianism in T. S. Arthur's *Ten Nights in a Bar-Room* (1854)," *Perspectives in American History*, 12 (1979): 364.

14. Young Men's and Young Ladies' Total Abstinence Society of Harrisburg, *Report*, 5, 8.

15. Tyrrell, *Sobering Up*, 206.

16. Quoted in John A. Krout, *The Origins of Prohibition* (New York, 1925), 108.

17. Samuel F. Cary, "The Story of the Bottle," in Samuel F. Cary, ed., *The National Temperance Offering, and Sons and Daughters of Temperance Gift* (New York, 1850), 25; *Western Temperance Journal*, Aug. 19, Sept. 15, 1841; *Morning Star*, June 1, 1842; W. H. Daniels, *The Temperance Reform and Its Great Reformers* (Cincinnati, Ohio, 1878), 101, 107.

18. Daniels, *Temperance*, 101, 107; Maxwell, "Washingtonian Movement," 416.

19. Maxwell, "Washingtonian Movement," 427; Tyrrell, *Sobering Up*, 162; Robert Louis Hampel, "Influence and Respectability: Temperance and Prohibition in Massachusetts, 1813–1852" (Ph.D. thesis, Cornell University, 1980), 241–42.

20. D. C. Burdick, *Evolution of Washingtonianism, or Society-Mirror* (Owego, N.Y., 1843), 14, quoted in Paul R. Meyer, Jr., "The Transformation of American Temperance: The Popularization and Radicalization of a Reform Movement, 1813–1860" (Ph.D. thesis, University of Iowa, 1976), 140–41.

21. *Western Christian Advocate*, Nov. 27, 1846; *Morning Star*, June 1, 1842; Krout, *Origins*, 202–4; Tyrrell, "Drink," 142–43, 161.

22. *Ohio Washingtonian Organ and Sons of Temperance Record*, Mar. 14, 1846 (on Jan. 23, 1846, the *Western Washingtonian and Sons of Temperance Record* merged with the *Ohio Temperance Organ* and on Jan. 31, 1846, changed its name to the *Ohio Washingtonian Organ and Sons of Temperance Record*; hereafter, both the *Western Washingtonian* and the *Ohio Washingtonian Organ* are cited as *Record*).

23. P. Peirce, *A History of the Introduction and Progress of the Order of the Sons of Temperance in the State of Ohio* (Cincinnati, Ohio, 1849), 47–48.

24. *Templar's Magazine*, June, 1851, 311.

25. *First Quarterly Report of the Auditor of the Washington Total Abstinence Society, with the Address of the President* (n.p., 1841), 13, quoted in Meyer, "Transformation," 142.

26. B. P. Aydelott, *The Church's Duties in the Temperance Cause* (Cincinnati, Ohio, 1865), 15; Ian R. Tyrrell, "Drink and the Process of Social Reform: From Temperance to Prohibition in Antebellum America, 1813–1860" (Ph.D. thesis, Duke University, 1974), 137–38; David Montgomery, "The Shuttle and the Cross: Weavers and Artisans in the Kensington Riots of 1844," *Journal of Social History*, 5 (1972): 421.

27. *Western Temperance Journal*, June 15, Dec. 31, 1841; *Morning Star*, Aug. 20, 24, 1842; Krout, *Origins*, 201; Tyrrell, "Drink," 159–60.

28. Fletcher, *Diary*, 2: 555 (Nov. 26, 1843); Blumberg, "Significance," 50–51, 64–65.

29. *Templar's Magazine*, June, 1851, 310–311.

30. Maxwell, "Washingtonian Movement," 429–30; Hampel, "Influence," 222.

31. Quoted in Maxwell, "Washingtonian Movement," 425, from John Marsh, *Temperance Recollections* (New York, 1866).

32. Peirce, *History*, 9; *Ohio Organ of the Temperance Reform*, May 27, 1853.

33. Donald W. Beattie, "Sons of Temperance: Pioneers in Total Abstinence and 'Constitutional' Prohibition" (Ph.D. thesis, Boston University, 1966), 75–76, 143, 438; Peirce, *History*, 10 and back cover; International Temperance Conference, *Centennial Temperance Volume* (New York, 1877), 550–51.

34. "S. F. Cary, M.W.P.," in Cary, ed., *Offering*, 29; Samuel F. Cary, *History of College Hill and Vicinity* . . . (n.p., 1886), 5; Charles T. Greve, *Centennial History of Cincinnati and Representative Citizens*, 2 (Chicago, 1904): 530; James H. Rodabaugh, "Robert Hamilton Bishop, Pioneer Educator," *Ohio State Archeological and Historical Quarterly*, 44 (1935): 95; A. H. Upham, "The Centennial of Miami University," *Ohio Archeological and Historical Publications*, 8 (1909): 338. For additional details, see Jed Dannenbaum, "The Crusader: Samuel Cary and Cincinnati Temperance," *Cincinnati Historical Society Bulletin*, 33 (1975): 136–51.

35. "Cary," in Cary, ed., *Offering*, 29.

36. *Garland*, Aug., 1853, 62.

37. *Biographical Encyclopaedia of Ohio of the Nineteenth Century* (Cincinnati, Ohio, 1876), 585.

38. G. Frederick Wright, *Representative Citizens of Ohio: Memorial-Biographical* (Cleveland, Ohio, 1918), 370; *National Cyclopaedia of American Biography*, 11 (New York, 1909): 480; "Cary," in Cary, ed., *Offering*, 30; *Biographical Encyclopaedia of Ohio*, 585.

39. *Record*, Jan. 2, 1847.

40. "Story of the Bottle," in Cary, ed., *Offering*, 27. For discussions of reformist attitudes in the antebellum years, see Sidney E. Mead, *The Lively*

Experiment: The Shaping of Christianity in America (New York, 1963), 90–133; Walter Hugins, ed., *The Reform Impulse, 1825–1850* (New York, 1972), 1–22; John L. Thomas, "Romantic Reform in America, 1815–1865," *American Quarterly*, 17 (1965): 656–81; Cross, *Burned-over*; William McLoughlin, *Revivals, Awakenings, and Reform* (Chicago, 1978).

41. *Biographical Encyclopaedia of Ohio*, 585.

42. Walter S. Glazer, "Taxpayers: 1850," *Cincinnati Historical Society Bulletin*, 25 (1967): 158; *Ohio Organ of the Temperance Reform*, Aug. 19, 1853.

43. *Record*, Oct. 25, 1845, May 9, 1846; Peirce, *History*, 12, 30, 39, 41.

44. Most of the temperance communities whose growth rates could not be included in these figures were too small in 1840 to be listed separately in the census, but were listed, often with substantial populations, by 1850. Several had already become major cities by mid-century (Xenia, Sandusky, Portsmouth). It is therefore likely that if these communities could have been included, they would have raised rather than lowered the average population growth rate for the Sons of Temperance locations. Of the 106 divisions listed in the *Record*, Jan. 30, 1847, twenty-nine were in Cincinnati or Hamilton County, fifty-seven others were on major transportation routes, thirteen more were within seventy-five miles of Cincinnati, three were in communities that could not be located, and four were not in any of these categories. Population statistics are from the *Sixth Census of the United States, 1840* and the *Seventh Census of the United States, 1850*.

45. Stephen Nissenbaum, in a study of Massachusetts communities around 1840, found a strong correlation between the extent of commercialization/industrialization and the degree of temperance agitation (results described in correspondence with the author); see also Tyrrell, *Sobering Up*, 12–13 and *passim*.

In a New York vote for or against liquor licensing in 1846, the median vote against licensing in towns under 1,000 population was 58 percent; in towns between 2,000 and 3,000, 61 percent; and in towns over 4,000, 64 percent. Towns that voted for license had gained only .5 percent population between 1840 and 1845, while towns that voted against license had grown 6.4 percent. Towns that were not on canals or railroads had median votes 60 percent against license, those on canals only, 62 percent, on railroads only, 61 percent; on both canals and railroads, 65 percent (W. J. Rorabaugh, "Prohibition as Progress: New York State's License Elections, 1846," *Journal of Social History*, 25 (1981): 428.

For Vermont, Paul Goodman found that for every 1 percent increase in the proportion of farmers in the population, the support for prohibition in 1853 declined by .8 percent and that for every 1 percent increase in the incidence of manufacturing labor, support for prohibition increased .46 percent (results described in correspondence with the author).

For Virginia, see Pearson and Hendricks, *Liquor*, p. 98.

For Mississippi, see William Graham Davis, "Attacking 'the Matchless

Evil': Temperance and Prohibition in Mississippi, 1817–1908" (Ph.D. thesis, Mississippi State University, 1975), 1–11.

For Ontario, a study has found that temperance reform was active primarily where "the processes of growth and modernization were most pronounced," and that at the inception of the movement "resistance was most pronounced in the rural parts of the province . . ." (Frank Laurie Barron, "The Genesis of Temperance in Ontario, 1828–1850" (Ph.D. thesis, University of Guelph, 1976), 92, 133).

For Ireland, a study of the Father Mathew temperance movement of the late 1830s and 1840s has found: "It was from the towns, small though they were in proportion to the rural population that the Mathewite movement . . . emerged. The Mathewites were urban-based with a small activist group in each town acting as a central focus of activity" (H. F. Kearney, "Fr Mathew: Apostle of Modernization," in A. Cosgrove and D. M. McCartney, eds., *Studies in Irish History Presented to R. Dudley Edwards* (Dublin, 1979), 172).

For England, Brian Harrison has written that "teetotalism in nineteenth-century England stood for 'urban intelligence as against agricultural rusticity'" (Brian Harrison, *Drink and the Victorians: The Temperance Question in England, 1815–1872* (London, 1871), 149).

For Georgia, see W. J. Rorabaugh, "The Sons of Temperance in Antebellum Jasper County," *Georgia Historical Quarterly*, 64 (1980): 263–79.

For North Carolina, see Tyrrell, *Sobering Up*, 276–78.

For the connection between temperance reform and social dislocation in two small but rapidly growing communities, see Don H. Doyle, *The Social Order of a Frontier Community: Jacksonville, Illinois, 1825–70* (Urbana, Ill., 1978), 137–39, 212–17, 223–26; and Stuart Blumin, *The Urban Threshold: Growth and Change in a Nineteenth-Century American Community* (Chicago, 1976), 145–47. The temperance movement maintained strength in urban areas into the late nineteenth and early twentieth centuries: see Norman H. Clark, *The Dry Years: Prohibition and Social Change in Washington* (Seattle, 1965), 114–22; James H. Timberlake, *Prohibition and the Progressive Movement, 1900–1920* (Cambridge, Mass., 1963), 150–52; Jack S. Blocker, Jr., *Retreat from Reform: The Prohibition Movement in the United States, 1890–1913* (Westport, Conn., 1976), 10.

46. Harry N. Scheiber, *Ohio Canal Era: A Case Study of Government and the Economy* (Athens, Ohio, 1969), 221; Glazer, "Taxpayers," 156–60. Population: 46,382 in 1840, 115,538 in 1850; industrial output: $18 million in 1840, $54 million in 1850.

47. Doyle, "Voluntary Associations," 336, 346; Harrison, *Drink*, 32; Robin M. Williams, Jr., *American Society: A Sociological Interpretation* (New York, 1960), 498; Rowland Berthoff, "The American Social Order: A Conservative Hypothesis," *American Historical Review*, 65 (1960): 507, and *An Unsettled People: Social Order and Disorder in American History* (New York, 1971), 274; Sam Bass Warner, Jr., *The Private City: Philadelphia in Three Periods of Growth* (Philadelphia, 1968), 61–62; Noel P. Gist, *Se-*

cret Societies: A Cultural Study of Fraternalism in the United States (Columbia, Mo., 1940), 143; Arthur J. Vidich and Joseph Bensman, *Small Town in Mass Society: Class, Power and Religion in a Rural Community* (Princeton, N.J., 1968), 22–25.

48. Rorabaugh, "Sons in Jasper County," 272.

49. Robert V. Wells, "Women's Lives Transformed: Demographic and Family Patterns in America, 1600–1970," in Carol Ruth Berkin and Mary Beth Norton, eds., *Women of America: A History* (Boston, 1979), 24; *Ohio Washingtonian Organ and Sons of Temperance Record*, Feb. 14, 1846; Beattie, "Sons," 164, 398; *Cincinnati Commercial*, Feb. 11, Mar. 23, Nov. 17, Dec. 2, 1847, Feb. 13, 1849; *Ohio Organ of the Temperance Reform*, Feb. 11, 1853.

50. Theo. A. Ross, *Odd Fellowship: Its History and Manual* (New York, 1895), 2–3.

51. Scheiber, *Canal*, 212–46.

52. Peirce, *History*, 118.

53. Cary, *Historical Sketch*, 11; Peirce, *History*, 118.

54. *Record*, Aug. 7, 1847; Peirce, *History*, 88

55. *Record*, July 31, 1847; Peirce, *History*, 97.

56. Sons of Temperance of North America, *Journal of the Proceedings of the National Division of the Sons of Temperance of North America, 1849*, 6–7; Beattie, "Sons," 286–87.

57. *Cincinnati Commercial*, Nov. 3, 1847.

58. W. J. Rorabaugh, "Estimated U.S. Alcoholic Beverage Consumption, 1790–1860," *Journal of Studies on Alcohol*, 37 (1976): 360–61 (figures are calculated for the population aged fifteen and over); Norman H. Clark, *Deliver Us from Evil: An Interpretation of American Prohibition* (New York, 1976), 20.

59. *Templar's Magazine*, Dec., 1859, 381.

60. *Cincinnati Commercial*, Apr. 6, 1846.

61. *Templar's Magazine*, Apr., 1851, 249.

62. The linkage rate for occupations (144 of 164) was 87.8 percent. More than half of the Sons in the building trades had demonstrated upward occupational mobility by 1856; for example, carpenters had become lumberyard proprietors or contractors. Robert Hampel has found that in Beverly, Mass., between 1847 and 1857, 80.6 percent of the local Sons of Temperance were skilled workers, and in Salem, Mass., 62 percent were skilled workers (Hampel, "Influence," 298–304). Paul Meyer has examined Sons of Temperance membership lists from divisions in Boston and Salem and has found 48 percent and 67 percent of the members respectively were skilled laborers (Meyer, "Transformation," 212). The Sons of Temperance membership list used for this study includes every member mentioned in the *Record*, in Peirce, *History*, or in Sons of Temperance of North America, Grand Division of Ohio, *Proceedings . . .* (Cincinnati, Ohio, 1847–48), for the period from 1845 to 1850. For discussions of occupational categories, see Clyde Griffen, "The Study of Occupational Mobility in Nineteenth-century Amer-

ica: Problems and Possibilities," *Journal of Social History*, 5 (1972): 310–30; and Michael B. Katz, "Occupational Classification in History," *Journal of Interdisciplinary History*, 3 (1972): 63–88.

63. The occupational distribution of Cincinnati's labor force is derived from a compilation of occupations employing ten or more, from the comprehensive list in Charles Cist, *Sketches and Statistics of Cincinnati in 1851* (Cincinnati, Ohio, 1851), 49–51.

64. Of the remaining Cincinnati Sons, 9 percent were commercial employees, 1 percent were in public service, and 2 percent did not list occupations in the city directory.

65. Rutherford B. Hayes, *Diary and Letters of Rutherford Birchard Hayes*, ed. Charles R. Williams (Columbus, Ohio, 1922), vol. 1, diary entries for Nov. 4, 19, 1850.

66. Peirce, *History*, 47–49; *Record*, Mar. 28, Apr. 11, 1846; Beattie, "Sons," 156; Tyrrell, "Drink," 168.

67. Peirce, *History*, 23.

68. *Record*, June 20, 1846, Aug. 9, 1845; Peirce, *History*, 9, 23.

69. Krout, *Origins*, 211.

70. *Templar's Magazine*, Sept., 1850, 17–20, Oct., 1850, 33–35; Cary, *Historical Sketch*, 14; Tyrrell, *Sobering Up*, 214.

71. *Templar's Magazine*, Oct., 1850, 37.

72. Peirce, *History*, 119; Cary, *Historical Sketch*, 11, 15–16.

73. *Cincinnati Commercial*, Nov. 3, 1847.

74. Peirce, *History*, 116–17.

75. *Ohio Organ of the Temperance Reform*, Apr. 22, 1853.

3

The Shift to Prohibition

The temperance movement underwent a profound transformation in the middle years of the nineteenth century. As late as the mid-1840s there was little to indicate that drink was about to become one of the dominant political issues of the day. Yet within the space of a few years the focus of temperance activism shifted from socially oriented organizations like the Washingtonians and the Sons of Temperance to powerful public political coalitions that ran statewide election campaigns with their own slates of candidates.

The turn to political action signaled not only a realignment in the tactics and organizational structure of the temperance movement but also a major change in its social philosophy. From its inception through the peak years of the fraternal phase, temperance reform had been based primarily on the principles of moral suasion. Reformers sought to convert society to temperance principally through argument, persuasion, education, and example. Yet by 1853 the temperance movement throughout the country had abandoned moral suasion and instead sought a temperate society through the legislative power of state governments. It had become a movement for prohibition, the outlawing of all alcoholic drink.[1]

Washingtonianism and fraternal temperance in the 1840s had been, in large part, responses to the social and economic changes that accompanied the rapid urban growth and commercialization of the United States. But they were concerned

principally with the personal lives of their members and prospective members, and drew upon the effects of social dislocation on the individual. By the late 1840s, however, the basic
concerns of the temperance crusade altered in the face of new
and frightening problems confronting the community as a
whole. The pace of change in basic economic and social structures grew ever more rapid, and its effects were suddenly intensified toward the end of the decade by massive waves of
immigration from Ireland and Germany. As a result, many
communities at mid-century were beset with widespread social
disorder in the form of burgeoning slums, growing numbers of
impoverished residents, marked increases in crime, and frightening epidemics of disease, as well as more frequent incidents
of Sabbath-breaking, rowdiness, and disturbances of the peace.

Temperance activists had long believed that social disorder was almost entirely the result of the use of alcohol. They
attributed the heightened level of disorder to increased alcoholic consumption, and their earlier confidence in the steady
progress of temperance reform quickly turned to despair as
they concluded that the movement was in fact losing the battle
against alcohol. Many began to wonder whether the evil of
drink could ever be eradicated through example and persuasion only. In addition, other factors—the emergence of a disease concept of alcoholism among reformers, the growth of a
powerful, centralized drink industry, the inaccessibility of immigrants to moral suasion appeals, the inadequacy of fraternal
temperance, the experience of the temperance movement in the
antilicensing campaigns of the 1840s, and the increasing willingness of a public frightened by disorder to consider drastic
measures of control—all helped to propel temperance activists
away from moral suasion and toward legal prohibition.

The decade of the 1840s experienced the highest urban
growth rate of any decade in American history. The percentage
increase of urban population for those ten years was nearly
half again as large as the rate during the 1830s (92.1 percent
compared to 63.7 percent), and much of the growth in the for-
ties must have come after recovery from the depression of
1839–43. The rate of increase was highest in the Midwest,

where the proportion of urban dwellers in the region more than doubled (3.9 to 9.2 percent).[2]

Although migration from rural areas of the United States continued to account for much of the urban growth, foreign immigration, particularly from Ireland and the German states, reached unprecedented levels in the late 1840s. Nearly one-third as many immigrants arrived in just one year, 1847, as arrived in the entire period between 1819 and 1840 (235,000 compared to 743,000.) The vast majority of these new immigrants settled in America's growing urban communities. Over one and a half million immigrants arrived in the United States during the decade, which, given the total population of the country in 1840, would be proportionally equivalent to roughly 20 million immigrants arriving during the 1980s. Significantly, the immigrants of the 1840s were not only culturally dissimilar from native-born Americans—nearly four-fifths (78 percent) were either Irish or German—but they generally came with less money and fewer skills than had earlier immigrants.[3]

The floods of poor migrants and immigrants to urban areas accelerated the development of a class of urban working poor. Cheap wage labor helped to produce a period of dramatic economic expansion after the return of prosperity in 1843. Between that year and 1860, domestic trade multiplied tenfold, and the total value of U.S. imports and exports rose over fivefold. At the same time class and ethnic differences produced tensions within communities. Without adequate intracity transportation systems, urban density rose precipitously within the limits of the old "walking city." Cheap housing for laborers sprang up near the docks, warehouses, and manufactories, while the filth, noise, disease, and disorder of those areas drove wealthier citizens toward the community's outskirts.[4]

Urban blight and congestion, residential segregation along class and ethnic lines, competition for jobs, demands on inadequate public welfare systems: all these factors led to marked increases in American social disorder at mid-century. Individual crimes of violence and theft rose sharply, as did the cost of poor relief. Major cities established their first full-time professional police forces, boards of health, and fire departments, and tightened regulations for poor relief eligibility. Poverty and crime became the pre-eminent public concerns of urban communities by the late 1840s and early 1850s.[5]

Cincinnati, like many other American communities at mid-century, was confronted with the poverty, slums, crime, and other disorder that had resulted from rapid immigration, population growth, and economic expansion. The city's industrial output increased from $18 million to $54 million during the 1840s, real estate values grew from $5 million to nearly $33 million, and the population, 46,000 in 1840, stood at 115,000 at mid-century, an average yearly increase of about 7,000 inhabitants. Even these figures of total population growth, remarkable though they are, do not reflect anything like the true number of people who lived in the city at some time during the decade and then moved on, or who passed through as transient workers on the river, canal, railroad, or wagon routes.[6]

Hemmed in by a semicircle of hills, the city could not expand geographically to meet the housing demands of the new residents. Population density therefore soared and ugly congested slums sprang up, particularly along the waterfront in wards 3, 4, and 6 (see Figure 1). The wealthy began to abandon the plush downtown areas of ward 5 and the western ward 2 between Third and Fourth Streets, moving beyond the heavily populated flat portion of the city to the spacious carriage-commuting areas of Clifton, Mt. Adams, Mt. Auburn, and Walnut Hills.[7]

The residential areas of the city became increasingly segregated not only by class but by ethnicity. Foreign-born residents accounted for 44 percent of Cincinnati's population in 1850; of these, most were either German (26 percent of the city total), or Irish (12 percent of the city total). The Irish settled primarily close to the waterfront, in wards 1, 2, 3, 4, and 6. Germans situated themselves predominantly in wards 9, 10, 11, and 12, an area north of the Miami Canal that quickly became known as the "Over-the-Rhine" district.[8]

These immigrant newcomers had fewer skills and were less prosperous than earlier immigrants; they often lived in the worst housing and took the lowest-paying jobs. Understandably, they also accounted for a disproportionate amount of those on the city welfare rolls; two-thirds of those granted in-

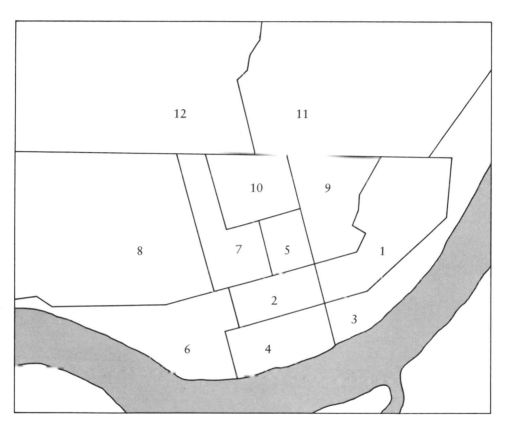

Figure 1. Cincinnati wards, c. 1851.

door relief (food and shelter in the Cincinnati Hospital) in 1848 were foreign-born. The most destitute were the Irish, who, as peasants fleeing the potato famine in Ireland in the late 1840s, often arrived penniless. Irish alone, 12 percent of the city's population, made up 40 percent of the cases of indoor relief in 1848. By 1853, four-fifths of relief recipients were immigrants, despite a new rule requiring applicants to have resided in the city for at least one year.[9]

Immigrants also were associated with criminal activity out of proportion to their members. In 1845, only 28 percent of the inmates in the Hamilton County jail were foreign-born. By 1848 the figure stood at 54 percent. City arrest records first specified nativity in 1863, when immigrants accounted for 65 percent of the total.[10] Some of the poorest, most squalid immigrant slums developed reputations for spawning murder, brawling, robbery, prostitution, gambling, and public drunkenness. The German "Sausage Row" (Cassily's Row) "would furnish facts sufficient for a book of the darkest and most fiendish crimes," according to one account.[11] The Irish saloons along the wharf's "Rat Row" were prolific sources of brawls, stabbings, and shootings. Most notorious of all was "Gas Alley," a predominantly Irish section of ward 6, abutting the city gas works, "filled with wretched hovels," the *Commercial* reported, containing "more haunts of vice and depravity, in their most immoral forms, than at any other point within the city limits. Alcohol is the undisputed king of these domains, and reigns supreme, having loathsome Prostitution for his queen consort, and Murder and Theft for his prime ministers."[12]

Although some of these figures and accounts may reflect prejudice directed against immigrants, it is also probable that the foreign-born did generate higher crime rates in the community. Young adult males, who commit an inordinate share of the crimes in most cultures, made up a disproportionately large share of the city's immigrant population. Moreover, many of these young males had no families with them, or had no plans to settle permanently in the city, and thus felt fewer familial and communal restraints on their behavior. Finally, the destitute condition of many of the foreign-born no doubt drove some to acts of crime.[13]

The influx of immigrants in the late 1840s greatly intensified the impact of the social disorder bred by rapid growth
and expansion. Rising crime and poverty had, by mid-century,
become constant topics of public concern. Many residents began to perceive not only an increase in the proportion of poor
people in the city but a change in the type of people found in
poverty. In addition to the "unfortunate and virtuous poor" [14]
—the widows, orphans, elderly, and handicapped—who were
considered chronically indigent through no fault of their own,
they also saw able-bodied men and women living on the edge
of poverty and easily driven to charity during economic hard
times. The Cincinnati Hospital, which administered both indoor and outdoor relief (handouts of food and firewood), reported in 1847 that the "increase of our cities,—the increase
of our Foreign Commerce,—the increase of manufactures, in
fine, all that sort of civilization, which drives men from the
cultivation of the soil, more or less tends to enlarge the class of
the Poor." By rendering men "more dependent on the fluctua-
tions of Trade and Government," the advance of commercial
civilization was especially enlarging the "class . . . denominated
the Out Door Poor," those "whom any sudden depression of
society will greatly increase, and any advance in prosperity will
decrease." [15] The writer of this report, however, was the exception at the time; few others were willing to blame increased
poverty on economic development. Most sought other expla-
nations for the destitute condition of the able-bodied poor.

The poor were not only increasing and changing in type,
but they were living at a level of poverty unlike anything
known in the past. Those few well-off citizens who ventured
into the city's slums saw whole families, devoid of hope, living
in unimaginable degradation, filth, and squalor. A *Commercial* reporter peered into a "small, dirty, dilapidated" tenement
room, filled with "confused heaps of filthy rags for beds, and a
meagre supply of old and broken furniture. The room seemed
to serve for all the cooking, eating and sleeping that was done
by the family." The children there were growing up "breathing
foul air, drinking filthy water and surrounded by a pestilent
moral atmosphere." [16] One impoverished mother informed a
shocked Methodist minister that she had "kept herself and

four children on dry bread for a whole week, and only thirty-seven and a half cents worth of it at that."[17] A *Commercial* editorial captured both the shame and the terror of these slums when it wrote of their inhabitants: "None care for them; they know it, and consequently disregard their own fates as well as the world's opinions. They feel they are doomed to the wretched squalor of their present state of misery and neglect, and . . . writhe out their woeful day of reckless indifference, like a den of pent-up serpents, amongst themselves."[18]

This dismal scene of intense poverty aroused the humanitarian concern of many Cincinnatians who increasingly involved themselves in efforts to aid the needy. However, the development of a degraded, desperate class of poor stimulated not only philanthropy but fear as well. Slums, those dens of "pent-up serpents" in the *Commercial*'s words, held an implicit threat of danger to the community, a danger that became explicit and concrete through the sudden increase of crime in Cincinnati during these years.

In 1845 all of Hamilton County reported only 873 arrests. By 1853 the number had risen to 6,769 in the city alone. Arrests for felony crimes against persons had climbed from 115 in the county to 409 in Cincinnati, and for felony crimes against property from 188 to 486. This might be attributed in part to the gradual development in these years of a modern police force, which replaced the city marshal and night watch system. However, local murders, always featured prominently in the daily newspapers, rose from only three in 1846 to twenty-two in 1854.[19]

Whatever the actual increase in lawlessness, citizens perceived a dramatic rise in both violence and immorality. "Some fifteen years ago," claimed the *Cincinnati Enquirer* in 1853, "a murder in Cincinnati was but a yearly event. . . . Now, how changed! . . . in our city scarcely a week floats off that the bowie knife or the pistol ball has not laid a human being low with the dead."[20] The *Commercial* believed that "as matters now stand, no man is safe in the streets; even *boys* sport their pistols! Strumpets have a wide range in the most prominent localities, and insult respectable ladies; vagabonds assail innocent men in the streets or go unmolested to brickbat or stone respectable houses."[21] "We know of no city in the Union," it wrote later, "where vice has increased to so alarming an extent, within the last few years, as this."[22] The respected and wealthy physician Daniel Drake, assaulted by a blackjack-wielding "footpad" directly in front of his home, wrote to his daughter: "Our city seems greatly infested with bad men."[23] The *Commercial* estimated that Cincinnati harbored at least 3,000 professional criminals.[24]

Poverty and violent crime were the foremost but by no means the only aspects of social disorder to concern Cincinnati's residents. They also complained of increased juvenile delinquency, prostitution, gambling, rowdiness, Sabbath-breaking, disturbances of the peace, and noxious filth and pollution in the water, in the air, and on the streets. One of the most frightening problems was epidemic disease; the worst cholera epidemic in Cincinnati's history scourged the city in the summer of 1849, claiming over 4,000 lives.[25]

Poverty, violence, crime, immorality, and disease profoundly disturbed Cincinnati's inhabitants by the early 1850s. The desperate plight of the poor stirred humanitarian consciences. Sordid and corrupting behavior outraged public morality. The burden of taxes weighed heavier on all property owners. And fear, the threat of physical danger, undermined many a citizen's complacency and security.

Temperance crusaders had long believed that most social problems emanated from the use of alcohol. The first annual report of the American Temperance Society in 1827 had noted "the relation between the sale of spirituous liquors and the production of pauperism, crime, madness, and death. . . ."[26] Cincinnati physician Daniel Drake, in an 1841 Washingtonian address, berated those in the drink trade for seeking profit "in the consumption by society of that which poisons its prosperity, generates disorder and idleness, impoverishes families, & stocks our poor houses, jails & penitentiaries with wretches and criminals. . . ."[27] Temperance reformers had been concerned about social problems such as poverty and crime since the earliest days of the movement, and had long promised that universal temperance would greatly reduce these problems.

But by mid-century the pace of mass immigration, urban growth, and economic expansion had created an unprecedented level of community disorder, which was increasing at an alarming rate. The link between social problems and alcohol ceased to be just one concern of the temperance movement and instead became a central, overriding preoccupation.

The frightening disorders confronting Cincinnatians at mid-century presented temperance reformers with a disturbing dilemma. If, as they believed, most social problems emanated from the use of alcohol, then increasing disorder seemed to indicate increasing alcohol consumption. First-hand accounts usually bore out this conclusion; the *Commercial*, for example, reported in late 1847: "That the tide of intemperance was for years rolled back, statistics and observation prove—that it is now advancing with fearful rapidity is equally proved by statistics and observation."[28] Temperance activists, rather than making progress toward their goal of a truly temperate society, appeared instead to be losing ground in the battle against drink. Yet, with disorder severely threatening the stability, morality, security, and humaneness of the community, temperance reform seemed more urgently needed than ever before. The social problems which demonstrated to the temperance reformers their failure in the past also proved to them that their future success was vitally necessary for the well-being of American society.[29]

Although responding primarily to the problems of their own community, Cincinnati's reformers were well aware, through the national fraternal temperance organizations and through the steady exchange of news items among temperance journals, that similar problems existed throughout the country. They therefore usually saw their crusade as an attempt not merely to rescue their community from disorder and decay but to save the entire nation from destruction. Cincinnati, like all America's large cities, was "a great cancer and its deadly influence is involving all that is good and hopeful in the body politic, and the body ecclesiastic for a hundred miles around," wrote Samuel Cary in the Cincinnati-based *Ohio Organ of the Temperance Reform*.[30] Cary pointed to Babylon, Nineveh, Alexander's empire, and Rome as "nations, once prosperous and powerful under the benign influence of temperance principles, [which] were reduced to effeminacy and poverty, through excessive indulgence . . . [in alcohol]."[31] The social disorder of mid-century convinced the temperance crusaders that, more than ever before, America's future greatness stood at stake in the fight against drink.

Temperance activists had no doubt that the problems besetting the city were induced by liquor. When word of the spread of cholera reached Cincinnati in 1849, temperance reformers circulated claims of the benefits which would result from adopting the total abstinence pledge to combat the disease: "Temperance and cleanliness constitute the great secret of health and if these are strictly adhered to we will have no reason to fear cholera or any other disease as an epidemic."[32] In the aftermath of the disease the head of the city's Temple of Honor noted with satisfaction that "not one single member of our National Temple, and very few of the members of our Order, have been carried off by this terrible scourge."[33] Temperance reformers' claims that drinking created a predisposition to cholera have in fact been borne out in part by modern medical findings. The chronic gastritis and other digestive irregularities that often accompany heavy drinking do make the body somewhat more vulnerable to the disease.[34]

Crime and alcohol were also directly linked in temperance thought. Some people were obviously more prone to violent behavior when drunk. Criminals reported that they drank before committing crimes to steel their nerves. Intemperance, according to temperance activists, engendered sloth and dissolution, which in turn encouraged a life of crime. Overall, criminals as a class appeared to be unquestionably within the grip of alcohol's evil power. The *Record* claimed that "two-thirds of all crimes committed in the State" were the product of intemperance.[35] Samuel Cary believed that "if all the liquor of this city could be annihilated at once . . . we should have but little business for our police court, or use for the rookery or jail."[36] Judges and lawyers within the temperance movement attested to the link between crime and alcohol from their own professional experiences. The frequent accounts in the daily newspapers of brawls, assaults, and various heinous crimes committed by those either intoxicated or known to be heavy drinkers seemed to make the relationship incontrovertible.

Poverty was also clearly linked to alcohol in the minds of temperance advocates. Examples abounded of wealthy men, or young men of promise, who had sipped from the bottle and ended destitute in the gutter. Workers, if they saved what otherwise might be spent on the drink habit, could accumulate capital, which might eventually move them up the economic and social ladder, or at least help cushion them during hard times. Sobriety was, in addition, an admirable and beneficial work habit, promoting industriousness and winning the good will of employers. "Intemperance is the leading cause of pauperism in every community," Unitarian minister and temperance activist A. A. Livermore told his congregation.[37] Another temperance advocate, Captain Charles Ross, director of the city infirmary and overseer of Cincinnati's public poor relief, believed that "if the use of intoxicating drinks can be done with, 5 percent on the amount now levied and disbursed will be amply sufficient in this city for poor purposes, *if not an entire abolition of the whole concern.*"[38]

Drink, the reformers believed, lay at the root of most other growing social evils. Juvenile delinquency resulted from parental neglect and from "the wickedness of street life,"[39] both promoted by liquor. Insanity was another fruit of intemperance. Drink led to madness either directly by destroying reason or indirectly by creating emotional despair through destruction of health, family, and prosperity.[40] Sabbath-breaking, gambling, prostitution, and disturbances of the peace all had their origins in the effects of alcoholic beverages.

The social problems generated by drink, moreover, were expensive. Livermore lamented that "during the present year, taxes have risen to $18.50 on a thousand, a good portion of which has gone to pay for pauperism and crime, created by spirituous liquors. . . ."[41] Eliminating intemperance, claimed another reformer, would "prevent the disorders of your city, and empty your prisons and alms-houses, and diminish your taxes fifty per cent. . . ."[42]

To a community troubled and burdened with social changes

"The Beginning and the End: Wine at the Dinner; The Club; Billiards; Respectable Bar; Grogery; The Last of All, Alms House/Potters Field." (from Stebbins and brown, *Fifty Years History*)

"Bar of Destruction." (from James Shaw, *History of the Great Temperance Reforms of the Nineteenth Century*, 1875)

"Poor Drunkard." (from Shaw, *History*)

"Specimen of the Work Done Inside." (from Shaw, *History*)

THE UNLICENSED ROBBER.

Highwayman: " *Your money OR your life.*"

THE LICENSED ROBBER.

Rumseller: " *Your money AND your life.*"

"The Unlicensed Robber/The Licensed Robber." (from Daniel Dorchester, *The Liquor Problem in All Ages*, 1884)

it could not fully comprehend, the temperance reformers presented an explanation both plausible and comprehensible. Most prominent and articulate Cincinnatians generally agreed with them. Newspaper editors, clergymen, businessmen, local officials, even those most vociferously critical of the organized temperance movement, all readily admitted that excessive use of alcohol was a prolific source of social evil. It would have been difficult to find anyone of respectable position at mid-century who opposed the abstract principle of "temperance."

But, for many, temperance still meant moderation, not total abstinence. If someone of high social standing wanted to enjoy a glass of fine wine with dinner, or if a laborer desired a tankard of beer after work, why should they deny themselves because of the inability of others to control their drinking? In this view, occasional moderate drinking set a good example, since it demonstrated that truly moral men could triumph over temptation without aids. Inebriation was the failing of the individual, a sign of moral weakness. "Drunkenness comes from a depraved appetite, and a blunted moral sense," wrote the *Cincinnati Times*. "All outward evils are the result of internal evil or error, spiritual, moral or intellectual—for diseases correspond to the lusts and passions of the mind."[43] Nathan B. Marsh, superintendent in 1854 of the new city infirmary for the poor, asserted that "pauperism is begotten of drunkenness, nursed in the lap of self-indulgence, and taught lies and laziness, ingratitude and wastefulness. . . . I find that however plausible their demeanor, all [the poor] possess some moral defect. . . ."[44] These critics concluded that society owed little to the drunkard, and instead would be wise to "punish drunkards and drunkenness as severely as possible. . . ."[45]

In contrast, most temperance advocates by mid-century assigned the culpability for drunkenness to the drink manufacturers and sellers and, ultimately, to the society that bestowed upon them social respectability and legal protection. Drunkards themselves were blameless, the victims of the drink trade's evil rapaciousness. Even in the early years of temperance reform, when drinking was seen by all as a personal moral failing, drink selling was nevertheless frowned upon. As early as 1833 a national temperance convention had declared that the traffic in spirits was immoral and deserved severe condemnation. After the shift to total abstinence in the mid-1830s, attacks on the morality of all drink selling became frequent, but were still accompanied by condemnations of drinkers. As one Cincinnati leader remarked, "the traffic [in intoxicating beverages] is as bad as the use."[46]

The Washingtonians, with their sympathy for the drunkard, began to see drinkers as the tempted prey of greedy drink sellers. Moreover, when many drunkards obviously sincere in their desire to reform nevertheless fell back into their old ways, Washingtonians began to understand that constant inebriation was a disease, not just a bad habit. Daniel Drake classified alcohol as a narcotic in 1843, and a year later compared its effect to that of opium; both, he stated, "modify our physiology in such a way, that we are miserable when deprived of them. . . ."[47] The *Record* in 1846 compared drinking to hydrophobia and questioned why Americans did not show as much sympathy for the victims of drink as they did for the victims of rabies, and the same hatred for the "mad dog" liquor seller as for his canine counterpart.[48] Although as late at the 1870s most physicians continued to view alcohol dependency as a moral failing, temperance reformers generally understood alcoholism as a disease by the mid-1840s, and believed that no one, however moral, was necessarily safe from its ravages. As the *Record* warned its readers, "We know not the powers and caprices of our own minds."[49] A moderate drinker at any time might "go hence rapidly to a drunkard's hell."[50] The only secure course was total abstinence.

Temperance activists therefore bitterly opposed the idea that moderate drinking set a good example. Wine at weddings, dinner and evening parties, the use of alcohol as a medicine: here lay the seeds of destruction as described in a Cincinnati temperance sermon. Next came moderate drinking, daily indulgence, public dinners, oyster suppers, and gambling rooms. "The public bar is the last and lowest scene—the drunkard's hell. . . ."[51] By the time drinkers might realize their peril, it was too late; the enslaving effect of alcohol had taken over, and they were "in bondage to the Devil, . . . a more degrading and damning servitude than that which the poor negro is subjected to."[52] Far from being personally responsible for their plight, drunkards were instead totally helpless in the clutches of drink. Many who wanted to reform simply could not. "We know of scores of poor, wretched inebriates," the *Organ* reported, "whose seared eyes weep over their degradation, and whose every word and look, and even their filthy rags, beseech us to take away from them the temptation."[53] As the effects of alcoholism became clearer to the temperance reformers, they despaired of rescuing drunkards from their uncontrollable need as long as the drink sellers could still tempt and ply them with alcohol. Only the elimination of all liquor selling, some concluded, could save drunkards from their addiction. This changed attitude toward alcoholism, which shifted responsibility for personal behavior away from the individual and toward society as a whole, undergirded the temperance movement's abandonment of moral suasion and shift to advocacy of legal prohibition.

In addition, the influx of immigrants during the 1840s further eroded temperance reformers' belief in the efficacy of moral suasion. It not only seemed useless for helping confirmed inebriates, but increasingly it appeared inadequate as a method of warning steady drinkers, potential drunkards, of their peril. In the metropolis of Cincinnati immigrants lived and often worked in separate sections of the city, read their own newspapers, elected their own politicians, sent their children to their own schools, and frequently spoke no English. Merely to reach these isolated groups with temperance teachings was a formidable problem, and to convert each one through moral suasion to a life of total abstinence seemed an overwhelming task. The temperance forces thus faced another impasse, another apparent failure for the tactics of the 1840s.

As temperance reformers grew more aware of the difficulties inherent in the moral suasion approach to liquor reform, they also began to suspect that they faced another, more insidious obstacle: the "Rum Power." The Washingtonian revival had shifted the moral onus of drink from the imbiber to the seller, and most liquor retailers were undoubtedly hostile to temperance reform. But the Rum Power, as it came to be thought of by the crusaders, constituted a much greater force than simply the individual opposition of a multitude of saloon keepers. Instead, it appeared to be "a secret and organized band" of distillers, brewers, wine makers, wholesalers, and retailers, heavily financed, highly efficient, and bent on political corruption, deceitful propaganda, and the harassing and besmirching of temperance activists.[54] Acting in coordination, the liquor traffickers became a formidable enemy to reform. Their effectiveness was enhanced by their ability to operate behind the scenes through "secret cabals"[55] and "secret auxiliaries,"[56] away from public scrutiny. They commanded "untold wealth,"[57] and they used it, vaguely but ominously, "to put down temperance men."[58] The mix of fact and fiction in these fears is impossible to determine. Temperance rhetoric portrayed the drink industry as such an awesomely organized and dramatically conspiratorial enemy that the descriptions inevitably sound unrealistic, even paranoid. In 1858 Samuel Cary wrote, "What makes the whisky influence so insatiable? . . . the secret is that the adversaries of prohibition come in solid column: they are united when the craft is in danger. Political ties are like a spider's web when the trade is in peril. . . . The liquor power is unquestionably the mightiest power in the Republic. It can make or re-make officers, from President to constable."[59]

Cary's rhetoric is certainly exaggerated, but his underlying assessment should not be totally discounted. The manufacture and trade of alcoholic beverages had become an important part of the local economy by mid-century. The number of whiskey distilleries had increased from three to thirty-eight during the 1840s, and the value of their product rose from $145,000 to nearly $3 million. The production of other distilled spirits, wine, ale, and beer accounted for an additional $2 million of manufactures, while another $2 million worth of whiskey passed through the city each year in trade. Drink manufacturing employed nearly 850 workers directly; in addition, an estimated 1,200 saloon keepers and hundreds of other construction, transportation, and commercial workers profited indirectly from the industry.[60]

The drink trade did command both money and political influence, it did fear the effect of the temperance movement, and it did organize to combat temperance reform. Cincinnati's liquor importers, manufacturers, dealers, brewers, and wine producers joined together openly in 1855 to form the "Free Traders Association," in order to support antiprohibition candidates and "for the purpose of resisting all assaults upon our personal rights and liberties, and for the protection of our property, and character from insult."[61] How much more might have been done in secret cannot be determined. In any case, the specter of the Rum Power had a strong effect on temperance reformers. They began to see the drink trade as a mighty and entrenched enemy that would continue to spread corruption and ruin for its own evil gain unless it were rooted out and totally destroyed.

By mid-century, then, a variety of influences impelled the temperance movement toward a radical change in its tactics. Drunkards, the reformers had come to believe, were incapable of helping themselves. They were enslaved victims of the liquor trade, and desired liberation as avidly as the slaves of the South. But, just as the abolitionists had failed to free the slaves through moral suasion, so too did the temperance reformers find moral suasion insufficient to liberate the drunkard from the Rum Power, implacable in its greed, powerful in its wealth and political influence, respectable in social standing, and, above all, protected by the law. The decline of the fraternal temperance movement and the inaccessibility of the new immigrants made moral suasion appear all the more hopeless. Most important, social disorder injected a sense of extreme urgency into the movement. All society stood direly threatened and only a speedy and complete temperance reform held out hope for stability, morality, safety, and a truly humane society. New and perhaps drastic measures were needed to attack and cut off intemperance at its source.

The problems, failures, and impasses of Cincinnati's temperance movement in the late 1840s engendered a search for some new approach, some tactical breakthrough, that would once again put the movement on the offensive. Samuel Cary, the leader of the temperance crusade in the city and the state, was the first to point the way. In a tremendously influential pamphlet published late in 1847 entitled *Cary's Appeal to the People of Ohio*, Cary anticipated by several years the future direction of the movement.

The pamphlet began with a fairly straightforward attack on the "traffic in intoxicating drinks [and] those who are engaged in it." The drink trade, Cary asserted, "multiplies paupers, maniacs and criminals. It increases taxation, and endangers the security of life and property. It furnishes a place of resort for idle and vicious persons, perils the peace and quiet of neighborhoods, and furnishes schools of vice for the young."[62] These were common themes in temperance rhetoric and not in themselves surprising.

However, Cary soon left these familiar subjects behind. The rest of the pamphlet elaborated his startling assertion that "moral appliances alone, cannot arrest the traffic." In the next section, entitled "The Traffic Must Be Branded as Criminal," Cary concluded that it was imperative to declare the sale of intoxicating beverages "a crime and punish it as such." The long-standing acceptance of liquor selling in society, and the respectability of its retailers, did not make it any less a crime: "The African Slave trade was once not only recognized as a lawful trade, but the guilty thieves who stole negroes from the coast of Africa were many of them church members; now they are hung up as pirates." One of the injustices of society was that there were laws to punish thieves, murderers, gamblers, swearers, and Sabbath-breakers, but none to punish the sale of liquor, the root cause of these evils. Society must "consign the incorrigible rumsellers to the prisons now occupied by their ruined victims."[63] Cary's *Appeal*, in short, demanded a tactical change from moral suasion to legal coercion. The goal would be prohibition, the outlawing of the sale of alcohol.

Cary was by no means the first temperance reformer to propose some form of prohibition. As early as 1826 Lyman Beecher in his *Six Sermons* had suggested that society might eventually need to banish "strong drinks from the list of lawful articles of commerce. . . ."[64] The idea of banning hard liquor continued to be proposed from time to time. Cincinnati's *Western Temperance Journal* published a letter in 1841 that recommended passing "a law . . . prohibiting the sale of ardent spirits." But, as the letter writer noted, many considered such a proposal "a wild scheme." [65] Most in the movement continued to believe, in the words of the *Morning Star*, "that the principles of temperance, like the principles of religion, recommend themselves. They need no assistance from government, but merely ask that government should let them alone. . . ." [66] Even those who felt that some form of prohibition would be justified usually added that public opinion would not yet support an attempt to pass such a law.

By the late 1840s appeals by temperance activists in the East for prohibition laws were becoming more frequent. Cary's pamphlet, however, came from the acknowledged leader of Ohio's own temperance movement and, as such, created a wave of reaction and comment. [67] The Hamilton County Temperance Union, an organization controlled by the Cincinnati area Sons of Temperance, adopted the pamphlet in 1848 as a statement of its official position, and had 100,000 copies printed and distributed. The *Appeal* was later reprinted widely throughout the country.

The Ohio temperance movement beyond Cincinnati was not yet ready to endorse the extreme position of advocating legal prohibition. At a sparsely attended quarterly session of the state's Grand Division of the Sons of Temperance in July, 1848, supporters of prohibition, primarily from Cincinnati, pushed through a resolution calling for the sale of intoxicating drinks to be made illegal and punishable by imprisonment. Members in the rest of the state criticized the action, and at the much larger annual session that October delegates repealed the resolution on a vote of sixty-four to thirty-five. Nonetheless, temperance newspapers throughout the country commented on the original resolution, and a few saw it "as a stepping stone to future permanent action upon the liquor traffic." [68]

The Cincinnati temperance activists waited several years for their fellow Ohio reformers to reach the conclusion that legal coercion was required. Beyond the Queen City, social problems were not yet so pressing. Although immigrants settled throughout Ohio, Cincinnati had a higher proportion of them than any other community in the state. In the smaller, more homogeneous towns and cities persuasion through direct contact and example still seemed possible. The decline of the Sons of Temperance was not apparent statewide until after 1849, and many clung to the belief that the order would yet overwhelm all opposition to temperance. Moreover, although the movement in the rest of the state looked to Cincinnati for leadership, it looked eastward as well, to New York, Pennsylvania, and New England. Ohioans were hesitant to be pathfinders in temperance tactics; they wanted first to be sure that the movement throughout the country was headed in the same direction. They were also unwilling to commit themselves to any statewide political action before they had some sign from the voters that public opinion would support them and would give prohibition a chance for success. Even in Cincinnati many who endorsed the idea of prohibition would have balked in 1848 at the direct political involvement necessary to accomplish it. Finally, a movement for statewide prohibition was unlikely to develop until the more attractive option of locally imposed restraints on the liquor traffic had been tried and found wanting.

Temperance activists overcame many of their reservations about prohibition as a result of their experiences in just such campaigns in the late 1840s. The fight against granting local licenses to sell liquor is a complex issue in temperance history. Paradoxically, although the anti-licensing ferment appeared to be a part of the temperance crusade, in fact its main impetus and support came from people who were hostile to the organized temperance movement and even to the principle of total abstinence, but who nevertheless feared the community problems they associated with drunkenness. These opponents of licensing primarily wished to prevent the spread of cheap, public, largely immigrant, working-class saloons into their wards and neighborhoods.[69] Temperance activists, on the other hand, although opposed in principle to liquor licensing, did not expect much practical result from the ending of licensing, and took only a peripheral part in the campaign for its abolition.[70]

Nonetheless, the fate of the anti-licensing agitation significantly influenced the future development of the temperance crusade. The experiences of that campaign taught temperance reformers not to trust allies who were not fully committed to the movement's principles, and not to compromise with their enemies. Thus, by the time of the state prohibition campaign in 1853, temperance leaders appeared more single-minded and inflexible than they might have had they not become involved in the license controversy.

The licensing issue spanned the period from the late 1830s through the 1840s. During those years many of Cincinnati's better-off citizens became alarmed at the steady encroachment of working-class residences into areas, particularly in wards 1, 2, and 5, which had until then been fashionable. As many on the edge of these neighborhoods began to abandon their downtown homes and flee to the suburbs, a general fear set in of a decaying inner city. One way to hold the line, they believed, was to stop the spread of the coffee houses. Many of the opponents of licensing drank alcoholic beverages, particularly brandies, cordials, and wines, but only in their homes or at expensive restaurants and hotel taverns. Some of these wealthy citizens planned to exempt the plush establishments which they frequented from restrictions either by allowing licenses to be granted only to "respectable" applicants, or else by imposing a uniformly high license fee, beyond the ability of the working-class coffee houses to pay. These "high-license" advocates, as they became known, were thus only opposed to the unrestricted, unselective granting of licenses.

The city's temperance movement, on the other hand, was committed to denying all licenses, no matter how respectable the applicant. The issue was primarily a symbolic one to the teetotalers: society must withdraw its sanction of liquor selling. What would happen then was uncertain. The *Record*, speculating on what might result from the abolition of liquor licensing, concluded that unlicensed drinking houses could either be prosecuted or be left alone. Prosecution would present severe problems, as penalties were not heavy and enforcement might be lax, uneven, or ineffective. If, on the other hand, the saloons were left unmolested, the *Record* hoped that they might decline owing to the withdrawal of community sanction and because unrestricted liquor selling would increase competition, which might in turn reduce profits. Yet encouraging the spread of unregulated drinking establishments did not seem an attractive alternative either. Without really taking a position on enforcement, the journal voiced its main concern, the fear that an anti-license City Council would reject most licenses but approve a few for some "*genteel hotels.*" Such a course, attacking "the '*small fry*' to the neglect of the *big fish,*" would be wrong and disastrous, bringing the indignation of "every honest republican."[71] Thus the alliance between the temperance movement and the other opponents of licensing was shaky from the outset, as the two groups differed in their social bases, in their motivations, and in their goals.

Opposition to liquor licensing in Cincinnati began in the late 1830s, when high-license advocates successfully persuaded the Cincinnati City Council to deny all liquor license applications and renewals except those for taverns and hotels. However, public dissatisfaction with this preferential treatment ran high, so that local authorities made little attempt to enforce the license law. The city's temperance movement criticized restrictive licensing as "one-sided and unfair"[72] and likely to lead to an "odious monopoly"[73] of the drink trade. In the spring of 1841 temperance activists decided to run a ticket for City Council that would support "the true principle" and cut off all licensing.[74] The *Western Temperance Journal* scorned those who, while professing friendship to the temperance cause, cried "What! go against all dram-selling at once—allowing us not even our tavern and hotel bars!"[75] The temperance ticket failed badly, and licenses were granted freely by the new council. Licensing continued to be an important issue in local elections between 1841 and 1845, but no-license advocates never won more than a third of the council seats.[76]

The first move in the escalation of the attack on licensing after 1845 was directed toward the state rather than the local level. Opponents of licensing submitted petitions to the legislature in the winter of 1845 requesting that power over licensing be given to the townships and precincts within each county, and to wards within each city, rather than to the county and city governments. The petitioners hoped they could then cut off the spread of saloons in their neighborhoods. When the petitions were ignored, anti-license advocates adopted the strategy of recommending that supporters vote only for legislative candidates in that autumn's election who pledged themselves to support the proposed change in law. The Hamilton County Temperance Union decided in August to endorse this tactic.

However, only the candidates of the antislavery Liberty party in Cincinnati supported the proposal. One stated that he considered intemperance "as (next to slavery) the greatest curse of the country. . . ."[77] At the other extreme were the Democratic candidates Flinn and Reemelin. When the *Record* inquired about their position on the issue, both submitted replies outlining their full support for liquor licensing and opposition to any change in the existing law. Caught in the middle was the Whig party. Most temperance activists were Whig, and it is likely that most of the high-license advocates were as well. But since the party also contained many opponents of the campaign, it feared that any stand might alienate some of its followers. The Whig nominees simply did not respond to the *Record*'s inquiries, hoping that if they took no position, most of the party's supporters would remain loyal. The *Record*, however, was committed to the principle of endorsing only those who were pledged affirmatively on the proposed law, and had no alternative but to urge support for the antislavery candidates.

Alliance with the Liberty party, considered by most voters at the time to be a fanatic fringe movement, soon became embarrassing for the city's temperance advocates. The Democratic *Cincinnati Enquirer*, amused at the discomfort of the reformers, indulged in some political histrionics. The temperance leaders were debasing "that God-sanctioned enterprise [temperance] to the ignominious cause of *Political Abolitionism*."[78] The *Record* stopped short of endorsing the Liberty party candidates by name, recommending only that the temperance men should "vote consistently with [their] principles, irrespective of party." Nothing could be gained, it added in an oblique reference to the Whigs, in supporting "those who will equivocate for the purpose of conciliating those who are opposed to us."[79] After the election the *Record* concluded: "It is true, we have not accomplished much, so far as the success of temperance candidates is concerned, but we have accomplished much in bringing temperance men to *act consistently* with their principles."[80] The campaign failed statewide, and the subsequent legislature rejected even a toned-down proposal to give a majority of petitioning voters in the wards, townships, and precincts a veto power over licenses issued by the city or county.[81]

The focus of anti-license activity then shifted back to the local level. In the spring of 1846 anti-license forces in Cincinnati tried to push the issue to the forefront of the City Council elections. The temperance movement did not act on the campaign until after council candidates had already been nominated. A city temperance convention met and endorsed a slate of candidates who were believed to favor ending licensing. After the election the *Commercial* reported that nineteen Whigs and eleven Democrats had won. "As regards temperance, 16 are anti-Coffee House [against licensing], 12 for licensing, and two not known. It is said that [three] . . . , reckoned with the Temperance men, are for high licenses. . . ."[82] A few days later, however, the *Commercial* noted: "There is much inquiry as to whether the new Council will or will not grant licenses. We do not think anyone can tell until the question comes up before the new organization. We shall see a stormy time—mark that."[83] The *Record*, however, felt certain that the anti-license forces had won a victory with a majority of seventeen to thirteen, "so that for the coming year *no licenses* will be granted in this city."[84]

The confidence of the temperance forces was shattered when in June the council began to pass license applications, and worst of all, with affirmative votes from a well-known Son of Temperance. Outraged and mortified, the *Record* claimed that such action, though not specifically prohibited, nonetheless violated the pledge and was grounds for expulsion. It added that the brotherhood was not infallible, and that men seeking "their own ambitious and personal ends" might well "steal the livery of the *Order* to serve the devil. . . ."[85]

It remained to be seen whether the new council would vote for all licenses or simply for those of the wealthiest and most influential applicants. In August the editor of a German newspaper applauded the council for granting licenses freely, and the *Record* noted that it united "with the German Editor in commending the liberality of the City Council. They eschew favoritism, and seem determined that there shall be no monopoly in this dirty work. We never could see any good reason for permitting a favorite few to peddle poison, and deny the right to many. The German, or Frenchman, or Englishman . . . has just as good a right to make drunkards in a small way, as the more wealthy, but not more *honest* American. . . ."[86]

Thus the city's temperance movement, uncomfortable in its alliance with the wealthy high-license advocates, attempted to put some distance between the two positions. Because of their dislike for high licensing, and because of their embarrassment over the actions of the errant councilman, the temperance forces were no longer content merely to endorse candidates thought to be anti-license but who might actually be weak in their commitment or actually for high license. In the following spring the temperance activists became fully involved for the first time in the anti-license campaign.

As the 1847 City Council elections approached, temperance leaders went to work in their wards to see that the Whig ticket had as many men as possible firmly pledged to vote against all licenses. At the Whig convention in March several of the city's best-known temperance advocates were present as delegates: attorneys Peter B. Manchester and John A. Collins, soon to be co-editor of the *Record*; Henry V. Horton, a jeweler and former publisher of the *Ohio Organ*; and Samuel Trevor, a life insurance agent and long-time member of the Cincinnati Chamber of Commerce. At least three other members of the Sons of Temperance were also delegates to the fifty-man convention. After the candidates were chosen, the *Record* urged voting only for "well-established temperance men."[87]

The activity of the reformers had a clear effect on the composition of the Whig ticket. Of the three council members noted as high-license advocates by the *Commercial* the previous year, only one was renominated. In the election a firmly anti-license council was chosen. As license applications and renewals were subsequently submitted to the new body, the division was consistently seventeen to thirteen against granting them. All seventeen no-license votes were Whig. Of the other thirteen, ten were Democrats and three were Whigs.[88]

Immediately problems arose over enforcement, as the *Record* had anticipated. Cincinnati's police forces were still divided into a fairly extensive night watch and a scant day police consisting only of the city marshal and his two deputies. The enforcement of the licensing laws placed a heavy burden on the day police. By June five or six people a day were being fined for "selling spirituous and malt liquors" without a license. The *Commercial* called for more day police: "When we realize that the Marshal has to see to the enforcing of *all* ordinances, one of which (the [ban on unlicensed] coffee house[s]) is sufficient for one man, what time or opportunity can he have to protect our citizens and their property from the lawless persons who flock here?"[89]

Furthermore, the highest fine allowed by law, $9 and costs, was hardly a strong deterrent. Licenses had cost $50, and even if liquor sellers were apprehended and fined at the rate of five or six per day, an entire year of enforcement would still not prove very costly to the city's approximately 400 coffee house keepers. The fine was not even enough to discourage new coffee houses from opening unlicensed, and certainly not enough to drive those already established out of business. By August the *Record* reported that the marshal had stopped enforcing the law requiring a license to sell alcohol.[90] Democratic councilman A. J. Pruden of ward 3 could claim by February, 1848: "This is a temperance Council. Licenses have been, in all cases, refused, and what is the result? Why the city has lost a large portion of its revenue, and there are now one hundred and fifty more coffee-houses than there were a year ago under the license system."[91]

As the next council election approached, dissatisfaction appeared within the Whig ranks over the virtual commitment of the party in the previous year to the no-license position. The mayor and the city marshal, both Whigs, issued a statement claiming that "within the last year, intemperance has increased at a fearful rate." They believed that "the quantity of liquor drank now, is greater than the quantity drank a year since, and the number of houses where liquor is retailed greatly increased."[92]

In short, the anti-license campaign had backfired. Whigs in some of the city's wards apparently agreed. Of the seventeen Whigs on the 1847 council who had voted no-license, only seven were renominated. One of these lost re-election, and another declared his support of high license, but the other five continued to oppose all applications to the new council. Two of the three who had supported license were renominated and re-elected. Eleven new Whigs were elected to the council, five of whom subsequently voted in favor of all licenses. Democrats on the council increased from ten to twelve. The Democrats and the pro-license Whigs now re-established a heavy majority for liquor licensing. A Democratic councilman claimed, shortly after the election, that "many members owe their seats in Council to pledges in favor of license."[93]

Several of the new Whigs on the council, however, were for high license. They began to submit amendments to coffee-house applications raising their license fee. The Democrats countered by advocating very high license fees for the wealthy downtown hotels and taverns while struggling to keep the fees for the coffee houses as low as possible. The resulting confusion and controversy often tied up meetings of the council for hours. In a typical debate Democrat A. Giffen of ward 10 defended a license petitioner as "a poor man, who had a small place up there in 'New Amsterdam,' and depended upon the small profit it yielded for his support." He attacked the proposed amendment (raising the license fee from $50 to $75) as typical of the attitude of the "codfish aristocracy" in the city. If "any of the big genteel houses, which are making their thousands each year, come in for license, they can get it at the same price [proposed for] . . . this poor man. . . . It is not fair. Let the petitioners be taxed according to their means."[94]

In an attempt to compromise, the council proposed that the Committee on Coffee Houses and Taverns recommend a fee for each application, based on the ability of the petitioner to pay. But high-license Whigs kept objecting to the amount set for some, Democrats to the amount set for others. By June the

Commercial's reporter was simply noting with disgust after council meetings that amendments were offered on nearly every application and that "the usual amount of gas was expended on these licenses" which took up "about one half the night. . . ."[95] Generally, however, the Democratic position was successful. Many licenses were granted for as little as $25, while a few went for as much as $200. Gradually attention to the issue diminished on the council. Between September, 1848, and August, 1849, 504 licenses were granted, at an average fee of $47, bringing $23,704 to the city in revenue.[96]

Attacks on local liquor licensing policies elsewhere in Ohio and in other states in the late 1840s followed the same pattern of short-term success followed by disillusionment and failure. The abolition of license simply led to nonenforcement of the laws against selling alcoholic beverages without a license. Cities lost revenue, and coffee houses were opened with no regulation. Eventually a backlash set in, and communities restored liquor licensing.[97]

The Cincinnati anti-licensing campaign altered the attitudes of the city's temperance activists in several ways. Because of their unpleasant experience with high-license advocates, they became wary of allying themselves with anyone not totally committed to their own tactics and goals. During the later prohibition campaign they were more scrupulous in choosing their allies. The temperance reformers also learned to view the Whig party as a fair-weather friend, unreliable on temperance issues. Finally, the crusaders became convinced that, if they were to attack the drink trade through legal means, halfway measures that allowed for favoritism, loopholes, and lax enforcement would in the end do more harm than good. In the fight for prohibition they would resist compromise.

The anti-licensing campaign was a complete failure at the local level only for those high-license advocates whose sole concern had been to stop the spread of coffee houses. Temperance activists, however, were delighted by the removal, albeit temporary, of official sanction for liquor selling. They sensed the psychological advantage to be gained by putting the drink trade on the defensive. And by 1850 they also glimpsed fresh support among the general public for their attack on the respectability of distillers, brewers, and saloon keepers. The problems of disorder produced a readiness in the rapidly growing areas of the state to fix the blame for social problems directly on the local liquor merchant.

The writing of a new state constitution in 1850 provided an ideal opportunity for the temperance movement to revive the anti-license fight at the state level. A constitutional ban on licenses, advocates believed, would eliminate the politicking that had undermined anti-licensing at the local level. In the elections for delegates to the constitutional convention, temperance forces actively organized support for nominees sympathetic to the goal of an anti-license clause in the new constitution. In Cincinnati a ticket of pro-license Democrats barely defeated an anti-license independent slate. Although in seven of eleven city wards majorities voted for the independent ticket, the Democratic candidates won so decisively in a few German and Irish sections, sweeping over 80 percent of the vote in two heavily German wards, that they carried the election.[98]

Anti-license advocates did better in the rest of the state. The constitutional convention, spurred on by petitions signed by more than 20,000 Ohioans, drafted a clause forbidding local governments to grant any licenses to traffic in intoxicating liquors. But fearing that the anti-license provision might defeat the entire document, the convention submitted the clause separately to the voters for ratification.

The temperance movement continued to oppose licensing on the grounds of principle. Temperance reformers enthusiastically campaigned for the anti-license clause but were careful to caution voters not to expect practical results should the campaign be successful. Samuel Cary stressed in his addresses that liquor would continue to be sold even without licensing, and the constitutional clause would impose "no restraint, but only takes away sanction."[99]

The no-license section carried in Hamilton County, and won statewide on a close vote, with 113,239 votes in favor and 104,255 opposed.[100] The vote greatly encouraged the temperance forces. In their first statewide ballot campaign they had successfully demonstrated their organizing abilities. More important, they now saw a strong sentiment throughout the

state supporting their concern over drinking and its consequences. "A temperance public sentiment is rising up," wrote
one of Cincinnati's reformers, "which can never be put down
until the accursed business of rumselling shall be smitten to the
dust."[101] Only five years earlier a temperance advocate had
written that the movement was not seeking to make "rumselling a penitentiary offense, however much we may consider it a
crime worthy of such punishment, because it would not be justified by public sentiment, and would therefore remain a dead
letter."[102] Now, however, events suggested that public attitudes
might well have changed. The anti-license vote indicated such
a shift, and it closely coincided with a watershed in the course
of the temperance movement: the passage in Maine of the nation's first prohibitory law.

The law approved in Maine on June 2, 1851, forbade the
manufacture and sale of all intoxicating liquors within the
confines of the state, provided for search and seizure, and encouraged enforcement by awarding all fines to the prosecuting
officers. Drawn to the specifications of Portland's prohibitionist mayor Neal Dow, the Maine Law was tough and uncompromising. For temperance crusaders it seemed a dream
come true. Throughout the country many reformers put aside
previous reservations about the feasibility and advisability
of supporting prohibition. Although some remained uncon-
vinced, by and large the temperance movement became a prohibitionist movement.

Cincinnati temperance activists, most of whom had endorsed the principle of prohibition since 1848, leapt into action at the August, 1851, county temperance convention. They
heartily applauded Maine's example, called for a similar law in
Ohio, but divided on the next step. A majority wanted to run
an independent prohibition slate in the fall elections for the
state legislature, endorsing any major party candidates who
would pledge to vote for the law but nominating their own
candidates where necessary. Others thought this course precipitous, and argued against entering into dangerous political
involvements before first exhausting the safer route of peti-

tioning the legislature. Dissension was so strong that the effort for separate candidates dissolved before the election.[103]

Petition campaigns throughout Ohio raised 145,000 signatures for a prohibitory law by the following February. A state temperance convention, convened in Columbus that month, passed numerous resolutions addressed to the state's lawmakers espousing the need of prohibition.[104] The convention stopped short of passing a resolution calling for independent political action if the legislature did not produce a prohibitory law, but only because such a declaration might have proved badly timed. But by the fall of 1852 it was clear that the legislature would take no action on the petitions. Temperance groups throughout Ohio began to prepare for a full statewide campaign in 1853 to elect a legislature favorable to prohibition. The temperance movement was about to become a major force in the arena of Ohio politics.

The shift to prohibition not only reflected the changed concerns of the temperance movement and the public at midcentury, but it also shaped the basic focus of temperance activity for the next eight decades. From the passage of the Maine Law in 1851 to the repeal of the Eighteenth Amendment ending national prohibition in 1933, the goal of prohibition dominated temperance thought. The movement went through many more phases and changes in its basic concerns, and at times returned to moral suasion as a major tactical weapon. But once committed to the concept of prohibition, the temperance crusade never repudiated it, and thus became inextricably tied to the world of political alliances, maneuverings, voter appeals, and lobbying strength. Henceforth its fortunes would rise and fall partly in response to the complex interplay of forces at work in the political realm.

Notes

1. The term "prohibition" in this study refers to the legal prohibition of the manufacture and sale of alcoholic beverages. Prohibition laws, therefore, are those intended to prevent all drinking. Other historians have used the term to apply as well to the control or elimination of liquor licensing and

to the control of the quantities in which liquors could be sold, as in the 1838 Massachusetts "Fifteen-Gallon Law" (see Ian R. Tyrrell, *Sobering Up: From Temperance to Prohibition in Antebellum America, 1800–1860* (Westport, Conn., 1979); and Robert Louis Hampel, "Influence and Respectability: Temperance and Prohibition in Massachusetts, 1813–1852" (Ph.D. thesis, Cornell University, 1980). I believe that this broader use of the term obscures important distinctions between regulatory efforts aimed at public drinking (and not always supported by temperance activists) and efforts to eliminate drinking entirely.

2. Eric E. Lampard, "The Evolving System of Cities in the United States: Urbanization and Economic Development," in Harvey S. Perloff and Lowdon Wingo, Jr., eds., *Issues in Urban Economics* (Baltimore, 1968), 108–12; Diana Klebanow, Franklin L. Jonas, and Ira M. Leonard, *Urban Legacy: The Story of America's Cities* (New York, 1977), 42.

3. *Historical Statistics of the United States, Colonial Times to 1957* (Washington, D.C., 1960), 57; Leonard Dinnerstein, Roger L. Nichols, and David M. Reimers, *Natives and Strangers: Ethnic Groups and the Building of America* (New York, 1979), 78, 87; Nora Faires, "Ethnicity in Evolution: The German Community in Pittsburgh and Allegheny City, 1845–1885" (Ph.D. thesis, University of Pittsburgh, 1980), 100.

4. Dinnerstein, *Natives*, 85; Klebanow, *Urban*, 81–83; Herbert G. Gutman, *Work, Culture, and Society in Industrializing America: Essays in American Working-Class and Social History* (New York, 1977), 13, 55; Bruce Laurie, *Working People of Philadelphia, 1800–1850* (Philadelphia, 1980), 28–30.

5. Klebanow, *Urban*, 84–95; David R. Johnson, "Crime Patterns in Philadelphia, 1840–70," in Allen F. Davis and Mark Haller, eds., *The Peoples of Philadelphia: A History of Ethnic Groups and Lower-Class Life, 1790–1940* (Philadelphia, 1973), 101; James Richardson, *The New York Police: Colonial Times to 1901* (New York, 1970), 51–52; John C. Schneider, "Public Order and the Geography of the City: Crime, Violence, and the Police in Detroit, 1845–1875," *Journal of Urban History*, 4 (1978): 185; Russell F. Weighley, "'A Peaceful City': Public Order in Philadelphia from Consolidation through the Civil War," in Davis and Haller, eds., *Peoples of Philadelphia*, 156–58; Roger Lane, *Policing the City: Boston, 1822–1885* (Cambridge, Mass., 1967), 70–71; Celestine Estelle Anderson, "The Invention of the 'Professional' Municipal Police: The Case of Cincinnati, 1788 to 1900" (Ph.D. thesis, University of Cincinnati, 1979), 122.

6. Harry N. Scheiber, *The Ohio Canal Era: A Case Study of Government and the Economy, 1820–1861* (Athens, Ohio, 1969), 221; Walter S. Glazer, "Taxpayers: 1850," *Cincinnati Historical Society Bulletin*, 25 (1967): 156–60.

7. Sidney D. Maxwell, *The Suburbs of Cincinnati* (Cincinnati, Ohio, 1870).

8. Charles Cist, *Sketches and Statistics of Cincinnati in 1851* (Cincinnati, Ohio, 1851), 47.

9. *Cincinnati Commercial* (hereafter cited as CC), Mar. 16, 1849; Cincinnati City Departments, *Annual Reports*, 1854, "City Infirmary, Clerk's Report," 40; Benhamin Klebaner, "The Myth of Foreign Pauper Dumping in the United States," *Social Science Review*, 35 (1961): 307–8; Dinnerstein, *Natives*, 92–93.

10. CC, Nov. 5, 1849; Cincinnati *Annual Reports*, 1864, "Report of the Chief of Police," 33. Even this figure is probably low, since by 1864 native-born children of immigrants, who would have been perceived as part of the immigrant community by other native-born Cincinnatians, would have been among those arrested. In 1858, 65 percent of the juvenile delinquents in the city's House of Refuge were native-born but only 20 percent had native-born parents (Cincinnati *Annual Reports*, 1858, "House of Refuge Annual Report," 12).

11. *Western Washingtonian and Sons of Temperance Record* (hereafter cited as *Record*), Jan. 16, 1846.

12. CC, July 20, 1853. See also *Cincinnati Enquirer*, June 24, 1853, and *Cincinnati Times*, quoted in *Ohio Organ of the Temperance Reform*, July 22, 1853.

13. Charles Cist, *Cincinnati in 1841: Its Early Annals and Future Prospects* (Cincinnati, Ohio, 1841), 32–33, 39; Gwynn Nettler, *Explaining Crime*, 2d ed. (New York, 1978), 120–22, 143, 148. Nettler, discussing ethnicity and crime in contemporary England, notes: "Drinking is associated with the high crime rates reported for Irish migrants to England. The Irish settler tends to be a single young man cut off from an Irish community. . . . For years Irishmen resident in England have had a rate of criminal conviction and recidivism higher than that of the majority population" (143).

14. Cincinnati *Annual Reports*, 1854, "Infirmary," 55–56.

15. CC, Jan. 22, 1847.

16. Ibid., July 12, 1853.

17. Bessie Bruce White, *A Story of the Cincinnati Union Bethel, a Social Service Agency since 1830* (Cincinnati, Ohio, 1952), 13–14.

18. CC, Sept. 26, 1851.

19. Ibid., Dec. 18, 1854, Nov. 5, 1849; *Record*, Nov. 7, 1845; Cincinnati *Annual Reports*, 1854, "Annual Report of the Mayor," 12; Anderson, "Police," 124.

20. *Cincinnati Enquirer*, June 25, 1853; Anderson, "Police," 124–25.

21. CC, Feb. 24, 1851.

22. Ibid., July 18, 1853.

23. Cincinnati Historical Society, Daniel Drake to Margaret Drake, Mar. 21, 1852.

24. CC, June 24, 1853.

25. Charles E. Rosenberg, *The Cholera Years: The United States in 1832, 1848, and 1866* (Chicago, 1962), 133–50; Alan I. Marcus, "In Sickness and in Health: The Marriage of the Municipal Corporation to the Public Interest and the Problem of Public Health, 1820–1870. The Case of Cincinnati" (Ph.D. thesis, University of Cincinnati, 1979), 75; CC, Mar. 18,

1854; Eugene H. Roseboom, *The Civil War Era, 1850–1873* (vol. 4 of *The History of the State of Ohio,* ed. Carl Wittke, Columbus, Ohio, 1944), 59.

26. Quoted in Ian R. Tyrrell, "Drink and the Process of Social Reform: From Temperance to Prohibition in Ante-Bellum America, 1813–1860" (Ph.D. thesis, Duke University, 1974), 53.

27. Daniel Drake, "Breweries vs. Foundries" (address delivered to Washingtonian Society, Louisville, Ky., 1841), MS, Cincinnati Historical Society.

28. CC, Nov. 3, 1847. W. J. Rorabaugh's estimates of alcohol consumption for the period indicate that, while not rising, consumption had leveled off after a dramatic drop during the years 1830–45 (see W. J. Rorabaugh, "Estimated U.S. Alcoholic Beverage Consumption, 1790–1860," *Journal of Studies on Alcohol,* 37 (1976): 357–64).

29. Roger Lane, in *Policing the City,* reaches a similar conclusion in regard to the temperance movement in Boston: "The temperance ideal was part of a wider vision of the progress of civilization, and specifically of Boston. And while in some respects this vision reached a height during the late 1840's, in others it was beginning to fade. The decline . . . for many . . . was precipitated by the evidence that there had been no social progress in Boston, a problem aggravated by the irony that the decade of reform overlapped the decade of the Irish coming" (70).

30. *Ohio Organ of the Temperance Reform* (hereafter cited as *Organ*), Mar. 4, 1853.

31. *American Temperance Magazine and Sons of Temperance Record,* vol. 1 (Nov., 1851). Cary's use of the term "effeminacy" to describe the result of excessive drinking indicates how temperance reformers attempted to subvert the popular image of drinking as masculine and manly. The relationship between alcohol use and gender roles deserves greater study.

32. CC, Apr. 16, 1849.

33. *Templar's Magazine,* Oct., 1850, 33.

34. R. J. Morris, *Cholera 1832: The Social Response to an Epidemic* (New York, 1976), 138–39.

35. *Record,* Nov. 7, 1845; Aug. 22, 1846.

36. *Organ,* July 22, 1853.

37. Ibid., May 27, 1853.

38. Ibid., Sept. 30, 1853.

39. CC, Mar. 28, 1845.

40. Officials of the Ohio state lunatic asylum reported that 14.5 percent of their cases in 1839 and 3.5 percent in 1847 were directly traceable to alcohol. They attributed the abrupt decline to the work of the temperance movement (James H. Cassedy, "An Early American Hangover: The Medical Profession and Intemperance, 1800–1860," *Bulletin of the History of Medicine,* 50 (1976): 408; Norman Dain, *Concepts of Insanity in the United States, 1789–1865* (New Brunswick, N.J., 1964), 326, fn. 10).

41. *Organ,* Aug. 19, 1853.

42. CC, Aug. 13, 1853.

43. *Cincinnati Times*, July 23, 28, 1853.

44. Cincinnati *Annual Reports*, 1854, "Infirmary," 55–56.

45. *Cincinnati Times*, July 28, 1853.

46. *Western Temperance Journal* (hereafter cited as *Journal*), Feb. 15, 1841; John A. Krout, *The Origins of Prohibition* (New York, 1925), 132–33.

47. Daniel Drake, "Diseases from the Habitual Use and Abuse of Alcoholic Drinks," Dec. 30, 1843, and "The Uses and Abuses of Opium," Feb. 17, 1844 (addresses delivered to Physiological Temperance Society of Medical Institute of Louisville, Ky.); Harry G. Levine, "The Discovery of Addiction: Changing Conceptions of Habitual Drunkenness in America," *Journal of Studies on Alcohol*, 39 (1978): 144, 154.

48. *Record*, Apr. 25, 1846.

49. Ibid., Aug. 23, 1845; A. Jaffee, "Reform in American Medical Science: The Inebriety Movement and the Origins of the Psychological Disease Theory of Addiction, 1870–1920," *British Journal of Addiction*, 73 (1978): 139. The word "alcoholism" did not come into use until around 1860.

50. *Record*, Jan. 2, 1847.

51. *Organ*, Apr. 22, 1853.

52. *Record*, Oct. 17, 1846.

53. *Organ*, Apr. 1, 1853.

54. *Record*, Sept. 13, 1845; Paul R. Meyer, Jr., "The Transformation of American Temperance: The Popularization and Radicalization of a Reform Movement, 1813–1860" (Ph.D. thesis, University of Iowa, 1976), 165–70.

55. *Record*, Feb. 21, 1846.

56. Samuel F. Cary, ed., *American Temperance Magazine and Sons of Temperance Offering*, 1 (Dec., 1851): 419.

57. "Ohio," *Journal of the American Temperance Union*, 17 (Sept., 1853): 141, quoted in Meyer, "Transformation," 168.

58. *Record*, Sept. 13, 1845.

59. *Crusader*, 3 (Aug., 1858): 80–81.

60. Cist, *1851*, 169–70, 180, 187, 252–53, 258–65; *New York Organ*, Jan. 26, 1850, quoted in Tyrrell, "Drink," 230.

61. CC, Aug. 15, Oct. 5, 1855.

62. Samuel F. Cary, *Cary's Appeal to the People of Ohio* . . . (Cincinnati, Ohio, n.d.), 1.

63. Ibid., 3–4.

64. Quoted in John G. Woolley and William E. Johnson, *Temperance Progress in the Century* (London, 1903), 115–16.

65. *Journal*, Feb. 1, 1841.

66. *Morning Star*, Aug. 30, 1842.

67. The city's newspapers referred to *Cary's Appeal* with no additional identification, assuming that readers were familiar with its contents. See, for example, CC, Feb. 17, 1848.

68. P. R. L. Peirce, *A History of the Introduction and Progress of the*

Order of the Sons of Temperance in the State of Ohio (Cincinnati, Ohio, 1849), 110–13.

69. William Baughin, "Nativism in Cincinnati before 1860" (M.A. thesis, University of Cincinnati, 1963), 71–72; Walter S. Glazer, "Cincinnati in 1840: A Community Profile" (Ph.D. thesis, University of Michigan, 1968), 258.

70. Skepticism about the possible benefits of license abolition extended beyond Cincinnati. Rutherford B. Hayes, living in lower Sandusky in 1847, wrote to his sister that he did not "consider it a matter of great moment whether spirituous liquor is sold *legally* in consequence of *lax* laws, as is now the case, or *illegally* in consequence of *lax* officers as would probably be the case (at least hereabouts) if no licenses were granted." He added that he would "vote 'anti' for the look and name of the thing" (Rutherford B. Hayes, *Diary and Letters of Rutherford Birchard Hayes*, ed. Charles R. Williams (Columbus, Ohio, 1922), vol. 1, Apr. 13, 1847).

71. *Record*, Apr. 18, 1846.

72. *Journal*, Mar. 1, June 1, 1841; Krout, *Origins*, 173.

73. *Journal*, Feb. 1, 1841.

74. Ibid., June 1, 1841; *Record*, Mar. 7, 1846.

75. *Journal*, Mar. 15, 1841.

76. Ibid., June 1, 1841; Glazer, "Cincinnati," 258. The 1843 council imposed new restrictions on drinking places (see Marcus, "Health," 131–33).

77. *Record*, Oct. 4, Aug. 9, Sept. 13, 1845.

78. Ibid., Oct. 18, 1845.

79. Ibid., Oct. 11, 1845.

80. Ibid., Oct. 18, 1845.

81. Ibid., Dec. 26, 1845, Feb. 28, 1846.

82. CC, Apr. 8, 1846; *Record*, Feb. 21, 1846.

83. CC, Apr. 13, 1846.

84. *Record*, Apr. 11, 1846.

85. Ibid., June 27, July 18, 1846. At the 1849 Sons of Temperance National Division meeting in Cincinnati, with Cary as chairperson, a resolution was passed giving subordinate divisions the "power to expel a member for voting in any way, directly or indirectly, to support the traffic in intoxicating liquors" (CC, May 22, 1849).

86. *Record*, Aug. 16, 1846.

87. Ibid., May 8, 1847; CC, Mar. 16, 1847, for delegate names.

88. CC, Apr. 7, May 28, 1847; *Record*, May 29, 1847.

89. CC, June 18, 1847.

90. *Record*, Aug. 7, 1847; CC, Mar. 1, 1845, June 18, 1847; Peirce, *Sons*, 46.

91. CC, Feb. 17, 1848, Aug. 23, Nov. 25, 30, 1847.

92. Ibid., Apr. 1, 1848.

93. Ibid., Apr. 21, 5, 20, 1848.

94. Ibid., Apr. 21, May 13, 1848.

95. Ibid., June 24, July 12, 1848.

96. Ibid., July 12, 1848, May 26, Sept. 12, 1849.

97. In Detroit license was abolished in 1846. Revenue fell but the sale of liquor continued unabated. In 1847 the City Council resumed licensing (Ronald P. Formisano, *The Birth of Mass Political Parties: Michigan, 1827–1861* (Princeton, N.J., 1971), 119). The state of Iowa enacted a law in Feb., 1847, allowing each county to decide independently whether or not to license liquor sales. Every county but one voted to end licensing. By 1849 the entire state was back to the old system of licensing (Dan E. Clark, "The History of Liquor Legislation in Iowa, 1846–1861," *Iowa Journal of History and Politics*, 6 (1908): 56–62). In New York the legislature passed a law in 1845 permitting the voters of towns and incorporated municipalities to abolish licensing (New York County was excluded from this law). Five-sixths of the towns and municipalities voted no-license, but two years later the law was repealed (John A. Krout, "The Maine Law in New York Politics," *New York History*, 17 (1936): 261–62). The Illinois legislature in 1851 abolished licensing and prohibited the selling or giving away of hard liquor in quantities of less than one quart. The law went unenforced and was repealed two years later (Cole, *Era*, 207). See also the *Record*, June 5, 1847, for disillusionment in the East over the failure of balloting on the license question.

98. CC, Apr. 4, 8, 1850.

99. *Western Christian Advocate*, May 21, 1851.

100. CC, June 18, July 8, 1851.

101. *American Temperance Magazine*, vol. 1 (Sept., 1851).

102. *Record*, Aug. 16, 1846.

103. CC, Aug. 14, Sept. 2, 8, 1851.

104. Ibid., Feb. 26, 27, 1852.

4

The Campaign for Prohibition

The entire nation experienced a decade of political upheaval in the 1850s. In the space of a few years the Whig party disintegrated, the ephemeral Know Nothings rose briefly to national prominence, and finally the northern-based Republican party appeared, capturing the presidency in 1860. Until recently, most historians believed that this political turmoil derived almost entirely from the issues of sectionalism and slavery, which dominated American life by the end of the decade and which ushered in the Civil War. Traditionally, historians dated the beginning of the breakdown of the second-party system from the passage in 1854 of the Kansas-Nebraska bill, which revived the slavery issue by threatening to introduce slave-holding into all the territories. But in the last fifteen years historical investigations at the state and local levels in the North have revealed that in many areas party structures had started to decay, and political allegiances to shift, well before the Kansas-Nebraska bill, and over issues not directly related to slavery. Party realignments, it appears, initially were not sparked by sectional controversies but by "ethno-cultural" issues, principally anti-Catholicism, nativism, and temperance.[1]

In Cincinnati the pattern of political change fits well into this revised interpretation of the period. The Whig party, ascendant in the early 1840s, gradually lost ground to the Democrats, who in turn dominated local politics by the early 1850s. The Democrats owed their majority position to the steadily increasing, and heavily Democratic, immigrant vote. But in 1852 a group of dissident German voters bolted the party, in part as an anti-Catholic protest. For a while this group of Germans held the balance of political power in the city. At the same time, the Whig party began to disintegrate after it failed to provide leadership on the issues—primarily anti-Catholicism and temperance reform—which a majority of non-Democrats came to view as the foremost political questions of the day.

When the temperance reformers launched their campaign for prohibition, they entered this turbulent political current and were carried along by it. The crusaders correctly sensed a surge in public receptivity to the idea of prohibition. However, this receptivity did not represent a deep-seated commitment to eliminate drinking. Rather, it sprang primarily from growing anxiety over social disorder, and from the hope that prohibition would alleviate social ills. The Maine Law, in the eyes of the public, would have to deliver on its promise to reduce crime and poverty. Moreover, since fear of Catholicism became the overriding concern of many citizens, prohibition would also have to serve as a unifying issue, a rallying point around which a new socially oriented anti-Democratic political majority could form. When it failed to meet both those expectations, the temperance cause was quickly shunted aside by its recent converts, and even by many long-time supporters. It languished for almost twenty years before it once more became a shaping force in American society.

The history of shifting political fortunes in Cincinnati in the two decades prior to the Civil War is largely the history of the growing influence and changing allegiances of the city's German voters. Germans began arriving in Cincinnati in large numbers during the 1830s, and their proportion in the population remained fairly steady through the next decade, amounting to 28 percent in 1840 and 26 percent in 1850. But their influence in the city grew tremendously in those years. By 1850 Germans constituted a majority of the population in wards 9, 10, 11, and 12, the "Over-the-Rhine" district, whereas ten years earlier they had not outnumbered the native-born in any ward. Since a disproportionate number of immigrants were adult males, they wielded even greater strength among potential voters.[2]

The German community had formed close ties with the local Democratic party as early as 1836. Between 1838 and 1844, the Whig vote in congressional elections declined from 65 percent to 50 percent, and both Whigs and Democrats attributed the change to the growing number of German voters in the city. In the early 1850s, when large numbers of non-Catholic Germans defected from the Democratic party over issues related to anti-Catholicism, their votes became pivotal in the balance of local political power.[3]

Cincinnati's Democratic party also counted the city's Irish as its loyal supporters. The Irish, however, did not become as important a factor in local politics. They were not nearly as numerous as the Germans: the census of 1850 counted 13,616 Irish-born residents, 12 percent of the city's population. Nor were the Irish as geographically concentrated, being scattered among the waterfront wards: outside the "Over-the-Rhine" area, only ward 4 had a majority of foreign-born residents. Moreover, the Irish were unwavering in their allegiance to the Democratic party. While German voters changed the outcome of several elections in the 1850s by shifting their votes, the Irish proved to be much less volatile, and therefore a less crucial factor in determining the outcome of specific elections.[4]

The Democratic party had gained supremacy by the late 1840s in citywide votes for state and national offices. But the City Council remained under Whig control throughout the decade, primarily because the Whigs refused to redraw Cincinnati's ward boundaries in a way that accurately reflected the rapidly growing population, predominantly German, in the northern part of the city.[5]

In 1850 Cincinnati finally incorporated the populous wards 11 and 12, which lay north of the old city line, and the added vote gave the Democrats a slight majority on the City Council in 1851. They quickly revised the city's ward boundaries, increasing the total number of wards from twelve to sixteen (see Figure 2). Under the new districting plan the heavily German wards 7, 9, 10, 11, and 12 and the German and Irish ward 13 became Democratic strongholds, while the partly

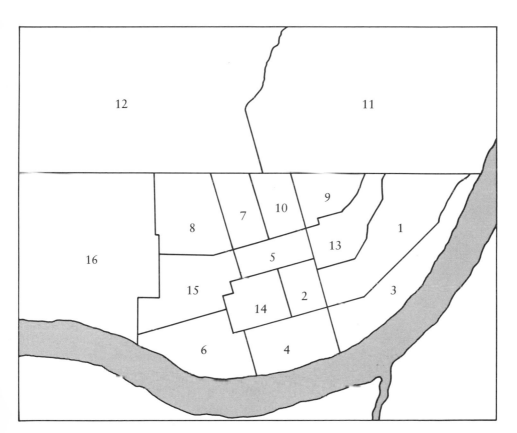

Figure 2. Cincinnati wards, c. 1852.

German ward 8 and the waterfront wards 3, 4, and 6 could be expected to fall fairly regularly into the Democratic column.[6]

The Democrats appeared to be in complete control of Cincinnati's politics by 1852. But in the summer of that year the party was rocked by the revelation that a secret fraternal society, the "Miami Tribe," existed within the local Democratic organization. Officially entitled Ohio Lodge Number One (Miami Tribe) of the Improved Order of Red Men, the society had been created a year earlier and included many of the city's top party leaders in its ranks. When word of the tribe's existence leaked out, its members professed that the order's only purpose had been to provide for congenial socializing. However, it soon became apparent that the tribe had engaged in another practice as well: that of drawing up and agreeing upon slates of nominees prior to the regular party convention. The Miamis intended that the lion's share of offices would go to native-born Democrats, with the remainder of the local party tickets apportioned carefully to Irish and Germans. The tribe planned to exclude both native-born Democrats who were tinged with antislavery associations and German Democrats who espoused "radical" doctrines.[7]

Radical Germans were a relatively recent addition to the city's political spectrum. After the 1848 revolution in Germany a group of refugees had appeared in the city, few in number but highly visible and controversial. These "Forty-eighters" were frequently agnostic or atheistic, anticlerical, and socialist. They founded radical newspapers, formed a Tom Paine society, established the Freimännerverein (Freeman's Society), and began the first Turnverein, an organization uniquely blending athleticism, rationalism, militarism, and extreme republicanism. Because they were politically skilled, articulate, and energetic, the Forty-eighters immediately began to exert influence out of proportion to their numbers, not only within the German community but throughout the city as well.[8]

The German radicals disliked organized religion in general, but most of all they despised the Catholic church. Thus on religious grounds they were the bitter enemies of their fellow Democrats, the Irish and German Catholics. Religious antagonisms had flared in February, 1852, when Hungarian patriot Louis Kossuth visited the city. Kossuth was a great hero to most non-Catholic Germans, who saw him as a living symbol of opposition to despotism and tyranny in Europe. Yet the Catholic hierarchy condemned Kossuth, and the *Catholic Telegraph* printed hostile attacks during his visit.[9] The Kossuth controversy caused many Protestant and Jewish Germans, particularly those who were relatively young and had arrived fairly recently from Europe, to join with the agnostics in condemning Catholicism as a dire threat to their hopes for Germany.[10]

The controversy surrounding Kossuth's visit demonstrated to the native-born leaders of the Democratic party that the strident anti-Catholicism of the radical Germans threatened the unity of the party. However, their strategy to limit the influence of the radicals through the Miami Tribe backfired. When the Miami scandal revealed that local Democratic leaders were secretly excluding the radicals from office, and seemingly catering to the Catholics, a large group of non-Catholic Germans quickly coalesced in opposition to the city's party hierarchy. Led by prominent radicals Charles Reemelin and *Volksblatt* ("people's paper") editor Stephen Molitor, and joined by antislavery Democrat Timothy Day, the group soon flexed its muscles at the party's county convention in August. There the "anti-Miami" delegates (also known as "Sawbucks") vociferously called upon every candidate for office to state whether or not he had been a Miami. Despite repeated denials by all nominees of any complicity in the tribe, the anti-Miamis managed to block the nominations of several men who were known members. A few Miami candidates did manage to get on the ticket, and for these offices the Sawbucks vowed to cross over to the Whigs in the fall election.[11]

The bolting Sawbucks wreaked havoc with the Democratic ticket in the October voting. For example, in the five Over-the-Rhine wards, the party's candidate for county commissioner, a Catholic who had admitted to attending "the Tribe twice upon solicitation,"[12] received an average vote 44.4 percent lower than the Democratic totals in the previous year's election, and 32.2 percent lower than the non-Miami candidate for auditor (see Figure 3). Anti-Miami defections were far

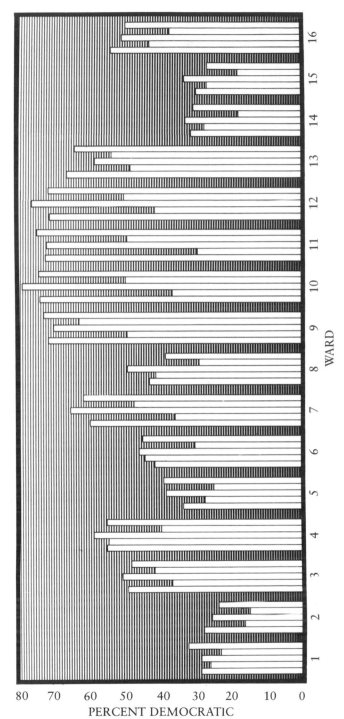

Figure 3. Percent Democratic vote by ward in five Cincinnati elections:

Column 1: Democratic state Senate candidates, October, 1851.
Column 2: "Miami Tribe" Democratic candidate for county commissioner, October, 1852.
Column 3: Franklin Pierce, Democratic candidate for president, November, 1852.
Column 4: Democratic candidate for mayor, April, 1853.
Column 5: Democratic state representatives, October, 1853.

"Over-the-Rhine" wards: 7, 9, 10, 11, 12.

smaller in the less heavily German wards, but the total drop in Democratic totals, about 14 percent citywide compared to the previous fall, was enough to defeat all four candidates tinged with Miami connections. And since some of the bolters refused to vote for any Democratic contender, many of the party's other candidates only narrowly escaped defeat.[13]

The German Sawbucks did not stay home on election day: voting was up in all wards and city vote totals ran about 1,000 ahead of the 1851 turnout. Nor did they cast their ballots for the Free Soil party, which opposed the extension of slavery into new territories, despite the antislavery sentiments of Timothy Day, a prominent anti-Miami. The Free Soilers received only about 1 percent of the vote throughout the city, and even less in the German wards. The Whigs were the sole beneficiaries of the defection, and they believed that the Miami split heralded new hope for their party in Cincinnati.

The Democrats won the majority of the races, but the Whigs nevertheless ecstatically claimed a triumph. Rutherford B. Hayes wrote to his uncle on election night that "every Whig in the city [is] either drunk or crazy over our victory." He added later that "every two minutes I hear some Whig cry, 'Hurrah for the Germans!' They gave us the victory."[14] Whigs envisioned that the bitterness of the October voting might grow into a Whig majority in Cincinnati for Winfield Scott in the November presidential balloting. Their hopes were short-lived, however, as the Sawbucks reasserted their loyalty to the Democratic party at all but the local level. Democrat Franklin Pierce easily defeated Scott in the city, and the Democratic margins returned to their 1851 levels in all wards (see Figure 3).[15]

The immediate consequences of the anti-Miami defection seemed minor and ephemeral. Yet the rift held great significance for the future of Cincinnati politics. Astute political observers realized that the "German vote" was not as monolithic as they had supposed. The Sawbucks had defeated the Democratic Miami candidates with little preparation or organization, and despite the complexity of the ticket-splitting procedure involved. Here, it seemed, was the Achilles' heel of the Democratic party in Cincinnati.

The Democratic hierarchy took immediate steps after the October election to heal the anti-Miami rift. Two members of the Miami Tribe, including Washington McLean, editor of the *Enquirer*, offered to resign from the state ticket of presidential electors (the offer was refused by the state central committee). The prevalent unity of the November balloting made the Democrats hopeful that the split was behind them. Their hopes were dashed when, within a few months, anti-Catholicism flared up once again, so violently that it changed the course of Cincinnati politics.[16]

In January, 1853, the *Catholic Telegraph* published a strong editorial condemning the public school system; in February, Cincinnati Archbishop John Purcell called upon the Ohio state legislature, then writing a progressive reform of the school code, to change the system of taxation for public school funds. Purcell demanded that Catholics either be allotted a portion of the tax money for parochial schools, or that those contributing money to a church school be exempt from school taxation. He argued that the public schools were not truly nonsectarian, since they taught Bible classes using the Protestant (King James) version of the Bible. Catholics, he concluded, were being taxed to support Protestant teachings.[17] Several hundred Cincinnatians, nearly all of whom appear to have been Irish, submitted a petition to the state legislature repeating the archbishop's arguments.[18] As a result of this Catholic initiative on school taxes, a heated controversy erupted in the city that not only reopened the split among Democrats but also severely damaged the Whig party organization.

Archbishop Purcell's actions were not an isolated occurrence. Rather, they reflected a growing assertiveness among Catholics, particularly Irish Catholics, both in Cincinnati and throughout the country.[19] Their new assertiveness had developed primarily out of a sense of increasing permanence and influence within their communities. The sheer number of Catholics in American cities following the flood of immigration in the late 1840s conveyed a feeling of power. A nineteenth-century Catholic historian, writing of the school issue in Cincinnati, explained the Church's aggressive stance by noting that "the Catholic body was growing in strength and influence,

. . . Catholic marriages in Cincinnati alone numbered, annually, 1261, and the baptisms, 3755." [20]

Tangibly increasing political strength, particularly within the Democratic party, augmented this awareness of local power. Cincinnati's Democrats paid homage to their loyal Irish Catholic supporters by holding the spring 1853 city convention on St. Patrick's Day rather than Andrew Jackson's birthday. In addition to numerical power and voting strength, Catholics felt more secure because of a marked decline after 1844 in the intensity of anti-Catholicism and xenophobia among native-born Protestants. [21]

Finally, Catholic immigrants became more assertive, particularly about schools, because many now saw themselves as permanent residents of their communities. Immigrants in the nineteenth century moved very frequently from city to city, [22] but by the mid-1840s a significant number had settled and made a permanent home for themselves. New families moving into the community could then readily take part in established social groups and feel allegiance to local political leaders. The most expressive symbols of Catholic permanence and collective strength in America were the cathedrals that many dioceses erected in the 1840s at great expense. Archbishop Purcell dedicated Cincinnati's St. Peter Cathedral in November, 1845. [23]

As Catholics in America became more settled, the problems of educating their children within the faith assumed greater significance. The public school system that developed in the 1830s and 1840s provided a clearly Protestant education and transmitted a Protestant culture. The most visible feature of this religious bias was the use of the King James version of the Bible in the schools. Most Protestants freely admitted that the common schools undermined the teachings of Catholicism. From their perspective that was one of the most valuable tasks the schools carried out. "Our cherished [American] civil institutions," editorialized Cincinnati's temperance journal for youth, "our habits of thinking and acting, are in direct opposition to Romanism and its teachings. . . ." [24] The common schools were "the true nurseries of sturdy republicanism," [25] and "republicanism," to most nineteenth-century Americans, was a term embodying all the qualities that underlay the nation's great virtue and strength. Catholic children "attending the same schools, sitting side by side with pure and open hearted American boys . . . naturally become imbued with our principles and Republican ideas," the journal concluded. "Here lies the cause of the Roman Catholic Priests' hostility to the common school system."[26] Catholics were thus caught between a public education with Protestant teachings and a Catholic education that was financially draining and that could not, in any case, expand fast enough to accommodate the rapidly growing Catholic school-age population.[27]

Catholic assertiveness did not stop with demands for school funds. Bishop John Hughes of New York, the first prelate to raise the school money issue, also delivered a number of highly publicized speeches on Catholicism, among them a talk on "The Decline of Protestantism and Its Causes," in which he stated that Catholicism meant "to convert the world—including the inhabitants of the United States. . . ."[28] The *Catholic Telegraph* in Cincinnati echoed Hughes's stance when it proclaimed that "the Catholic Church alone can save Republican institutions [in America] by her faith."[29]

The growing power of Catholics in America gave weight to the Church's assertive statements. Since most native-born Americans viewed the common schools as vital sources of American republicanism, attacks on the schools seemed to represent a threat to the nation itself. Protestants' dormant fears of papal plots to conquer and suppress the United States revived overnight. Moreover, anxiety over social disorder, the most pressing public issue of the time, was easily vented against immigrant Catholics, who seemed responsible for most of the disorder. Although the Cincinnati controversy focused on the school issue, accusations of undesirable Catholic social behavior and renewed Protestant fears of Catholic despotism fueled the debate.

Agitation on the school issue came primarily from Irish Catholics.[30] Cincinnati's German Catholics, who accounted for half the Church's membership in the city,[31] were notably less concerned about sending their children to the common schools. The Cincinnati petition to the state legislature requesting public school funds had essentially no German signatures, and German Catholics kept a low profile in the "school campaign" of that spring.[32] This may have been due in part to their distrust of the Irish-dominated church hierarchy which controlled parish schools, and particularly to their concern that Irish-run schools would not provide bilingual instruction.[33] Nevertheless, German Catholics, along with the Irish, suffered from the backlash of virulent anti-Catholicism that quickly spread throughout the city.

Protestant Cincinnatians responded with outrage to the Catholic school demands. Almost from the first, Protestant counterattacks exceeded the confines of the school issue itself, extending to accusations of deliberate subversion of American liberties and denunciations of Catholic social behavior. Cincinnati's Methodist journal, the *Western Christian Advocate*, remarked that Purcell seemed to have "no conception of the evil influence of drunkenness, Sabbath-breaking, profanity, and other vices among his own people." In the journal's opinion the real reason for Purcell's campaign was that "he sees that light and knowledge are doing their efficient work in the Popish church, in alienating multitudes of her children from her. . . ."[34] A well-known anti-Catholic lecturer spoke at length "of the prevalence of intoxication, gambling and profanity, among their creed." "Now, this is the class of people," he concluded, "that are called on in their zeal for purity, to break down our common schools."[35] The *Commercial* editorialized that the Catholic school demands were, although disguised, "a bold effort to unite here, as they [Catholics] have in other countries, the Church and the State. . . ."[36] The *Weekly Patriot* set out "to prove that Catholicity is treason,"[37] and the *Cincinnati Times* rose to the status of a major newspaper on the basis of its anti-Catholic stance during the school campaign.

The school issue dominated the city's local election campaign in the spring of 1853. As one speaker at a "free-school" meeting observed, "The old points of issue between whigs and democrats, had grown obsolete, and . . . the free school question was the only one of moment before the people."[38] As a result, party loyalties faltered and voting patterns shifted. The German vote divided once again, but this time the Whig party not only failed to recruit the dissident Germans but split itself. The Democratic party alone emerged intact, but seriously weakened by the renewed loss of German voters.

Four mayoral candidates and four major tickets made the election of 1853 one of the most complex in Cincinnati history (see Table 7). The members of the regular Democratic ticket, headed by mayoral contestant David T. Snelbaker, dodged the school issue as much as possible, claiming it was an inappropriate topic for a city election. The "Independent City Ticket," in reality a straight Whig organization slate, promoted Joseph S. Ross for mayor. Ross and the other Whig regulars mouthed anti-Catholic "free-school" rhetoric but generally hoped to avoid making the issue central to the campaign. Instead, they tried to redirect public attention to more traditional economic issues that had distinguished the Democratic and Whig party platforms in the past. The Whigs adopted the "independent" label in the hope of attracting bolting German Democrats, but their ticket proved unacceptable not only to the German dissidents but to all those who saw the school issue as the overarching issue of the election. The Whigs had chosen the same slate they would have run under any circumstances, whereas the prevailing mood of the electorate demanded candidates with solidly anti-Catholic, pro–free-school credentials. Furthermore, the national Whig party had attempted in the 1852 presidential campaign to appeal to Catholic immigrant voters in order to draw them away from the Democratic party and had thus severely damaged their credibility with anti-Catholics.[39]

"Free-School" mass meetings assembled on March 25 and 28. Although most of the participants had until then been Whigs, they stressed in their speeches that the school issue superseded party loyalty. The speakers were principally men named as candidates on an "Independent Free School Ticket," which had been assembled and circulated under the direction of James D. Taylor, editor of the vehemently anti-Catholic *Times*, and himself the Independent Free School candidate for mayor. The Free Schoolers endorsed part of the Whig slate, but besides substituting Taylor for Ross at the top of their ticket, they struck off several other Whig nominees and replaced them with their own candidates. The Free School slate found several Democrats (none of them prominent party men) to serve as

Table 7. Cincinnati mayoral candidates and election percentages, April, 1853.

Party or Ticket	Mayoral Candidate	Percentage of Total Vote
Democratic	David T. Snelbaker	39.6
Whig	Joseph S. Ross	19.2
Independent Free School	James D. Taylor	34.6
Anti-Convention Free School	F. T. Chambers	7

candidates, in order to stress that the movement was above party, and not simply a renegade Whig faction. However, no one on the ticket was German. Moreover, when the March 28 assembly received a message from free-school Germans who were meeting separately the same night, asking that they delay final action until joined by the German group, the request was shouted down. The incident highlighted what would prove a major weakness of the Independent Free School ticket: Taylor, his newspaper, and many of his supporters stood not only for anti-Catholicism but for anti-foreign sentiments as well.[40]

The subsequent German "Anti-Convention Free School" ticket ("Anti-Convention" signifying opposition to the slate chosen at the Democratic convention) rejected both Taylor and Ross as mayoral candidates, Taylor because of his nativist leanings and Ross because he was not strident enough in his free-school stance. Meeting at Turner's Hall, the dissident Germans (described by the *Times* as the "*ultra* Rhine") selected F. T. Chambers as their choice for mayor. They made up the rest of their ticket by selecting nominees from all three of the other slates, rejecting Taylorites with anti-foreign taint, Democrats with Miami or Catholic connections, and Whigs who were too bland on the school issue, until they had narrowed the field to a group acceptable to them.[41]

The final election results left everyone confused and no one satisfied. Snelbaker, the Democrat, won the mayoral race, but with only 39.6 percent of the vote. Taylor, the anti-Catholic leader, ran a very strong second with 34.6 percent. The Whigs had proclaimed frequently during the campaign that Ross was the only viable opponent of Snelbaker, and that Taylor would merely act as spoiler, handing the election to the Democrat. Ross's surprisingly low 19.2 percent, however, put the Whigs in the role of spoiler instead. Their candidate did not carry a single ward and lost to Taylor in all but three of the sixteen, including all the old Whig strongholds. Taylor's vote correlates much more strongly to previous Whig voting than does the vote for Ross, the regular Whig candidate, suggesting that the Free School slate picked up traditional Whig votes throughout the city, not just among certain segments of the population.[42]

Chambers won 990 votes, 7 percent of the total. But his vote did not represent the full strength of the dissident Germans. Many abandoned him in the end as a sure loser. A better indication of the German strength can be obtained by comparing two-candidate races, where the Anti-Convention Free School endorsement was the one variable. Such a comparison can be made between the voting for the office of auditor and that for marshal. The independent Germans placed on their ticket the Democratic candidate for auditor, but for marshal they chose the candidate who also appeared on the Whig and Independent Free School slates. The Democratic contestant for auditor, with dissident German support, won with 55 percent of the citywide vote; the Democratic contender for marshal, opposed by the German group, lost with only 43 percent of the vote. The bolting Germans had cost the party about 12 percent of the vote, nearly the same strength the Germans had mustered in the anti-Miami split. And once more their support had meant the difference between winning and losing for the Democrats.

The school election left a thoroughly muddied and confused political scene in its wake. The *Commercial* remarked that it had never "known an election in this city at which old party lines were so much disregarded."[43]

Despite Snelbaker's victory, the Free School forces took heart in the defeat of most Irish Catholic candidates for school board and city council, including one described as the "head and front of the Pope party."[44] The *Western Christian Advocate* headlined its report "Defeat of the Pope in Cincinnati," but cautioned that "the price of liberty is eternal vigilance. The foreign religious and political power in our midst is a government within a government. It is also well organized. The seat is at the vatican."[45] It seemed that anti-Catholicism might well continue to play a powerful political role in the city.

The Whig organization came out of the election shattered and totally demoralized. Although the Democrats clearly could be beaten by a united opposition, Ross's dismal showing demonstrated that the old Whig structure had neither the credibility nor the right issues to spark a new coalition under its banner. By July the *Times* was already claiming that the Whigs "no longer existed as an organization" in the city, even though their "remnants" still exerted some political influence.[46]

The Democrats, in turn, were smarting not only from the loss of four city offices but from their obviously increasing vulnerability to defections within their party. The vote in the Over-the-Rhine wards did not plunge as far as it had in the October, 1852, election, but the stigma of popery had caused Democratic totals in the other wards to drop more than they had over the Miami Tribe issue (see Figure 3). Democratic leaders needed to mollify the bolters on the Catholic issue, and yet they could not risk alienating their loyal Catholic supporters in the process.

The 1853 spring elections destroyed the old party structure within Cincinnati. The Democratic organization was left intact but weakened and on the defensive. The moribund Whig party, having failed to respond adequately to the new issues of social disorder and Catholic aggressiveness, lost its members in droves. But as the school issue subsided, the voters who had supported the Independent Free School ticket and the German Free School ticket were left with no focal issue, no rallying cry, no organization. The circumstances were favorable for a movement that would address itself to the social anxieties of the day and serve as a unifying force, pulling together all the elements of the populace dissatisfied with the old, unresponsive party system. It was in this political context that the temperance movement launched its all-out campaign for a prohibitory law.

Temperance activists in Ohio began 1853 determined to make liquor prohibition a prominent political issue in the state. On January 5 the state temperance convention resolved to vote only for candidates in the coming fall legislative elections who had pledged to support a Maine Law for Ohio. The Hamilton County temperance convention met in February and unanimously endorsed the state action. The 250 delegates initiated plans for a county organization that would produce "efficient and united action in every ward and township."[47] Temperance reformers throughout the state began to lay the groundwork for what was to be one of the most massive and influential nonpartisan political efforts in Ohio history.

The school issue that spring, however, sidetracked the Maine Law campaign in Cincinnati. Not only was temperance reform temporarily forgotten by the public as attention focused on the schools, but the reformers themselves became involved in the growing religious tensions of the city. Anti-Catholic sentiments surfaced in the *Ohio Organ for Temperance Reform.* At the same time its editor, Samuel Cary, launched an attack on the antireligious attitudes of the German radicals. By the end of the school campaign the temperance movement had managed to alienate further both Catholic and non-Catholic elements of the immigrant population in the city.

Temperance crusaders had increasingly found reason to resent the attitude of the Catholic church toward their reform. The Church for years had forbidden members to belong to any fraternal society that entailed pledges of secrecy: passwords or rituals that could not be repeated, even to a priest during confession. Catholics could not therefore join either the Sons of Temperance or the Templars of Honor. To members of these orders, the rule seemed arbitrary and destructive, preventing "many, otherwise good and honest citizens . . . [from being] spared the evils of intemperance. . . ."[48] On the issue of prohibition, the stance of the Catholic church was even more galling. When the *Catholic Telegraph* explained its reasons for raising the school question, it suggested that the controversy would "cause thinking men to reflect that at present, Maine Liquor Laws, State Education Systems, Infidelity, Pantheism, are not isolated measures . . . but parts of a great whole, at war with God."[49] The Church attacked prohibition because it believed that merely passing laws would not and could not change human behavior. The *Telegraph* classed the Maine Law campaigners as "quack" reformers, along with advocates of manifest destiny, slavery abolition, "European Red Republicanism," socialism, Fourierism, and women's rights.[50]

When the school issue aroused a feverish anti-Catholic mood throughout the city in the spring of 1853, many temperance advocates were among those infected. Moreover, since temperance followers had often criticized blind party loyalty when it had conflicted with their own cause, they must have been ready recruits to a similar call to conscience over the school issue.

Samuel Cary at first made no editorial mention of the school controversy in the *Organ*. His reticence did not suit the publisher, Caleb Clark, an ardent supporter of James Taylor, anti-Catholic mayoral candidate and editor of the *Times*. Clark began to write separate editorials for the paper, lauding the *Times* as "a right worthy champion of the hosts of America against the *Roman*, foreign and papistical legions of Despotism,"[51] and condemning the Catholic church for its "unholy crusade against our beloved [Sons of Temperance] Order."[52] Cary later appended his own opinions: he supported the free School forces, but not out of opposition to the Catholic church as such; he would oppose any Protestant church just as heartily if it wanted access to public school funds. Yet he then went on to criticize the Catholic church for not encouraging Bible reading among its members.[53] Cary was a deeply religious man, and his devout beliefs created controversy on another front.

Cary, like most Cincinnati citizens, had been astonished when, in January of that year, a huge torchlight procession of German radicals had celebrated the birthday of Thomas Paine, propagandist of the American and French revolutions and an anticleric. The celebration was organized by Friedrich Hassaurek, editor of the antireligious weekly *Der Hochwaechter* ["the high guardian"] and leader of the Freimännerverein. Two thousand, of whom only a handful were non-German, marched through the streets of the city and then listened to toasts and speeches praising not only Paine but other reformers who had attacked organized religion, such as Robert Owen and Frances Wright. The German radicals espoused a full program of social change, including women's rights, land reform, freedom from political corruption, and abolition of black slavery in the South and white wage slavery in the North. The touchstones of their radicalism, however, were opposition to monarchy and to all organized religion. They hated Catholicism most of all, but condemned Protestant churches as well for promoting dogma that restricted individual freedom of thought. Most considered agnosticism or atheism the only appropriate creeds for the Age of Reason.[54]

The Tom Paine celebration disturbed Cary deeply. Although he personally agreed with many of the German radicals' reform aims, he could not countenance any attack upon religion. "We were not before aware of the extent of the infidel clubs in this city," Cary wrote in the *Organ*. Paine, he added, was not only an infidel but "a notorious profligate, a libertine and drunkard." His followers were "disorganizers of society" likely to re-enact the bloody scenes of the French Revolution in America if they had their way.[55] Cary continued the attack a few issues later, referring to the "Free Thinker's Hall" (Turner's Hall), which had "two or three large bars connected with it which require seven or eight active men on the Sabbath, to wait upon the worshippers at the shrine of *free inquiry*. The *thousands* who assemble here on the Lord's day, to listen to the profane babblings of infidels, and engage in gymnastic exercises, find liquor indispensable to wash down the truth. . . ."[56] The temperance movement in Cincinnati thus began its Maine Law campaign in Cincinnati by directly offending the leaders of the most important bloc of swing voters in the city.

Maine Law advocates had been aware from the beginning of their campaign in Cincinnati that the German vote was crucial locally. The February county temperance convention had proclaimed that "a German mission is indispensable to success . . . ," passing that resolution immediately after approval of the state convention's actions. Delegates planned for a German temperance missionary, hired at $500 per year, and for a temperance journal to be published in German. One speaker asserted: "When there were 1,000 Germans in Hamilton County who would vote right on the Temperance question, political parties would put Temperance men on their tickets."[57]

The speakers were not thinking primarily of radical or Catholic Germans. Rather, they hoped to reach German Protestants (and perhaps Jews, although they were not mentioned) with the temperance message. They were encouraged, in particular, by the small but growing number of German Methodists in the city. Germans were first converted to Methodism in the United States; indeed, the first mission had been founded in Cincinnati by William Nast in 1838. When Germans converted to Methodism, they also adopted the teetotalism practiced by their American-born brethren. Nast himself spoke at the March, 1853, county temperance convention, applauding plans for a German temperance mission and encouraging the organization to seek German ministers who would open their pulpits to speakers in favor of the Maine Law.[58]

The Methodists, however, were a tiny minority even among German Protestants, and they were generally disliked by their fellow Germans. Perhaps the friendly attitude of Nast and his followers misled Cary into thinking that Protestant Germans would not be offended by his attacks on the radicals. But Germans were sensitive to any attack that might be considered nativist. Moreover, even among Protestant Germans who disliked the radicals' doctrines, many acknowledged Reemelin, Hassaurek, and Molitor to be leaders and representatives of the German community. The attacks in the *Organ* offended many nonradical Germans and undermined efforts to win even minimal German support for prohibition. The county organization eventually abandoned its ambitious German mission plans, and Cary wrote that he had been "severely censured for speaking strongly against the anti-Bible, Tom Paine, infidel movements."[59]

It is doubtful whether the Maine Law campaign could

have made any significant gains in the German community
even if its leaders had avoided attacking the radicals. Germans
were in the forefront of the opposition to prohibition throughout the country. Although German speakers did sometimes
condemn whiskey drinking and the evils of frequent inebriation, the consumption of wine and beer was an integral part of
German culture. Temperance reform was not widespread in
Germany at the time, and to immigrants it seemed both alien
and offensive to their traditions. Moreover, both brewing and
wine making were important sources of German employment
in the city, as were the coffee houses that sold those beverages.
So long as prohibition included wine and beer in its provisions,
active German support was probably out of the question. (In
later years German influence within the Republican party
brought about the exemption of beer and wine from the prohibitory laws of Iowa and Michigan.)[60] Of course, different degrees of opposition were possible, and the German response to
the campaign might have been milder if only prohibition had
been at issue. But once prohibition was identified with religious parochialism and what appeared to be anti-German nativist prejudice, Germans, and in particular the radicals,
quickly became the city's most articulate and organized opponents of the "despotic and fanatical" prohibition effort.

After the spring election temperance leaders hoped the
school issue would disappear quickly. Although it did fade away
as a focus of controversy, the political disruption it had caused
persisted. Moreover, later events were to demonstrate the continuing, and even growing, vitality of anti-Catholicism in the
city. For the time being, though, the field seemed once again
open for the prohibition efforts of the temperance movement.

In the rest of the state, many Ohioans had followed the
Cincinnati school campaign with great interest but without direct involvement. Temperance forces successfully made opposition to liquor selling a key issue in several local election campaigns elsewhere in the state during that spring of 1853, and
scored a number of victories for their endorsed candidates.
The *Organ* headlined the news "Temperance Triumphant!"
and asked, "Who says the people are not prepared for a pro-

hibitory law?"[61] The *Commercial* noted the resolutions of the Hamilton County temperance convention to press for prohibition in the fall elections, and predicted: "If these measures are prosecuted with energy, (and from the character of the men who are to lead them, we presume they will be,) there will be no slight temperance agitation in our city and county during the next six months."[62]

But neither prohibitionists nor political observers could have anticipated the damage done to Cincinnati's party structure in the spring election. Nor could they have foreseen that the Maine Law campaign would become not only the predominant public issue in the city and throughout the state but also the potential nucleus of a new major political party.

Temperance activists organized at several levels to reach the electorate during the months prior to the October election. Ward and township meetings, massive parades and public gatherings, nationally known speakers, and widely distributed journals were all integral parts of the Maine Law campaign in Ohio. Leaders within the cause put aside differences and cooperated closely within a tight hierarchical structure that reached from precinct leaders to the state executive committee. For six months the temperance movement in Ohio ran a massive and efficient political organization.

When prohibitionists had planned the campaign in early 1853, they intended to force the major political parties to run candidates pledged to support the Maine Law. But after the spring election the situation changed rapidly. Whig support had not only collapsed in Cincinnati but was declining rapidly throughout the state. Many Whig voters had been alienated from their party when it had appealed to Catholics in the fall of 1852. The party then confirmed its unreliability on Catholic questions when it sidestepped the Cincinnati free-school issue. Moreover, as historian Michael Holt has forcefully argued, another, less obvious factor entered into the sudden breakdown of the party system: events between 1848 and 1853 made it seem to people that the Democratic and Whig parties no longer offered them clear alternative positions on important issues. The adoption of new state constitutions and the advent of economic prosperity caused some old issues to be resolved and led the two major parties to espouse similar positions.[63] Rutherford B. Hayes wrote in his diary in September, 1852: "Politics is not longer *the topic* of this country. Its important questions are settled. . . ."[64] Just before the November election he admitted to his uncle: "The truth is there is no principle at stake in the election. It is only a preference for our party and our man."[65] In this political climate many voters were eager to support new groups or coalitions that appeared to address forcefully and effectively the new issues which surfaced in 1853. In Ohio they pressed for independent Maine Law tickets, Maine Law/Free Soil tickets, or Maine Law/Whig fusion slates headed by new faces, to run against the Democrats that fall.

With party lines severely disrupted, political observers began to look upon the statewide Maine Law organization as more than just a temporary, nonpartisan campaign structure. The *Times* reported that most citizens expected the old party system to die; they "took it for granted that there must be some great question" that would redivide the state into new political alignments, and many assumed that prohibition would be the "Shibboleth" that would bring about the new party structure.[66]

The idea of being a new political party worried the leaders of the prohibition campaign. By and large, these men were totally committed to the anti-liquor crusade and solely interested in passing a Maine Law in Ohio. They did make plans to run independent and fusion slates where it seemed necessary but otherwise continued to focus on encouraging prohibitionist candidates within the Whig and Democratic parties.

The state temperance convention executive committee, chaired by Samuel Cary, made policy for the campaign. Day-to-day decisions were also made by Cary, as head of the local committee, and by A. A. Stewart of Columbus, hired as general and financial agent.[67] While Cary made broad policy decisions, Stewart concentrated on the practical problems of raising funds and scheduling statewide speaking tours. He set a budgetary goal of $10,000–20,000 to be raised through county organizations, with three-fourths of the money to be credited back to the counties in the form of lecturing engagements and publications, the rest going to an executive committee general fund. Actual financing exceeded even these optimistic expectations, as more than $20,000 was raised and spent in the campaign. Stewart at one time had as many as seventeen speakers traveling in the state.[68]

The state organization distributed some pamphlets but concentrated on promoting short-term "campaign subscriptions" to the *Organ*. Between July and September the journal's total circulation quadrupled from 5,000 to 20,000. The executive committee also planned a "mass temperance convention" for Columbus June 29 and 30. The procession through the city which highlighted the convention stretched, according to one estimate, over two miles in length and contained nearly 10,000 marchers.[69]

In Hamilton County the temperance organization employed tactics at the local level similar to those used in the state campaign. In the spring and early summer frequent meetings at the ward and township level sparked enthusiasm for the cause. Cary and other city leaders spoke at a large temperance picnic on the Fourth of July. Nationally known orators from other states began to arrive in late summer and early fall, lecturing at Melodeon Hall. The executive committee for the county also engaged an old Washingtonian, John R. Williams, to hold "genuine temperance meeting[s] of the good old-fashioned kind" for the "river men" at the wharf every Sunday.[70] Throughout the campaign Sons of Temperance, Templars of Honor, and even nonfraternal prohibition advocates, especially clergymen, cooperated with one another and submerged their differences. With victory over the liquor trade at stake, the temperance movement closed ranks and set its sights on October 11, election day.[71]

Converting the Ohio temperance movement into a statewide political organization may have been a new departure for the reformers in 1853, but their campaign rhetoric sounded quite familiar. During the previous five years citizen concerns over the suffering, the immorality, the danger, and the costs generated by social disorder had sparked growing public interest in and support for prohibition. The specter of rising crime and poverty had, in effect, made passage of a Maine Law in

Ohio a realistic objective. Temperance activists shared the general public's concern over disorder. They also knew that their promise to eliminate social ills would be the pre-eminent selling point for prohibition, and would be the focal issue of the campaign.

The theme of social disorder—its causes, its consequences, and its cure—dominated the speeches, letters, articles, editorials, and pamphlets of the prohibitionists in 1853.[72] A typical *Organ* editorial stated: "Crime of all description is fearfully on the increase—the peaceable citizen is in danger of his life, whether on the highway, in the lane, or on the broad streets of our city. Our jails, watch-houses and poor-houses, all, all, are full to overflowing, old offenders having to be unloosed upon society, unwhipped of justice, to make room for new ones. . . . Murder, riot, and bloody assaults are so common to our courts that they have ceased to excite wonder."[73] Some judges and prosecuting attorneys estimated that 39 out of every 40 criminal cases they saw were caused by liquor. The solution to this horror seemed evident to temperance advocates, since in their eyes it was "undeniably true, that under the operation of such laws as prohibit the [liquor] traffic, crime is lessened, taxation is reduced, and order preserved in communities."[74] Prohibitionists flatly proclaimed that their success would mean an end to the most troublesome social ills of their day.

The opponents of prohibition never challenged the assumptions that drinking caused disorder, and that drinking and disorder were both growing at a frightening pace. Critics based their counterarguments instead on the efficacy, the fairness, and the constitutionality of the Maine Law itself. The *Commercial* accurately singled out the key questions: "Whether the legislature may legitimately exert its authority upon this subject? Whether the proposed remedy [the Maine Law] will effect the object intended [diminished drinking]? Whether such a legislative interference with private privileges and private appetites can be justified by any considerations of public expediency? Whether it it wise to attempt a moral reformation by such coercive means?"[75] Such questions troubled many thoughtful citizens who were undecided on the issue of prohibition.

Temperance crusaders responded harshly to all those expressing any doubts on the wisdom of total prohibition. The justifications for the Maine Law seemed self-evident to its dedicated supporters; they automatically doubted the sincerity of anyone who, once fully exposed to the temperance rationale, professed to remain unpersuaded. Moreover, the anti-license campaigns had convinced temperance activists that proposals for compromise were either the attempts of privileged or powerful groups to seek unjust favoritism, or were the deliberate efforts of the enemies of temperance to provide legal loopholes that would serve to destroy the entire law.

Perhaps most important, the drink reformers had for many years feared the secret "Rum Power" in Cincinnati. At the outset of the 1853 campaign Cary stated that temperance men in Hamilton County were "marked. There was a secret association which took note of them. . . ."[76] When in 1853 some city leaders who had formerly voiced support for temperance goals came out against the Maine Law, temperance advocates declared that they were finally getting a public look at those who privately had been part of, or had been subverted by, the Rum Power.

Thus unqualified support for the Maine Law became a litmus test for temperance activism, and those who had their doubts about the efficacy of the Maine Law found themselves harshly condemned. Prohibitionists, the *Times* noted, considered "that all who are opposed to the Maine Law are friends of intemperance, or, at least, not enemies of intemperance . . . and we regret it, because it shuts out many temperance men, by narrowing the platform so that they cannot work with their more zealous brethren."[77] In short, personal abstinence was no longer sufficient for one to be considered a friend of the temperance movement. As Cary wrote in the *Organ*: "It is not enough, dear reader, that you should live a life of total abstinence; you are required to enroll your name, join the army of temperance, and be prepared for a mighty struggle with a mighty foe."[78] In the course of the campaign this insistence on public support for prohibition had the effect of alienating some who had been sympathetic to organized temperance reform.

As opposition to the Maine Law coalesced, attacks on the proposed law fell primarily into five areas of argument: that the proposed law was unconstitutional; that it was unenforceable; that it unjustly included wine; that it would hurt the state's corn farmers; and that it was a Whig trick intended to undermine the Democratic party. Each of these arguments proved to be effective with some voters, and all were repeated continually by the opponents of prohibition.

In 1853 there were as yet few legal precedents to clarify the issue of constitutionality. In the years to come the courts in nearly every instance upheld the right of states to prohibit their liquor traffic. However, the question was still open in 1853. Moreover, each state differed in its constitutional provisions and in the specific wording of its prohibitory law, so that the legality of the law was always in doubt until after a state had passed prohibition and then tested it in the courts.[79]

The opponents of prohibition in Ohio claimed that the law attacked free trade, the rights of property and privacy (in its search and seizure provisions), and the liberty of choice guaranteed to all free people. When the argument got down to specific legal precedents, they ironically pinned their hopes on the anti-license clause of the 1851 constitution. Part of that provision stated: "the General Assembly may by law provide against the evils resulting [from liquor trade]. . . ." Critics argued that the clause implicitly recognized the existence of a liquor trade in the state, and that outlawing such trade entirely would therefore be unconstitutional.[80]

Prohibitionists took the ground that personal liberty extended only to the point where it began to damage the commonweal. They sometimes pointed to concrete examples, such as "the drunken driver of a stage coach," but more often to the general social costs of crime and poverty, to show that the liquor trade injured the community. The Maine Law, they argued, would be no more of an infringement on personal liberty than were laws against gambling and prostitution. As to the anti-license clause, they felt sure the record of the constitutional convention debates would prove that the clause had not been intended to protect the future existence of the liquor traffic.[81]

The constitutional argument against prohibition appealed strongly to German voters, who were sensitive to any perceived infringement of human liberties. At a German anti–Maine Law mass meeting in September, the theme of unconstitutionality underlay nearly every speech. In the words of one speaker prohibition laws "interfered in an unwarrantable manner with private rights, and were disgraceful." He urged "the people to be cautious as to who they elected Legislators, that their liberties might not be taken away or interfered with, . . . [or laws passed] striking at the most sacred privileges of free men."[82] Portraying the Maine Law as "despotism" proved effective in helping to stir the rancor of German voters.

In addition to the charge of unconstitutionality, critics of prohibition also claimed that the law would be unenforceable or would be enforced inequitably. The *Enquirer* argued that the Maine Law would be a "dead letter" in Ohio as soon as it was passed, and would therefore only teach disobedience to law.[83] The *Commercial* cited reports from Maine and Massachusetts which indicated that, although public "grog-shop tippling" had been greatly reduced, the rich still had easy access to alcoholic beverages: wine and brandy in hotels, and whatever they wanted for private consumption. In fact, anyone could obtain alcoholic beverages if he was willing to go to dishonest physicians and druggists who could prescribe them for "medicinal purposes." If this were true in the "favorable conditions" of Maine, what could be expected in Cincinnati? For many potential supporters of the prohibition cause, the charges that it would mean favoritism for the rich and that it would undermine respect for the law were particularly troublesome issues.[84]

Supporters of the Maine Law did not deny that enforcement would be difficult, especially in Cincinnati, where prohibition would have to overcome the dual obstacles of a police force notorious for its drunkenness and a large population of "citizens of foreign birth and *habits*" who were less "tractable" on the question of drink.[85] But, wrote a local temperance spokesman in a series of letters to the *Commercial*, just because the Maine Law would not be totally effective immediately did not make it unworthy of passage. Laws against licentiousness, gambling, and larceny were not completely effective in stopping these crimes, but they were good laws nonetheless. In states where the Maine Law had been passed, the writer claimed, it was doing much good even though not fully enforced, and was "diminishing crime, pauperism, rowdyism, &c., to a very considerable extent." Some of these states had large Irish populations in their cities, who were "more excitable and lawless, and more sensual in their mode of life, than any other class of immigrants." By contrast, most of Cincinnati's immigrants were Germans, "*in the main*, a quiet and orderly class." From the viewpoint of this temperance writer, the fact that the fugitive-slave law, to him "the most odious law in the land," had just been executed without tumult in the city proved that Cincinnatians were a law-abiding people, and that the Maine Law would eventually be effective there.[86]

Another continuing source of controversy in the campaign involved the inclusion of wine in the proposed prohibitory law. Temperance activists believed that distillers, brewers, and influential drink sellers were responsible for the "secret cabals" they thought operated clandestinely to undermine drink reform. But linked to these enemies of the cause, they claimed, were others even more insidious because they were more respected and more powerful. The "most formidable enemies that retain the field against the progress of temperance" were none other than "our moderate wine-drinking citizens." "We know," wrote a temperance spokesman, "that they are strong, very stong; that they occupy the highest walks of life, and fill almost every station of honor, trust, and emolument."[87] These members of Cincinnati's parvenu "mushroom aristocracy" insisted on drinking wine, according to the *Organ*, because they thought it "genteel and refined to have sideboard and tables loaded with costly decanters filled with the devil's drink."[88] Although they spoke from the lofty positions of civic leaders, these citizens were less concerned with community welfare, claimed temperance activists, than they were with protecting their own affectations, privileges, and financial interests in the wine industry.[89]

The deep-seated hostility of the temperance crusaders toward the local plutocracy was palpable nearly every time they spoke on the subject. The reformers delighted in pointing out that the opponents of teetotalism were largely the very richest and the very poorest in society, while the hard-working, productive citizens in between were the allies of the reform. Whereas the temperance cause had wrought a great change during the previous two decades in the drinking customs of the middle ranks of society, the consequences of intemperance were still to be found "among the rich—gout and plethory in broadcloth [and] in the hovels of the poor—rags and wretchedness. . . ."[90] The fight against drink would have to contend with a combination against it that ran from "the fashionable and wealthy manufacturer of wine, down to the most degraded vendor of rum who occupies the filthiest hovel. . . ."[91] By 1853, given the years of mutual hostility that preceded the Maine-Law campaign, temperance leaders could not have expected support for prohibition from the local elite. But once again prohibitionists seemed to provoke more active and steadfast opposition than might otherwise have been the case.

One could not mention the "wine-drinking aristocracy" in Cincinnati at mid-century and not immediately bring to mind the imposing figure of Nicholas Longworth. The wealthiest man in the city by far, Longworth was also the first to grow grapes and make wine in the Cincinnati region. Although he had made his fortune in real estate (and still owned so much city land that he paid the second-highest property tax in the nation), his passions were viticulture and oenology. He promoted the industry tirelessly, and was almost solely responsible for making the Cincinnati area the foremost American wine-making region of the time. Longworth's own sparkling Catawba wine was internationally renowned, he had encouraged many others to plant grapes and invest in wine making, and, as head of the Cincinnati-based American Wine Grower's Association, he was recognized as the country's principal promoter of the development of domestic wines.[92]

Nicholas Longworth had planted his first grape vines in the city in 1823. An early advocate of anti-spirits temperance, he always claimed that providing an alternative to hard liquor had been the primary motivation for starting his vineyard. He had broken with the reform when it was taken over by total-abstinence advocates, and had been at odds with it ever since. The Maine Law campaign, which advocated outlawing the wine industry, naturally aroused Longworth's ire. There is no knowing what influence he brought to bear privately, but he was so incensed that he took the uncharacteristic step of speaking out publicly on the issue.

In early August, 1853, Longworth submitted to the *Commercial* an open letter to Cary that touched off a public debate on wine in the pages of the paper. Cary's response came two days later, followed by a flurry of letters from both wine makers and temperance leaders. Longworth and his associates claimed that wine was a temperance beverage, too mild to cause inebriation (Longworth's Catawba was promoted as the wine which "exhilarates but does not intoxicate").[93] The only places in Europe where drunkenness did not abound, they claimed, were those areas where pure, unadulterated wine served as the principal beverage. The Wine Grower's Association appointed a committee of five "very respectable" doctors to investigate the effect of wine on the human system. Their report concluded that there was no "free alcohol" in wine, so that it could not intoxicate; that wine was as nutritious as flesh meats; and that it prevented the too-rapid decomposition of the blood when taken in winter by the laboring class after a frugal meal. The authors of the medical report left no doubt as to where they stood when they added that wine was recommended by the Savior, that the Maine Law would destroy Ohio's fledgling grape industry, and that it was, moreover, clearly unconstitutional.[94]

The prohibitionists flatly refused to consider excepting wine from the law should a legislature favorable to prohibition be elected. Wine, they asserted, contained alcohol, like whiskey or beer, and had exactly the same effects. Moreover, even Longworth's pure wine, they claimed, was frequently adulterated after it left his hands. Justice and equality forbade exempting "the drink of the aristocracy" while prohibiting the drink of "the 'wool-hatted,' hard-fisted poor. . . ."[95] The temperance activists issued their own medical report, authored by a professor of chemistry at the Cincinnati College of Medicine and Surgery, disputing every point in the wine growers' report. Finally, the Reverend Dudley Tyng wrote to explain that the wine of the Last Supper was a nonintoxicating wine (that is, grape juice). Indeed, as Cary detailed in his initial response to Longworth's letter, the Bible in numerous places condemned the use of intoxicating wines.[96]

Cary's letter in response to Longworth's not only outlined most of these arguments against wine but laced them with undisguised hostility. Longworth had argued that the local grape and wine industry would be ruined by prohibition. Cary answered acidly: "We protest against that wealth and splendor which are secured by the miseries, tears and blood of society."[97] These were harsh words to direct at the city's foremost philanthropist and most prominent citizen.

Subsequent letters from other temperance leaders tried to take a more conciliatory tone, and to suggest that the grape growers would find other profitable markets. But the entire wine controversy left many convinced that Cary and his fellow prohibitionists had erred badly in taking an uncompromising and even insulting attitude toward Longworth and his powerful associates. "General Cary—we still persist in calling him a very poor general—and other of the *fast* leaders of the movement," wrote the *Circleville Herald*, "must have the 'Maine Law,' and nothing else. They must make war on the manufacturer of wine. . . ."[98] The *Commercial* believed that the fundamental need of the community was for a law to close the grog shops and stop the sale of hard liquor. If so, "Why hang upon it other features calculated to provoke the opposition of classes of men? Why overload it with that which must inevitably either defeat its passage or its enforcement? Why make warfare where warfare is not needed, and create enemies of those who would otherwise be neutral if not friendly?"[99] Cary claimed later that exempting wine would have cost the cause at least as many votes as including it. But the fact was that the wine controversy, and the tone it took, made bitter enemies of some Ohioans with incalculable influence and prestige.

Germans and wine-drinking elites formed the nucleus of public opposition to the Maine Law within Cincinnati, but corn farmers were its primary foes in the rural areas of Ohio. A convention of corn growers in Portsmouth, Ohio, in 1851 had officially condemned any liquor-restriction laws whatsoever.[100] By 1853 they were convinced that passage of prohibition would destroy their livelihood. The *Times* thought that the law would be far more difficult to pass in Ohio than in New England simply because of the influence of the state's corn farmers: "From the first they have been accustomed to carry their corn in their own wagons to the very doors of the distilleries." Anyone who thought that hard-working, respectable farmers would give up a source of ready cash for as much as a third of their crop "in order that some lazy loafers shall be obliged to go without their bitters," wrote the *Times*, did not know human nature.[101]

The potential plight of the corn farmers was a particularly troublesome issue for prohibitionists. If corn prices dipped because of the Maine Law, all rural families who grew corn would have their livelihoods damaged, whether or not they themselves sold to distillers. Moreover, while some versions of the law in other states provided monetary compensation for those in the liquor trade, there was no way to aid injured corn growers. The *Organ* noted that from "listening to conversations in village towns and bar-rooms," one would think that prohibition would create "a huge quantity of surplus corn."[102] The reformers had, in the past, appealed to the morality of the farmers, and had implored: "Do not shrink from your responsibility, by saying that you must have a market for your grain. Better, far better for you that it should rot in your barns, than be thus made into consuming fire." This could not have been a very comforting thought for most farmers. By 1853 prohibitionists avoided such statements, and instead tried to counteract the fears of farmers by arguing that only one-seventeenth to one-twentieth of the corn crop went into whiskey production. Farmers themselves placed the amount at nearly a third

Nicholas Longworth, engraved by E. E. Jones from a daguerreotype. (courtesy Cincinnati Historical Society)

Nicholas Longworth (seated, right) and the Horticultural Society. (courtesy Cininnati Historical Society)

Nicholas Longworth's vineyards in the hills outside Cincinnati (from *Longworth's Wine House*, 1866)

Bottling, corking, and wiring Nicholas Longworth's "Sparkling Catawba Wine." (from *Longworth's Wine House*)

YOUNG LADY OFFERING HER LOVER WINE.

THE RESULT.

"Young Lady Offering Her Lover Wine/The Result." (from Stebbins and Brown, *Fifty Years History*)

"Temperance." (from Shaw, *History*)

of the crop. The actual figure was probably somewhere in between. Even the temperance figure of 5 percent, however, was more of their market than corn farmers cared to lose.[103]

Of all the accusations hurled at the Maine Law in Ohio, perhaps none was as damaging statewide as the claim by the Democratic party organization that prohibition was a Whig ruse, meant to obscure legitimate party issues and overthrow Democratic ascendancy. Party newspapers repeated this charge over and over. They claimed that nineteen out of twenty temperance leaders were Whigs, and they frequently singled out Samuel Cary as a well-known "bitter Whig" who hoped to ride the prohibition issue into office.[104]

Democratic leaders in Ohio could not be certain how much support the Maine Law campaign might draw from their own rank and file. Temperance meetings around the state seemed to be arousing the same kind of enthusiasm and disregard for party loyalties that the school campaign had generated in Cincinnati. There was no way to predict how successful the prohibition movement might be, and it was this very uncertainty that made the Democratic hierarchy so hostile to the movement. For years the distinctions between Democrat and Whig had been clearcut and stable, and Democrats had defined themselves as a party largely in terms of their opposition to Whig platforms and programs. Now that Democrats were dominant in the state, they feared any new issue or movement that might cloud party lines and undermine partisan loyalties. Their attempt to pin a Whig label on the Maine Law phenomenon was an attempt to keep the Whigs alive, to maintain in opposition a known enemy, one that would be sure to spark party feeling among the state's Democratic voters.

The temperance organization responded by going out of its way, as the Independent Free School ticket in Cincinnati had done that spring, to ensure that Democrats were as prominent as possible in its upper ranks. The *Organ* claimed that "three of the five members composing the State Executive Committee are Democrats. . . . Our State Agent, A. A. Stewart, Esq., is now and always has been a warm decided Democrat. . . . In Hamilton county . . . the Temperance Executive Committee is composed of ten Whigs and Free Soilers, and

TWENTY-EIGHT DEMOCRATS!"[105] The paper criticized "the wreck of the whig party" for its failure to support temperance measures in the past, and pointed out the continued opposition of the Whig press to prohibition.[106] Editorial assistants defended Cary while he was away on speaking tours, denying that he had any interest in seeking public office. The Hamilton County temperance executive committee even considered nominating only Democrats for the county Maine Law ticket, in order that it could not "with any consistency be denounced as a 'Whig trick.'"[107]

The surviving Whig organization in Hamilton County responded with dismay to the Maine Law movement, knowing that it would serve to split the party even further. The *Gazette* in April remarked that the campaign would prove "very annoying to the political managers of both parties," but that the Whigs would suffer the most.[108] At the county party convention in September, attempts to question prospective candidates on their Maine Law stance were shouted down with cries that they "need not answer as to anything but Whig principles."[109] As the election approached, the *Gazette* adopted a fatalistic attitude. The Maine Law, it noted, was the only "great measure" now agitated before the voters, "and about that the people are not divided according to their old political affinities." But, the journal added, "we know of no time when the Whigs could lose less by the introduction of this [prohibition] element into our politics than at present. . . ."[110] The Whigs were already well aware that they were about to place a distant third in the Cincinnati voting. In the city and throughout the state many diehard Whigs sat out the election and, in the words of the *Commercial*, simply "forgot to vote" on election day.[111]

The *Times* saw the Maine Law campaign as destructive of all party ties, even though the paper also anticipated an overwhelming Democratic victory. "All acknowledge," it claimed, "that there never was such political confusion in Hamilton county as there is at the present time. Old party ties have in great measure been rent asunder; and the only organizations that now exist, are founded upon an entire new issue—that of a prohibitory liquor law." Clearly the Democratic organization was still politically dominant, but it could no longer campaign effectively on the economic issues that had delineated its existence in the past. The "cry of 'banks' is lost in that of 'rum-shops;' of 'tariff,' in that of 'fanaticism.'" The Maine Law was "the only question discussed on the stump, and therefore it must be THE issue and nothing else." Despite the prospect of a Democratic sweep at the polls, the significant fact of the campaign was the "desertion from all party platforms." The Democrats were being swept along rather than defining the dominant political issue of the day. In this context the *Times* could declare that "party traces have lost their power . . . [and] old division lines are lost in the brilliancy of the new one."[112] Within Cincinnati the prohibition issue completed the destruction of the old political structure that the school issue had begun, preparing the ground for a new party system to spring up.

The public expectation that the Maine Law organization might itself develop into a major political party brought some new, if fair-weather, friends into the movement. Old temperance hands spoke of those who "had become Temperance men all at once—sprung up like mushrooms, in a night. . . ." They feared that these new converts viewed temperance "as a hobby on which designing men were to ride into office."[113] At the Hamilton County Maine Law convention to choose an independent prohibition slate for the election, many of these newcomers had their names put in nomination, but the delegates passed over them in favor of "tried and true" temperance men.

When 116 delegates convened the county Maine Law convention on September 13, the major issue they faced was whether to endorse nominees for all state offices or only for the legislature. Those who favored a full ticket argued that "sober men" should fill all offices, and that one of the objects of the convention was "to break up the arrangements of the dominant party. . . ." They were also influenced by the knowledge that the Free Soil candidate for governor would be Samuel Lewis, a Cincinnati temperance advocate of long standing. Opponents of a full ticket claimed that the only purpose of the Maine Law campaign was to elect a legislature favorable to prohibition. Anything further would appear to be "a squabble for the spoils. . . ."[114]

In effect, the debate was between those who thought the

Maine Law campaign should lead to the formation of a political party and those who believed that it should remain a non-partisan, single-issue movement. The latter position proved by far the most popular, and the convention named nominees for the House and Senate only. Had they decided to broaden their appeal, the temperance activists might have developed a fusion movement with anti-Catholics, ambitious former Whigs, and Free Soilers. By rejecting this approach, they remained true to their prohibitionist principles but lost the interest of the "mushroom" temperance activists who had seen the Maine Law campaign primarily as a potential nucleus for a new political movement.

Delegates at the convention carefully balanced the Maine Law ticket for Hamilton County in terms of the political backgrounds of the nominees. Of the eleven named (three for the Senate and eight for the House), five were Democrats (including one already on the Democratic ticket), five were Whigs (including three from that party's slate), and one was a Free Soiler. However, the Democratic organization quickly notified John Krauth, the one nominee on both the Maine Law and Democratic tickets, that "he must desert the Maine Law men, or they [the Democrats] will part company with him." [115] Krauth withdrew from the Prohibition ticket, as did two other well-known Democrats. The incident served further to underscore the total opposition of the Democratic organization to political temperance.

As the election approached, even temperance activists realized that their slate would be defeated in Cincinnati. Every major newspaper in the city had come out against the Maine Law. That the Democratic *Enquirer* and the Whig *Gazette* had done so was no surprise; but that the independent *Commercial*, long a warm friend of the temperance cause, had rejected prohibition as being impracticable, came as a hard blow. Worst of all, the *Times*, champion of the free-school campaign, threw its weight against the Maine Law, leaving temperance leaders "surprised and mortified." [116] Without the solid support of those who had put together the Independent Free School ticket in the spring, the prohibition candidates had little hope.

Moreover, the vehement opposition which the Maine Law campaign had aroused among German voters drew many anti-Miamis back into the Democratic party ranks. A mass meeting of the party, just before election day, perfunctorily passed a resolution opposing religious influence in the common schools. After that gesture in the name of unity, the speakers turned their attention entirely to the Maine Law, a pernicious proposal, they claimed, which would "trample on the dignity of men. . . ." One speaker drank a glass of wine at the podium, calling it "'Sam Cary's Oil.' Sam lived in the hills," he added, "and wanted to go to the U.S. Senate, and was determined to keep people from drinking, when they pleased, but he could not do it." Several of the speeches were made in German, and one man apologized for not yet being able to speak fluently in German, "but [he] hoped soon to be able to do so." [117] The ranks of the Democratic party appeared to have closed once again. A few members of the old Sawbuck group put forward an anti–Maine Law, anti-Miami independent ticket but it attracted little attention or support. [118]

The only gains the prohibitionists made during the campaign were with some church hierarchies and with the Free Soil party. The clergy seemed more at ease with temperance after it became a political rather than a proselytizing movement. The yearly regional conventions of the Methodists, the Quakers, and even the Episcopalians, who had been traditionally cool to the temperance movement, all passed strong resolutions in favor of the Maine Law; the *Presbyterian of the West* reported, "Our religious papers, we believe, are all on the right [pro–Maine Law] side." [119] Many clergymen in Cincinnati actively spoke out in favor of prohibition and even campaigned for the Maine Law ticket.

Cincinnati's Free Soilers met in convention on August 30. Most of the meeting was taken up with the question of whether to nominate Free Soil candidates for the state legislature, or to decline to nominate in anticipation of supporting the Maine Law ticket. A few speakers claimed that placing prohibition above antislavery would mean selling out their antislavery principles in favor of political expediency. But others insisted that "whiskey was the handmaid of slavery," and that if they

united with the prohibitionists against intemperance now,
"soon the time will come when [prohibitionists] will unite
with us against . . . [slavery]." The latter view prevailed, and
no Free Soil candidates ran against the temperance slate.[120]
However, Free Soilers in Cincinnati had never won more than
a tiny fraction of the local vote, and their role in the campaign
had little effect. It may even have hindered the prohibition
ticket, since opponents suggested that Maine Law advocates
were likely to be "zealots and ultras" on "all the 'isms' of the
day." Voting them into office would necessarily increase the
number of "unsound and injudicious men in the coming Legislature," who were likely to be radical reformers opposed as
well to slavery and to capital punishment.[121]

Not only in Cincinnati, but throughout Ohio, prohibitionists sensed by election day that the tide was running
against them. Cary, campaigning elsewhere in the state, admitted as much in a letter to the *Organ*. "If we fail at this election," he wrote, "the political parties will regret the failure as
much as we, before two years shall have passed. None need
flatter themselves that the friends of prohibition will give up in
despair, if defeated now."[122] But neither Cary nor the other
campaigners for prohibition were prepared for the extent of
the defeat they suffered at the polls on October 11, 1853.

"The latest intelligence indicates clearly that we are defeated badly," Cary wrote in the *Organ* three days after the
election. "There is no accounting now for this unexpected result. . . . We hope our friends will not be discouraged or dis-
heartened."[123] Statewide, only about one-third of the new legislature could be counted as friendly to prohibition, with most
of those coming from Free Soil/Maine Law fusion tickets of
the Western Reserve, the area in northeast Ohio that had long
been a hotbed of reform activity. Samuel Lewis, the Free Soil
gubernatorial candidate who had campaigned more on his advocacy of prohibition than on his antislavery sentiments, took
17.7 percent of the vote, running third behind the Democratic
(52.0 percent) and Whig (30.2 percent) candidates. The Whig
and Free Soil nominee for lieutenant governor, J. J. Allen, who
had received unofficial but widely publicized support from the

temperance forces, won 45.1 percent of the ballots cast compared to 54.9 percent for his Democratic opponent.[124]

In Cincinnati candidates for the Ohio House of Representatives who appeared on only one of the tickets won, on average, the following portions of the approximated total vote of nearly 14,000: Democratic, 56.7 percent; Independent Prohibitory Law, 30.0 percent; Whig, 8.9 percent; Independent, 4.7 percent.[125] Those who had run on both the Prohibition and Whig slates averaged 40.0 percent, or about the combined total of the two separate tickets. The Prohibitory Law ticket ran behind the spring percentage totals for Taylor (Free School mayoral candidate) in twelve of the sixteen wards, despite the fact that the Whig vote had once again declined precipitously.

After the fall election the Whig party was dead locally. It had taken only 8.9 percent of the vote, and had been reduced to this meager position by issues not directly connected with slavery. The prohibition campaign, although less important than the Catholic school fund issue in this respect, effectively continued the wholesale desertion from the Whig organization.

Table 8, compiled from an estimating procedure based on multiple regression analysis, suggests voting trends from the spring and fall elections. Nearly everyone who had voted Democratic in the spring mayoral campaign voted Democratic again in the fall. But among those who had voted non-Democratic in the spring, there was much greater variation. Only about half of the Taylor/Free School supporters went with the Maine Law ticket; most of the rest voted Whig. In marked contrast, most of those who had voted Whig in the spring went with the prohibition candidates in the fall; those who did not tended to move into the Democratic columns. Most of the Chambers/German Free School voters also went with the Democrats in the fall.

These results strongly support the basic conclusions suggested by qualitative evidence: that the Maine Law campaign reunited and even strengthened the Democratic party in Cincinnati, driving dissident Germans and even many former Whigs into the Democratic camp, and that it also failed to unite the anti-Democratic voters in Cincinnati under a single

Table 8. Voter distribution estimates.

		SPRING 1853			
		Free School	Whig	Democrat	Anti-Miami
FALL 1853	Maine Law	51.5% 40.2% .751	83.1% 103.0% .716	−4.5% 3.7% −.886	−23.8% −57.4% −.740
	Whig	32.5% 39.2% .886	6.6% −16.8% .282	−10.1% −6.4% −.868	16.1% 15.7% −.503
	Democratic	3.8% 7.3% −.894	20.9% 25.0% −.543	111.8% 100.5% .958	82.6% 118.6% .667
	Independent Democratic	12.4% 13.4% .149	−10.6% −11.0% −.443	2.8% 2.0% .003	24.9% 22.9% .289

Table 8 gives two estimates based on multiple regression analysis of how Cincinnati voters in the spring, 1853, mayoral election voted in the fall of 1853 for Ohio House of Representatives tickets. Each vertical column encompasses the total vote for one of the four spring mayoral candidates. The two percentage figures within each grid square are direct and indirect estimates of how that vote was distributed in the fall election (horizontal columns). The direct esimate is listed above the indirect estimate. For example, the upper-left-hand square refers to those who voted for the Free School candidate in the spring and then voted the Maine Law ticket in the fall. Thus the direct estimate is that 51.5 percent of all Taylor/Free School voters cast their ballots for the Maine Law slate in the fall. The third figure in each square is the product/moment correlation coefficient for the spring and fall votes represented by that square. Thus the upper-left-hand square shows that there is a correlation of .751 between the spring Free School vote and the fall Maine Law vote. See Appendix for an explanation of statistical methods used.

banner. As the unifying spearhead of a new, socially oriented political movement, the prohibition campaign had failed abysmally in Cincinnati. In the rest of the state, except the Western Reserve, Maine Law candidates almost invariably went down to defeat, and Democrats won what had been in the past safe Whig seats.

Why did prohibition fare so badly in Ohio when it appeared to be winning favor throughout the North, and when it had recently been overwhelmingly approved by another Northwest state, Michigan? The comparison with Michigan is instructive: there the question was submitted to the voters as a referendum, a process that was far less threatening to the Democratic party. As a result, many Democratic newspapers supported the Maine Law. Moreover, corn was not a major Michigan crop, nor were distilling, brewing, and wine making important industries. These factors undoubtedly made passage of prohibition easier in Michigan than in Ohio.[126]

Of more importance, even though prohibition failed in Ohio, the political effects of the campaign resembled those in states that passed the Maine Law. As it had in Ohio, Maine Law agitation contributed to the disruption of the second-party system, and to the decline of the Whig party, throughout the North.[127] Even in states where it was initially successful, prohibition soon ran into trouble. It was never effectively enforced in any major city, and was usually laxly enforced elsewhere in a prohibiting state within months of passage. Crime and poverty rates remained high. Several states repealed their Maine Laws, and others let them lapse into complete disuse. Most politicians of the Know Nothing party, and later those of the Republican party, did all they could to suppress the prohibition movement. Thus the Maine Law issue contributed to the realignment of American politics that occurred in the 1850s, but it failed to serve as the touchstone for the creation of a new party system.

In the aftermath of the fall election, Ohio prohibitionists were left bitter and dismayed. The defeat had been so complete and so humiliating that the campaign leaders despaired of ever passing the Maine Law in their state. Temperance activity came to a near standstill in the winter of 1853–54. Leaders directed blame for the defeat primarily at familiar targets. The *Organ* editorialized angrily on the combination of "political parties, 'Wine-Grower's Associations,' distillers, wholesalers, retailers, and '*namby-pamby*' editors" that had blocked the reform.[128] But often, in the months following the election, a new enemy was added to this list. Cary spoke of the success of their candidates in the Western Reserve, "where foreigners are not omnipotent. . . ."[129] In Cincinnati, he claimed, "take out the vote of the German wards" and the Prohibition ticket would have carried.[130] Increasingly, hostility to the foreign-born spread through the temperance movement, constricting its vision and undermining its autonomy. Over the next two years the bile of nativism and anti-Catholicism turned temperance reform into little more than an adjunct of the xenophobic Know Nothing party during the latter's meteoric political life.

Notes

1. For example, see Michael F. Holt, *Forging a Majority: The Formation of the Republican Party in Pittsburgh, 1848–1860* (New Haven, Conn., 1969), 121; Joel H. Silbey, ed., *The Transformation of American Politics, 1840–1860* (Englewood Cliffs, N.J., 1967), 2; Ronald P. Formisano, *The Birth of Mass Political Parties: Michigan, 1827–1861* (Princeton, N.J., 1971). For examples of the traditional view, see Arthur Charles Cole, *The Irrepressible Conflict, 1850–1865* (vol. 7 of *A History of American Life*, ed. Arthur M. Schlesinger and Dixon Ryan Fox, New York, 1934), 143, 272–73; Allan Nevins, *A House Dividing, 1852–1857* (vol. 2 of *Ordeal of the Union*, New York, 1947); Roy F. Nichols, *The Stakes of Power, 1845–1877* (New York, 1971), 42–58.

2. Charles Cist, *Cincinnati in 1841: Its Early Annals and Future Prospects* (Cincinnati, Ohio, 1841), 34, 37, 39, and *Sketches and Statistics of Cincinnati in 1851* (Cincinnati, Ohio, 1851), 47; Irwin F. Flack, "Who Governed Cincinnati? A Comparative Analysis of Government and Social Structure in a Nineteenth Century River City: 1819–1860" (Ph.D. thesis, University of Pittsburgh, 1977), 65.

3. William Baughin, "Nativism in Cincinnati before 1860" (M.A. thesis, University of Cincinnati, 1963), 38–39, 84–89, 93–95.

4. Cist, *1851*, 47.

5. The council did redistrict some wards, but the effect was to cut off and isolate the Germans, preventing them from gaining predominance in the old wards 1 and 5, where they accounted for 41 percent and 46 percent respectively of the population in 1840. The new heavily German wards 9 and 10 were carved off from the older wards, and henceforth voted overwhelmingly Democratic. The area north of Liberty Street, also preponderantly German, remained unincorporated until the end of the decade, when it became the new wards 11 and 12 (Cist, *1841*, 29, 37, and *1851*, 47).

6. *Cincinnati Commercial*, Mar. 6, 1851, Apr. 7, 1852 (hereafter cited as CC).

7. CC, July 14, 20, 1852; Louis R. Harlan, ed., "The Autobiography of Alexander Long, 1858," *Historical and Philosophical Society of Ohio Bulletin* (later the *Cincinnati Historical Society Bulletin*), 19 (1961): 122 (hereafter cited as *CHS Bulletin*); Baughin, "Nativism," 143.

8. Baughin, "Nativism," 55–56, 123–24; Nora Faires, "Ethnicity in Evolution: The German Community in Pittsburgh and Allegheny City, 1845–1885" (Ph.D. thesis, University of Pittsburgh, 1980), 553–57; Kathleen Neils Conzen, "Germans," in Stephan Thernstrom, ed., *Harvard Encyclopedia of American Ethnic Groups* (Cambridge, Mass., 1980), 410, 416.

9. William E. Gienapp, "The Transformation of Cincinnati Politics, 1852–1860" (unpublished seminar paper, Yale University, 1969), 7–18; Baughin, "Nativism," 134–35; Eugene H. Roseboom, *The Civil War Era, 1850–1873* (vol. 4 of *The History of the State of Ohio*, ed. Carl Wittke, Columbus, Ohio, 1944), 288.

10. Guido A. Dobbert, "The Disintegration of an Immigrant Community: The Cincinnati Germans, 1870–1920" (Ph.D. thesis, University of Chicago, 1965), 23–27; CC, Oct. 4, 1853; George C. Schoolfield, "The Great Cincinnati Novel," *CHS Bulletin*, 20 (1962): 51; Baughin, "Nativism," 123–24; Eugene H. Roseboom, "Salmon P. Chase and the Know Nothings," *Mississippi Valley Historical Review* (later the *Journal of American History*), 25 (1938): 335–50.

11. CC, Aug. 6, 1852.

12. Ibid., Aug. 6, 1852; Gienapp, "Transformation," 37.

13. CC, Oct. 18, 1852. The final vote in ward 12 was discarded on a technicality. For that ward, the nearly complete results reported by the *Commercial* on Oct. 15, 1852, were used.

14. Rutherford B. Hayes, *Diary and Letters of Rutherford Birchard Hayes*, ed. Charles R. Williams (Columbus, Ohio, 1922), vol. 1, Hayes to S. Birchard, Cincinnati, Oct. 12, 1852.

15. CC, Nov. 6, 1852. Only figures for ward *majorities* were reported in the newspapers. The average vote has been estimated using voter turnout figures from the following spring election. Any error in this method would throw off the averages in heavily Democratic and heavily Whig wards much more than in wards where the party votes were close. The resultant set of observations would then correlate less well with other elections. However, high correlations (.981 product/moment correlation between the Democratic votes in Nov., 1852, and Oct., 1851, .972 between Democratic votes in Nov., 1852, and Oct., 1853, .981 between Whig votes in Nov., 1852, and Oct. 1851, for example) indicate that the estimates for Nov., 1852, contain very little error. See also Michael F. Holt, *The Political Crisis of the 1850s* (New York, 1978), 126.

16. Roseboom, *Era*, 272.

17. *Catholic Telegraph*, Jan. 22, 1853 (hereafter cited as *Telegraph*).

18. *Cincinnati Times*, Mar. 23, 1853 (hereafter cited as *Times*). The

list of names had no recognizably German surnames, but may have contained some names of English Catholics.

19. Ray A. Billington, *The Protestant Crusade, 1800–1860: A Study of the Origins of American Nativism* (Chicago, 1964), 289–93; Michael F. Holt, "The Politics of Impatience: The Origins of Know Nothingism," *Journal of American History*, 60 (1973): 324; Formisano, *Birth*, 222–23; Andrew M. Greeley, *The Catholic Experience: An Interpretation of the History of American Catholicism* (Garden City, N.Y., 1969), 120–21. Pennsylvania, New York, Maryland, and Michigan were among the other states where Catholics agitated for a share of public school money.

20. John Gilmary Shea, *History of the Catholic Church in the United States . . .* (New York, 1892), 541.

21. Baughin, "Nativism," 98; Billington, *Crusade*, 238.

22. Jay P. Dolan, *The Immigrant Church: New York's Irish and German Catholics, 1815–1865* (Baltimore, 1975), 38–41.

23. Shea, *History*, 175.

24. *Garland*, June, 1853, 44.

25. Ibid., Apr., 1853, 28.

26. Ibid., June, 1853, 44.

27. Nancy R. Hamant, "Religion in the Cincinnati Schools, 1830–1900," *CHS Bulletin*, 21 (1963): 239–41; Dolan, *Immigrant*, 100–101, 104.

28. Quoted in Billington, *Crusade*, 290–91.

29. Quoted in Baughin, "Nativism," 131.

30. Dolan, *Immigrant*, 110.

31. German Catholics accounted for 49 percent of the marriages, 56 percent of the baptisms, and 55 percent of the deaths recorded by the parishes in 1852 (CC, Jan. 17, 1853).

32. *Times*, Mar. 23, 1853.

33. Catholic churches throughout this period were divided into Irish and German churches. In 1843 some German Catholics in Cincinnati attempted to become incorporated as "The German Catholic Congregation of Cincinnati." Archbishop Purcell consulted with local German priests (their role in the division is unclear) and prevented a schism.

34. *Western Christian Advocate*, Mar. 30, 1853.

35. CC, Apr. 4, 1853.

36. Ibid., Mar. 26, 1853.

37. Quoted in Gienapp, "Transformation," 25.

38. CC, Mar. 26, 1853.

39. *Times*, Mar. 24, 1853; CC, Mar. 29, 1853; *Cincinnati Enquirer*, Apr. 8, 1853; Gienapp, "Transformation," 26–31; Holt, *Crisis*, 123–26.

40. CC, Mar. 26, 29, 1853.

41. *Times*, Apr. 5, 1853.

42. *Cincinnati Enquirer*, Apr. 9, 1853. The Pearson product/moment correlation coefficient (r) between the ward by ward vote for Taylor and the

Nov., 1852, Whig vote was .915; between the vote for Ross and the Nov., 1852, Whig vote, the correlation was .446.

43. *CC*, Apr., 7, 1853.

44. *Ohio Organ of the Temperance Reform*, Apr. 8, 1853 (hereafter cited as *Organ*).

45. *Western Christian Advocate*, Apr. 13, 1853.

46. *Times*, July 19, 1853.

47. *Organ*, Feb. 25, 1853.

48. Ibid., Apr. 1, 1853. During the 1840s Catholic temperance organizations formed in many cities. Their membership was overwhelmingly Irish Catholic; German Catholics were hostile to temperance reform even within the confines of the Church, and quarrels erupted between German and Irish clergy over the issue. Irish Catholic temperance seems to have developed primarily in those cities where leadership emerged from the local clergy; it was not officially promoted by the church hierarchy. Although these organizations have been little studied, the indications are that they had some of the same features as the fraternal temperance organizations, and that mutual benefit features were of particular importance. The organizations seem to have appealed primarily to upwardly mobile Irish who had emigrated from the urban areas of Ireland that also produced Father Mathew's very successful temperance movement in Ireland.

Many Catholic prelates in the United States were suspicious of or hostile toward both the Mathewite crusade in Ireland and the Catholic temperance groups in the United States. When Father Mathew visited the United States between 1849 and 1851, he met with little cooperation from the Catholic clergy; one bishop complained that the Capuchin monk's public appearances were arranged by and made in conjunction with "sectarian fanaticks [and] Calvinistic preachers and deacons. . . . The appearance of fellowship between a Catholic priest and such men can hardly be without evil results" (quoted in Joan Bland, *Hibernian Crusade: The Story of the Catholic Total Abstinence Union of America* (Washington, D.C., 1951), 38).

Irish Catholic temperance groups disappeared everywhere in the United States after the shift of the temperance movement to prohibition in the early 1850s, and the Irish were as nearly unanimous as the Germans in opposing the Maine Law campaigns. Perhaps because no one in the Cincinnati Catholic hierarchy championed the temperance cause, and also because of the high proportion of German Catholics in the city, the Catholic temperance movement never developed in Cincinnati. On Catholic temperance in the 1840s, see Bland, *Hibernian Crusade*, 10–38; Faires, "Ethnicity," 387–93; Kathleen Neils Conzen, *Immigrant Milwaukee, 1836–1860: Accommodation and Community in a Frontier City* (Cambridge, Mass., 1976), 159–60; Dolan, *Immigrant*, 128–29; Patricia Simpson, "The Drunk and the Teetotaler: Two Phases in Temperance Reform among the Irish Working Class of Pittsburgh" (unpublished manuscript, University of Pittsburgh), 55–82; Paul J. Kleppner, "Lincoln and the Immigrant Vote: A Case of Religious Polarization," *Mid-America*, 48 (1966): 190; Vic Walsh, "'Drowning the Shamrock': Drink and Temperance" (unpublished manuscript, University of Pittsburgh); H. F. Kearney, "Fr Mathew: Apostle of Modernization," in A. Cosgrove and D. M. McCarthy, eds., *Studies in Irish History Presented to R. Dudley Edwards* (Dublin, 1979), 172; James R. Barrett, "Why Paddy Drank: The Social Importance of Whiskey in Pre-famine Ireland," *Journal of Popular Culture*, 11 (1977): 156.

49. *Telegraph*, Mar. 19, 1853.

50. Ibid., July 9, 1853. The *Telegraph*'s opinion of the temperance movement was echoed by a German Catholic priest in Cincinnati, who considered the movement an example of the "fanaticism, intolerance, and ultra-views on politics and religion" that bred in the United States, and he classed drink reform with "spiritualism, mormonism, free-lovism, infidelity, and materialism . . ." (quoted in Zane Miller, unpublished manuscript, University of Cincinnati).

51. *Organ*, Mar. 11, 1853.

52. Ibid., Apr. 1, 1853.

53. Ibid., Apr. 8, 1853.

54. *Times*, Jan. 31, 1853; Schoolfield, "Novel," 51.

55. *Organ*, Feb. 11, 1853.

56. Ibid., Mar. 4, 1853.

57. Ibid., Feb. 25, Mar. 11, 1853.

58. Faires, "Ethnicity," 401–2, 429–31; *Organ*, Mar. 11, 1853.

59. *Organ*, Apr. 15, 1853.

60. John G. Woolley and William E. Johnson, *Temperance Progress in the Century* (London, 1903), 140–41; D. Leigh Colvin, *Prohibition in the United States* (New York, 1926), 47; CC, Oct. 23, 1853; Conzen, *Immigrant Milwaukee*, 210–14; Dolan, *Immigrant*, 128; William G. Shade, "'New Political History': Some Statistical Questions Raised," *Social Science History*, 5 (1981): 181–91; Susan E. Hirsh, *Roots of the American Working Class: The Industrialization of Crafts in Newark, 1800–1860* (Philadelphia, 1978), 104–5; James B. Sellers, *The Prohibition Movement in Alabama, 1702 to 1943* (Chapel Hill, N.C., 1943), 36–37; David E. Schob, *Hired Hands and Plowboys: Farm Labor in the Midwest, 1815–60* (Urbana, Ill., 1975), 145–47; Faires, "Ethnicity," 255–56.

61. *Organ*, Apr. 15, 29, 1853.

62. CC, Mar. 23, 1853.

63. Holt, *Crisis*, 105, 106–15.

64. Hayes, *Diary*, 1:421–22, entry for Sept. 24, 1852.

65. Ibid., 1:425–26, Hayes to S. Birchard, Oct. 7, 1852.

66. *Times*, July 18, 1853.

67. *Organ*, Apr. 1, 15, May 13, July 29, 1853.

68. Ibid., July 29, Aug. 26, Oct. 28, 1853; CC, Oct. 10, 1853.

69. Ibid., May 20, July 15, 22, Aug. 12, Sept. 23, 1853.

70. Ibid., Mar. 11, Apr. 29, July 15, 29, 1853; CC, July 26, Sept. 2, 21, 1853; *Cincinnati Enquirer*, June 30, 1853.

71. *Organ*, June 3, 1853.

72. See, for example, ibid., Jan. 21, 28, Feb. 11, Mar. 4, Apr. 1, June 13, 24, July 15, 22, Aug. 12, 19, Nov. 4, 1853; CC, Aug. 8, 13, 18, 1853.

73. *Organ*, Sept. 9, 1853.

74. Ibid., July 1, 15, 1853.

75. CC, Jan. 7, 1853.

76. *Organ*, Feb. 25, 1853.

77. *Times*, Sept. 5, 1853.

78. *Organ*, Feb. 25, 1853.

79. Five of the thirteen states which passed prohibitory laws prior to the Civil War had their laws struck down by the state courts. But in all cases the grounds were minor or technical. Four of the five states revised or rewrote their laws to meet judicial objections and in only one of these was the statute voided a second time. Maine, Vermont, Rhode Island, Michigan, Connecticut, New York, New Hampshire, Tennessee, Delaware, Illinois, Indiana, Iowa, Wisconsin, and the territory of Minnesota all passed prohibitory laws prior to the Civil War. New York, Indiana, Michigan, Rhode Island, and Massachusetts had part or all of their laws repealed. All but New York repassed prohibition. Indiana's law was overturned a second time. Woolley and Johnson, *Temperance Progress*, 139–40; John A. Krout, "The Maine Law in New York Politics," *New York History*, 17 (1936): 271; Ernest H. Cherrington, *The Evolution of Prohibition in the United States of America* (Montclair, N.J., 1969; originally published 1920), 136–38.

80. CC, June 23, 1851, Oct. 23, 1852, Aug. 24, 25, 1853.

81. Ibid., Aug. 15, 24, 25, Oct. 4, 1853; Samuel F. Cary, "An Address to the People of Ohio, in Behalf of a Law to Prohibit the Liquor-Manufacture and Traffic . . ." (Cincinnati, Ohio, 1852), 4.

82. CC, Sept. 9, 1853.

83. *Cincinnati Enquirer*, July 6, 1853.

84. CC, Aug. 10, 11, Sept. 19, 1853.

85. Ibid., Aug. 15, 18, 1853; on police force drunkenness, see ibid., Jan. 6, 1851, Oct. 18, 1853; *Organ*, July 29, Dec. 23, 1853; Cincinnati City Departments, *Annual Reports*, 1854, "Mayor's Annual Report," 9.

86. CC, Aug. 15, 18, 1853.

87. *Western Christian Advocate*, Mar. 25, 1852.

88. *Organ*, Dec. 30, 1853.

89. *Ohio Washingtonian Organ and Sons of Temperance Record*, Oct. 24, 1846, Jan. 2, Mar. 7, 13, 1847.

90. Cary, ed., *American Temperance Magazine*, vol. 1, no. 1 (July, 1851). Mary P. Ryan, in *Cradle of the Middle Class: The Family in Oneida County, New York, 1790–1865* (Cambridge, Mass., 1981), discussing temperance associations in Utica, N.Y., during the 1840s, notes that the temperance press "was particularly deferential to the 'producing classes,' to farmers, artisans, and workingmen. Conversely, the editors were known to cast a disdainful glance upon the city's 'upper ten.'" (134).

91. *Western Christian Advocate*, Apr. 16, 1851.

92. John von Daacke, "Grape-Growing and Wine-Making in Cincinnati, 1800–1870," *CHS Bulletin*, 25 (1967): 197–211; Louis Leonard Tucker, "'Old Nick' Longworth, the Paradoxical Maecenas of Cincinnati," *CHS Bulletin*, 25 (1967): 249. Longworth's employees in his vineyards were predominantly Germans; he also leased land to German grape growers and sold most of his wine to the Cincinnati German community (Schob, *Hired Hands*, 145–47).

93. CC, Oct. 27, 1852, Aug. 2, 15, 1853.

94. *Organ*, Sept. 16, 30, 1853.

95. Ibid., Nov. 11, Aug. 12, 1853; CC, Aug. 8, 1853.

96. CC, Aug. 4, Sept. 28, 30, 1853; *Times*, Sept. 20, 1853.

97. CC, Aug. 4, 1853.

98. *Organ*, Nov. 11, 1853; CC, Sept. 23, 1853; *Times*, Sept. 20, 1853.

99. CC, Sept. 21, 1853.

100. *Western Christian Advocate*, Sept. 15, 1851.

101. *Times*, June 20, 1853. On the opposition of farmers to prohibition in other states, see Arthur C. Cole, *The Era of the Civil War: 1848–1870* (vol. 3 of *The Centennial History of Illinois*, Springfield, Ill., 1919), 209–10; Holt, *Crisis*, 300, fn. 21; W. J. Rorabaugh, "Prohibition as Progress: New York State's License Elections, 1846," *Journal of Social History*, 14 (1981): 429–30. On the opposition of farmers in England to the temperance movement there, see Lilian L. Shiman, "Crusade against Drink in Victorian England" (Ph.D. thesis, University of Wisconsin, 1970), 110.

102. *Organ*, June 10, 1853.

103. *Western Washingtonian and Sons of Temperance Record*, Jan. 16, 1846; *Organ*, June 10, July 15, 1853; Roseboom, *Era*, 224; CC, May 3, 1853; Asa E. Martin, "The Temperance Movement in Pennsylvania prior to the Civil War," *Pennsylvania Magazine of History and Biography*, 49 (1925): 224.

104. *Organ*, Aug. 12, 1853, responding to an *Ohio Union* editorial reprinted in the *Enquirer*. See also responses to Democratic editorials in the *Organ*, July 1, Aug. 19, Oct. 7, 1853.

105. *Organ*, Oct. 7, June 10, 1853.

106. Ibid., July 1, June 3, 1853.

107. CC, Sept. 14, 1853; *Organ*, Aug. 12, 19, 1853.

108. *Cincinnati Gazette*, Apr. 11, 1853.

109. CC, Sept. 5, 1853.

110. *Cincinnati Gazette*, Sept. 30, 1853.

111. CC, Oct. 17, 1853.

112. *Times*, Oct. 7, 1853.

113. CC, Sept. 15, 1853; *Times*, Aug. 12, 1853.

114. CC, Aug. 23, Sept. 15, 1853.

115. *Times*, Sept. 14, 1853.

116. *Organ*, July 29, 1853; CC, Aug. 10, 1853.

117. CC, Oct. 8, 1853.

118. Ibid., Sept. 9, Oct. 11, 1853; *Times*, Oct. 7, 1853. A Maine Law

campaign in Wisconsin also reunited the Catholic and non-Catholic Germans of Milwaukee under the Democratic party banner (see Conzen, *Immigrant Milwaukee*, 213–14).

119. CC, Sept. 12, 1853; *Organ*, Sept. 30, Oct. 7, 1853.

120. CC, Sept. 1, 10, Oct. 10, 1853. An Ohio Free Soiler wrote to Salmon P. Chase during the campaign: "You are aware that nearly every Free Soiler is a Maine Law man" (Salmon P. Chase Papers, Library of Congress, R. W. P. Muse to Salmon P. Chase, July 12, 1853, quoted in Stephen E. Maizlish, "The Triumph of Sectionalism: The Transformation of Politics in the Antebellum North, Ohio, 1844–1860" (Ph.D. thesis, University of California, Berkeley, 1979), 345, fn. 217). In the areas of the state where the Free Soilers were stronger, they generally formed fusion tickets with the temperance forces and campaigned more on prohibition than on opposition to the expansion of slavery (see Theodore Clarke Smith, *The Liberty and Free Soil Parties in the Northwest* (New York, 1897), 271–72; Frederick J. Blue, "The Ohio Free Soilers and Problems of Factionalism," *Ohio History*, 76 (1967): 29; Holt, *Crisis*, 131). On coalitions between prohibitionists and antislavery forces in other states, see Edward O. Schriver, "Antislavery. The Free Soil and Free Democratic Parties in Maine, 1848–1853," *New England Quarterly*, 42 (1969): 84–85; Cole, *Era*, 208–9; Holt, *Crisis*, 131.

121. CC, Sept. 10, 1853.

122. *Organ*, Oct. 7, 1853.

123. *Organ*, Oct. 14, 1853.

124. Ibid., Oct. 28, Nov. 4, 1853.

125. The approximated total vote for each ticket was determined by averaging the votes of the candidates who appeared on only that ticket. See Appendix for an explanation of the statistical method used to arrive at Table 8.

126. Formisano, *Birth*, 229–31.

127. For discussions of the disruptive effect of the prohibition issue on the political alignments of other states, see Kevin Sweeney, "Rum, Romanism, Representation, and Reform: Coalition Politics in Massachusetts, 1847–1853," *Civil War History*, 22 (1976): 128–32; Holt, *Crisis*, 131; Rorabaugh, "Prohibition as Progress," 431–33; Paul Goodman on prohibition vote in Vermont, 1853, correspondence with the author.

128. *Organ*, Nov. 11, 1853.

129. Ibid., Oct. 28, 1853.

130. Ibid., Nov. 11, 1853.

5

Political Temperance in Decline

The issue of prohibition dominated Ohio public life in the fall of 1853; four years later it was practically a forgotten topic. The *Templar's Magazine* in 1857 mused on "the impulsive temperament of the people of the present age. One day, or one year, they manifest great interest in some particular movement—the next, they appear indifferent toward it."[1] By the late 1850s party leaders were carefully avoiding or ignoring the prohibition issue, which had proven itself divisive and therefore politically unattractive. Most citizens had also lost their interest in outlawing the drink trade. Many states with Maine Laws had failed to enforce them effectively, so that public confidence in the practicality of prohibition had diminished; moreover, the growth of the sectional crisis and a lessening of concern over social disorder made prohibition seem of secondary importance. In only four years the temperance movement plunged from the peak of its nineteenth-century popularity to its nadir.

The Ohio temperance movement remained committed to a legal, and therefore political, solution to the liquor problem after 1853. But the total failure of the Maine Law campaign signaled that the prohibition issue could not, in the immediate future, dominate state politics. Temperance activists blamed foreign-born voters for their failure, and concluded that the best hope for future passage of the Maine Law lay in breaking the political power of the immigrants. When the Know Nothing party rose to prominence in 1854 and 1855, temperance reformers became active supporters, and they were highly influential in pushing the new party beyond its original emphasis on anti-Catholicism toward a broad nativist stance. As a result, the Know Nothing party quickly lost the support it had at first received from non-Catholic German voters, a loss which contributed greatly to the party's rapid decline. The nascent Republican party, recognizing the divisiveness of both prohibition and nativism, insistently suppressed both, and focused instead on the unifying issue of opposition to slavery expansion.

During the period of the late 1850s and the 1860s, organized temperance reform reached a low ebb of activity and influence. Yet those same years produced crucial changes both within the temperance movement and in the broader social context of the anti-drink crusade, changes which led to a new era of temperance reform ushered in by the Woman's Crusade of 1873–74.

The question of prohibition dominated Cincinnati public life in the summer and fall of 1853; anti-Catholicism lay dormant during the Maine Law campaign. Catholics avoided the school fund issue, and non-Catholic Germans returned to the Democratic fold in opposition to the temperance ticket. But the hatred and fear of the Catholic church that had flared in the spring continued to smolder under the surface. Anti-Catholicism soon re-erupted with even greater intensity, and this time led to the formation of an ongoing political organization, the Know Nothing party.

When discussing the brief political career of the Know Nothing party, historians have frequently used the terms anti-Catholic and nativist as if they were nearly interchangeable.[2] In cities such as Boston, where nearly all the foreign-born were also Catholic, there was an inevitable blurring of anti-foreign and anti-Catholic sentiments. The experience of Cincinnati, however, demonstrates that these two attitudes should be thought of as distinct and separate, if sometimes linked, phenomena. The Know Nothing movement in Cincinnati grew directly out of the anti-Catholic fervor of the spring 1853 school campaign. During its most successful period in the city, the

Know Nothing party openly courted, and won, the support of non-Catholic German immigrants. Only later did the party shift to an anti-foreign as well as an anti-Catholic stance. One prominent cause of this tactical shift was the growing influence in the Know Nothing hierarchy of temperance activists who believed that prohibition would never become a reality in Ohio until the political power of foreigners, including the non-Catholic Germans, was destroyed.

In December a visit to the city by the papal nuncio Archbishop Gaetano Bedini reignited Cincinnati's anti-Catholicism. Bedini, according to popular belief, had been responsible for the massacre in Bologna of Italian revolutionaries. The radical German paper *Der Hochwaechter* suggested that "the Butcher of Bologna" deserved summary justice while in Cincinnati. On Christmas Eve the Freimännerverein organized a massive procession to Archbishop Purcell's house, where Bedini was staying, in order to burn the nuncio in effigy. The police, most of whom were Catholic, charged the crowd. A riot ensued in which one German was killed and many others wounded. Public opinion in the city ran overwhelmingly against the police. Citizens expressed outrage at what they perceived to be an attack on "a lawful and constitutional manifestation of religious and political opinion."[3] On January 14 a crowd of 5,000, mostly native-born Cincinnatians, marched through the city and burned Bedini in effigy without interference from the police.

In the spring of 1854 anti-Catholicism once again swept through the city and provided much of the initial impetus for the formation of the first Cincinnati lodges of the secret Order of the Star Spangled Banner, or the "Know Nothings," as they came to be called. By July there were seven lodge rooms in the city, each the meeting site of two or three different Know Nothing lodges meeting each week. Cincinnati became the hotbed of Know Nothingism in Ohio. Statewide, the order had 50,000 members by October, 1854, and 120,000 by February, 1855.[4]

The Know Nothing cause was specifically political in its objectives, and as such it embodied more than simply an attempt to save "the country from Popish misrule."[5] It also captured the disillusionment felt by many toward the entire political system's cronyism, unresponsiveness to new issues, and apparent inability to come to grips with the rapid social and economic changes that had overtaken American society. Know Nothingism was a deliberate attempt to create a new party from the fragmented, but potentially dominant, opponents of the ruling Democratic party. Anti-Catholics, prohibitionists, former Whigs, free soilers, and non-Catholic Germans all looked for a way to ally themselves within a reform party that would address itself to pressing public issues of the day.[6]

The Know Nothing party seemed to be a perfect vehicle for this alliance. Its potential was immediately apparent when a "Union Reform" ticket, stressing anti-Catholicism, free schools, and an end to political corruption, unexpectedly won most of the races in the spring 1854 city election. The *Enquirer* charged that the ticket had been "made out by a half dozen persons meeting in a secret and clandestine manner. . . ."[7] The city's first Know Nothing lodges were still organizing in secret, and their effect on the election is unknown. It seems likely, however, that the organizers of the Union Reform ticket were by and large the same people who were establishing the Know Nothing order in the city. Significantly, the *Gazette* reported that the non-Catholic Germans were consulted on the makeup of the ticket.[8]

By summer, the existence of the Know Nothings was public knowledge. The order was immediately thought of as the second major party locally, and observers gave them a good chance to beat the Democrats in the fall. The main factor once again would be the votes of the non-Catholic Germans. On the major issues the German bloc and the Know Nothings were quite compatible: both opposed "Jesuitism and Popery," advocated political reform, and opposed the Kansas-Nebraska bill. This last issue, which had grown to tremendous importance nationally in the preceding months, had reawakened many northerners' fears of the spread of slavery into the territories. Although anti-Nebraska sentiments were strong among both the dissident Germans and the Know Nothings, the issue was not as important locally in the fall campaign as was the Catholic question.[9]

Despite this mutuality of interest on the major issues, the dissident Germans were nonetheless wary of the Know Nothings. Although the order stressed anti-Catholicism, it refused to admit all foreigners (even English and Scottish immigrants) as members. Some well-known nativists—including those whom the Germans had opposed on the Free School ticket—were among its members, as were many prominent prohibitionists. Moreover, the Democrats tried to head off a German/Know Nothing alliance by stirring up old economic issues, accusing the Know Nothings of being agents of the banks and the railroads.[10]

With the loyalties of the non-Catholic Germans in doubt, Charles Reemelin, one of the most radical German leaders, precipitated a new clash within the Democratic party at its county convention. Reemelin attacked the Democratic county office holders for "reckless extravagance"; ridiculed an anti–Know Nothing resolution by stating that "in your very midst exists the worst and meanest of all secret political organizations of conspirators [the Miami Tribe]"; and finally accused H. H. Robinson, editor of the *Enquirer*, of printing a "falsehood." At that point Robinson leapt to his feet shouting, and pandemonium broke out. Some delegates cried, "Down with the d[amne]d Dutchman." One of the best-known party leaders charged furiously toward the speaker's stand. When Reemelin turned and fled the building, the attacker cried out, "The reign of the d[amne]d Dutch is over by G[o]d!"[11]

Even after this confrontation at the Democratic convention, some political observers still doubted that the Know Nothings could win the support of the dissident Germans. The *Commercial* ran a humorous interview with a ficticious Know Nothing, asking him: "And what, think you, is to be the political effect of this Teutonic Hegira . . . ?" The imaginary Know Nothing spokesman answered: "That can't be told. . . . To tell the truth, we've said rather too much about native born citizens, and Anglo Saxon blood, and talked somewhat carelessly about Protestantism and all that sort of thing, to make much headway with the Dutch." He added that "there is said to be an infallible recipe for German votes, but as the candidates on all sides are trying it, the results may be rather mixed." "What is it?" "Lager Bier!"[12] This fictional conversation pointed out the predicament facing Cincinnati's Know Nothing movement. To win the crucial German votes in the city, the party had to suppress the nativist and temperance sentiments of some of its own supporters. For the fall election the party was able to quash these issues, and campaigned solely on opposition to the Catholic church, political corruption, and the Kansas-Nebraska bill. As a result, the Know Nothings were successful in winning the support of the city's non-Catholic Germans.

At the state level, opponents of the Kansas-Nebraska bill focused their efforts on the candidacy of Joseph R. Swan, who had been nominated for Supreme Court judge at a July "fusion" convention of anti-Nebraskaites and Know Nothings. But in Cincinnati, the stronghold of the state's Know Nothing movement, anti-Catholicism and political reform surpassed the slavery question in importance and attention.[13] The "American Reform" ticket, always referred to in the newspapers as the Know Nothing slate, endorsed Swan but ran prominent Know Nothings for all the local offices.

The city Know Nothings swept to a massive victory over the Democrats, winning nearly two-thirds of the Hamilton County vote. Significantly, there was very little ticket splitting. The ward-by-ward vote for Thomas Spooner, state leader of the Know Nothing order and candidate for city clerk, closely matched the vote for Judge Swan. Voters did not try to distinguish between anti-Nebraska and anti-Catholic nominees, but saw the Know Nothing party as representing both positions. Rutherford B. Hayes wrote that "Anti-Nebraska, Know Nothings, and a general disgust with the powers that be, have carried this county by between seven and eight thousand majority! How people do hate Catholics, and what a happiness it was to thousands to have a chance to show it in what seemed a lawful and patriotic manner."[14]

In all five Over-the-Rhine wards the Know Nothing percentages were higher than the combined totals of the Free School, German Free School, and Whig mayoral candidates in the spring 1853 election. When the *Enquirer* claimed that "the large vote cast by foreigners in favor of the Know-Nothing ticket" gave that party its victory, a reader indignantly replied that "in justice to the Catholic voters of this city," the paper should have made it clear that the foreigners in question "were Irish Orangemen, Scotch and English Tories, Infidel Germans, and lastly, the Christ-killing Jews. No wonder, with such a compound of bigotry, that the lovers of the Constitution, law and liberty, should be defeated."[15] Clearly, the Know Nothing party had successfully suppressed the anti-foreign elements in its midst, and had reaped its reward in the election.

But the Know Nothing/German alliance was tentative at best. One German wrote: "We will try the Know-Nothings this time for reform, and then if they be humbugs, we will try some new sort of Know-Nothings next time."[16] Since the party was successful that fall, it might have been expected to continue its course of stressing anti-Catholicism, political reform, and opposition to the Kansas-Nebraska bill, hoping to win the whole-hearted support of the dissident German voters. But by the spring of 1855 city election, the tenuous union had abruptly ended after the Know Nothing party adopted a strident nativist tone which alienated former German supporters and which led to a disastrous electoral defeat.

Shortly before the spring election a "Foreign Protestant," writing to the *Commercial*, described the predicament of "citizens of his background": they were caught, he claimed, between "two ultra parties," one standing for popery and the other for opposition to all foreigners.[17] Charles Reemelin and Friedrich Hassaurek led a meeting at Turner's Hall in which they accused the Know Nothing party of abusing foreigners "*en masse*," and urged all Germans to support the Democratic ticket.[18] The *Commercial* noted that whereas the Know Nothings had gotten "almost the entire Israelite vote in the last election," that party's radical doctrines and ferocious attacks on the foreign-born had now alienated the city's Jews.[19] By election day it seemed likely that German votes would tip the balance of power back toward the Democrats. Know Nothing rowdies, including several hundred from Kentucky, formed into mobs when rumors spread of fraudulent voting in the Over-the-Rhine wards. They seized and destroyed the ballot boxes in wards 11 and 12 and tried to do so in ward 9. Fighting went on for days after the election. Germans erected barricades on three bridges over the canal into the German wards, and when nativist mobs tried to storm them, two were killed and several more were wounded.[20]

The ballots destroyed in wards 11 and 12 turned out to be crucial in determining whether the Democrats or the Know Nothings had won. Clerks at the polls testified that the Democratic ticket had been winning overwhelmingly in those wards before the mob attacks, and the court declared the entire Democratic slate elected. The *Commercial* editorialized that the Know Nothing party had come "out of the contest severely chastised if not annihilated."[21] The validity of this assessment was soon confirmed by a precipitous decline in the popularity and power of the Know Nothing party.

Why had the Know Nothings abandoned the safe, successful course of anti-Catholicism and embarked instead on their ill-fated attack on all foreigners? The answer lies in the different and conflicting objectives sought by the varied groups that made up the leadership of the party. The Know Nothings had never been homogeneous or more than superficially united. Throughout the North the party contained a strong reform element, an element stressed by the *Commercial*'s fictitious Know Nothing interviewee: "Have you not, at some time," he asked his interviewer, "been a roaring Abolitionist, or a Temperance man, ready to burn all negro-sellers and rum-drinkers at the stake?" The interviewer answered that he had not. The Know Nothing commented: "I'll warrant you never dreamed yourself a moral earthquake . . . with a determination to blow the universe to atoms, with the hope of improving it," and concluded that the interviewer would never make a good Know Nothing.[22] The problem lay in the fact that some reformers saw the Catholic church as the main obstacle to their social reforms, and therefore looked upon the non-Catholic Germans as valuable allies; others, principally prohibitionists, viewed all immigrants, not just Catholics, as inimical to their goals.

Much of the anti-Catholicism in the Know Nothing party can be seen as an outgrowth of its reform spirit. The Catholic church school fund initiative had genuinely alarmed educational reformers who thought of parochial schools as backward and harmful to children, and who believed the public schools to be a source of American character and a key to upward mobility. Many American-born as well as German-born republicans hated the Catholic church for actively subverting attempts at nonmonarchical representative government in Europe, and believed it would readily do the same in the United States if given a chance. For these Know Nothings, anti-Catholicism was a liberal credo, aimed at the church hierarchy rather than at Catholic laymen, who were thought of as misguided.

Many Know Nothings, however, were motivated by considerations other than reform. The *Commercial*'s imaginary Know Nothing admitted to this, adding that the party contained "a goodly number of gentlemen whose tastes are purely physical, whose patriotism exhibits itself in . . . a tendency to load themselves with broadsides of portable artillery and cutlery, and whose religious and civic virtues are prone to become effervescent in the form of brickbats and blasphemy, employed as means for the conversion of 'our adopted fellow-citizens' from the errors of Romanism." This element of the party was not only anti-Catholic but also nativist, "going it strong for our native land and Anglo-Saxon blood . . . and kicking up a rumpus generally." (The 1855 election riot in Cincinnati certainly proved this to be true.) However, noted the Know Nothing, these rowdies were the only ones in the party that did not want political office. All the rest aspired to be pillars of the state: "We have more pillars than places to put them—ten to one. . . . Why, we are a perfect bag of political saltpetre. Everybody wants to save the State, and knows he could if he had half a chance."[23]

The overall picture that emerges of the Know Nothing party is not of a unified political movement but rather of a catch-all, including reformers of various stripes, particularly prohibitionists, free soilers, and free schoolers, with many aspiring to political office. The party leaders, in turn, depended upon the votes of a "rowdy" faction of the party. Those perceived as the rowdies by the party leaders were primarily native-born unskilled workers who competed with the foreign-born for jobs and urban living space. That competition, always intense in the mid-nineteenth century, peaked in 1854 when a drought and the development of railroad trade displaced Cincinnati river workers just as prewar European immigration reached its highest level. These Know Nothings were motivated more by economic hardship than by reform ideals. As a result, according to the *Commercial*'s Know Nothing, "no two of us agree precisely as to what Know Nothingism is."[24] But the most marked division among the leaders was between those who saw non-Catholic Germans as potential allies, and those, primarily temperance activists, who saw all German and Irish immigrants as enemies.[25] By the spring of 1855 the temperance leaders had allied themselves with the rowdy nativist wing of the party, and had wrested control from the anti-Catholics who had shaped the party's winning strategy the previous fall.

The break between the Know Nothings and the non-Catholic Germans came when the party announced its ticket for the 1855 spring election. As Rutherford B. Hayes wrote, "the rowdies nominated" the ticket.[26] James D. Taylor, editor of the *Times*, won the endorsement for mayor. Taylor's ties to the nativist element in the city had made him unacceptable to the German dissidents in 1853 when he had run for mayor on the Free School ticket. His position at the head of the ticket in 1855 could only be taken as a direct insult to them and a repudiation of their support. Moreover, another well-known nativist received the nomination for police judge, and temperance activists won endorsement for the positions of treasurer, commissioner, and civil engineer. In several wards prohibitionists monopolized the Know Nothing nominations for City Council. The Germans quickly condemned this shift to nativism and prohibitionism, declaring they would once again support the Democratic ticket. Anti-Catholics tried to salvage some offices by creating a "Citizen's Ticket" composed of candidates from both parties, but excluding all the Know Nothing candidates with nativist or temperance credentials. The *Commercial* claimed that the "Citizen's Ticket" had been "received with favor by all the classes of our German Protestants," but the similar vote totals for all the Democratic candidates indicate that hardly any German voters were persuaded to split their votes.[27]

Cincinnati temperance activists were so convinced that prohibition would have to wait until the power of the foreign-born voters was broken that they let the issue lapse in the spring election. Taylor had vehemently opposed the Maine Law in 1853, but prohibitionists supported him nonetheless, abandoning their long-standing policy of voting only for candidates openly pledged to prohibition. Indeed, they asked only that candidates state their intention to enforce the weak liquor laws already on the books.[28]

The 1855 spring election demonstrated once again to both temperance and nativist groups the political power of Cincinnati's non-Catholic German voters. The election had the effect of cementing the bond between the two groups. Temperance activists were prominent in the list of planners for the Know Nothing Fourth of July parade that summer, and the city's Sons of Temperance lodges marched in the parade just behind the American Protestant Association lodges. A journalist noted Samuel Cary's assertion that those assembled "had no war to wage against any persons, but, as Americans, they would vigilantly watch the ark of liberty. . . . Americans had nothing to fear from without. . . . The great dangers they had to fear were internal." [29] The Fourth of July parade demonstrated the extent to which temperance had been subsumed within nativism. The temperance movement in Cincinnati no longer functioned as an independent political element; it had linked its future irrevocably to nativist-oriented Know Nothingism.

The nativists and prohibitionists had won control of the Know Nothing party in 1855, but the spring election defeat and rioting in Cincinnati ensured that they took command of a sinking ship. If the party could not stay in power in Cincinnati, the center of Ohio Know Nothingism, then it had no hope of carrying the entire state. Those with political aspirations as well as those alienated by Know Nothing nativist lawlessness and rowdyism shifted quickly to the nascent Republican movement, which focused on opposition to the expansion of slavery and avoided other controversial issues.[30]

At the Know Nothing party convention in June, 1855, delegates decided not to nominate a party ticket for the fall state election, believing that their best hope for reversing their declining popularity lay in forming a fusion ticket with the Republicans. At the fusion convention in July the two parties worked out an elaborate compromise whereby the convention platform would avoid mention of any issues other than slavery and a free soiler would be chosen as the gubernatorial candidate at the head of a "Republican" ticket. All other eight places on the state ticket would go to Know Nothings, and the state Republicans would support all local Know Nothing tickets. In this compromise the Republicans undoubtedly saw a chance to beat the Democrats on the slavery issue alone, under the banner of their new party, thereby establishing slavery as the pre-eminent issue in state politics and the Republican party as the dominant political organization. The Know Nothings foresaw winning control of the state under the auspices of a less controversial party organization which they believed they could then push in the direction of their issues, by virtue of having incumbent Know Nothings in all but one of the state offices.[31]

The one hitch in this compromise was the insistence of the Republicans that Salmon P. Chase be the nominee for governor. Chase had spoken out strongly against Know Nothingism in the past, was known as an abolitionist, and had old ties with the Democratic party. The Know Nothings were in the majority at the fusion convention and many of them balked at the arrangement. Chase was nominated on the first ballot, although the Hamilton County delegation voted seventeen to fourteen against him.[32]

At the Know Nothing rank-and-file level, particularly in Cincinnati, there was an outcry against Chase's nomination. The *Times* editorialized that the order had been betrayed by its leaders. A bolter's convention met in August and nominated former Governor Allen Trimble to oppose both Chase and the Democratic candidate William Medill. The Cincinnati Know

Nothing ticket, true to the fusion compromise, formally endorsed Chase, but local party sentiment ran strongly for Trimble. Cincinnati rallies for Trimble abandoned the bland free-soil Republican platform and instead endorsed stricter naturalization laws, the primary goal of the nativists.[33]

One result of the Chase/Trimble split was to undercut Republican efforts to win the non-Catholic German vote in Cincinnati. The fusion compromise platform, which had avoided any hint of nativism, had convinced a few radical German leaders to campaign for the Republicans. However, the unwillingness of most local Know Nothings to stand by the compromise and to limit themselves to the free-soil issue served to void the platform's appeal to Germans. And the platform was the only selling point the new party had in the German community; otherwise, the Germans were being asked to support eight state and sixteen local Know Nothing candidates, and Chase. Although a free soiler, Chase inspired little enthusiasm among the Germans, since he refused to condemn the Know Nothing nativist position during the campaign and moreover was a temperance advocate of long standing, having endorsed prohibition in 1853. Chase noted after the election that he had lost votes "on both sides—on the American because not a member of the order & on the naturalized because connected with Kns on the ticket."[34] The Germans voted the Democratic ticket, and consequently the state Republican and local Know Nothing ticket went down to defeat in Cincinnati. Chase ran third in the city with 17.6 percent of the vote compared to 29.7 percent for Trimble and 52.8 percent for Medill.[35]

Statewide, Chase won the gubernatorial race, but by a narrow margin. The rest of the Ohio Republican ticket won easily. However, the influence the Know Nothings assumed they would have within the new party by virtue of controlling most of the state offices failed to materialize. Nativism and prohibitionism had proved too controversial and divisive as political issues, and Republican strategists were determined to suppress them in order to win over the non-Catholic German votes.

In Cincinnati the Germans were at odds once again with the old Miami Tribe leadership by January, 1856, both because the Miamis refused to budge on their pro-Catholic, pro-Nebraska, pro-Pierce stance and also because they were unwilling to give the radical Germans any share in the Democratic leadership. After the Democratic nominating convention for city offices in March, a new break between the two factions seemed likely. A majority of the delegates, led by a solid block of Irish Catholics, voted down every potential candidate for office who had ever been a Know Nothing supporter, thereby effectively excluding non-Catholic German candidates from the ticket. One candidate warned, "There were 7,000 Democrats of this city in there [the Know Nothing lodges], and you can't elect your ticket without . . . [their] votes. . . ."[36] However, the Irish faction refused to compromise with the non-Catholic Germans.

Despite the growing hostility between the Germans and the Democratic hierarchy, German leaders delayed making another break with the party until they had won a clear commitment from the Republicans to eliminate all prohibitionist and nativist influence from their legislative program and from their party leadership ranks. Stephen Molitor, a prominent German radical in Cincinnati, wrote to Governor Chase shortly after the city's March Democratic convention, deploring the fact that "the Jesuitical influence was prominent" at the meeting but warning that "the whole ticket will be elected" because of continuing Know Nothing and Maine Law sentiments apparent within the Republican party. He noted that Germans had been especially offended by "the passage of the temperance bill in the Senate, particularly the rejection of the amendment about wine and beer. It had its effect at the primary meetings and at the City Convention, and afforded to demagogues a dangerous weapon. Should the said bill pass the house and become a law, I am afraid the republican movement among the Germans will be an utter failure throughout the State."[37]

The warnings of Molitor and other Germans had their effect. In Cincinnati the Citizen's Reform ticket organized by local Republicans for the spring elections stressed that, of the eight candidates fielded, three had never been Know Nothings and two were foreign-born citizens. The ticket campaigned on a narrow anti-Catholic platform and won enough support in the German wards to elect two of its candidates. In the following months it became clear that the Republicans had effectively subdued the vestiges of prohibitionism and nativism in the party and were reaping the reward of German support. By June German Republican leader Friedrich Hassaurek could claim: "The people of the wards for whom I speak, are, a majority of them, Germans, but they are *all right*. When it comes to the polls you will see that 'over the Rhine' will give a nearly unanimous vote for Fremont and Dayton [the Republican presidential ticket]. . . . In October, 1855, these wards didn't turn out in their full strength on the side of Freedom. There was then a question entangled with that of freedom, and my friends didn't wish to prevent black slavery by making white slaves of themselves. This is no longer." [38] Samuel Cary wrote to a friend a few months later that, although the Republicans had the power in the state legislature to pass a prohibitory law, they "are afraid they will lose their foreign vote and thus lose power if they interfere with lager beer & whiskey." [39] Whereas all eight of the candidates below Chase on the 1855 state ticket had been Know Nothings, not a single one was still on the slate two years later when Chase and the Republicans swept to a new victory. [40]

The Republican leaders were willing to risk alienating Maine Law and Know Nothing voters in order to win over the Germans because they assumed that the nativist/prohibitionist element in the party had nowhere else to go even if their issues were suppressed and the German voters courted. Not only was the Democratic party anathema to most Know Nothings and prohibitionists, but sectionalism was beginning to assume such overwhelming importance that it seemed necessary to most voters to put aside other issues for the time being. When the 1856 national convention of the American (Know Nothing) party refused to take a stand against the expansion of slavery, many northern delegates, including three-fourths of the Ohio contingent, walked out. The Ohio state council of the party endorsed the action and then voted to ally officially with the Republican party. Temperance and nativist leaders such as Samuel Cary and former Know Nothing state leader Thomas Spooner campaigned actively for the Republicans even though they were and would remain barred from the party's positions of authority.[41]

A minority of the American party in Ohio endorsed the national American ticket headed by former President Millard Fillmore. This rump nativist party was centered in Cincinnati, where Know Nothings ran a local as well as a state ticket. In the city fear that sectional hostility would cut off southern trade and result in lost jobs overlapped with the fear of job competition with immigrants. The Republicans, however, felt confident of soon winning over even these die-hards. The *Gazette* remarked that the "Fillmore men" could be expected "to cast their votes hereafter to defeat . . . [the Democratic] party."[42]

The three way campaign in the city proved to be beneficial in a sense to the Republicans, since they were now seen by the non-Catholic Germans as distinctly separate from the Know Nothings. All the prominent German dissident leaders campaigned actively for the Republicans, and managed to inject some anti-Catholicism into the campaign along with the party's free-soil rhetoric. The Republicans made huge gains in the Over-the-Rhine region, actually beating the Democrats by large margins in wards 10 and 11. The Democratic *Enquirer* bitterly remarked: "The Irish born—indeed all other of our naturalized citizens, except the Germans—have proved faithful to their party and their principles. They have not deserted their friends."[43]

Citywide, the Democratic totals fell far below an outright majority, although in the three-way campaign they still managed to win a plurality of the votes. In a typical contest, that for Supreme Court judge, the Democratic candidate won 43.0% of the total vote, the Republican 32.4%, and the Know Nothing 24.6%. In a regression analysis of this Know Nothing vote with several past city votes, the Pearson product/moment correlation coefficients were .773 for the spring 1853 Free School mayoral vote and .911 for the fall 1853 Independent Prohibitory Law ticket vote. Since the 1853 Free School, 1853 Prohibition, and 1856 Know Nothing votes were the purest electoral expressions in Cincinnati of anti-Catholicism, prohibitionism, and nativism respectively, the figures support the conclusion that there was a stronger link between prohibitionism and nativism than there was between anti-Catholicism and nativism.[44]

The state and national elections of 1856 were the last gasp of the Know Nothing movement. Afterward its remains in the North were largely incorporated into the Republican party. The temperance movement in Ohio was, by then, several steps removed from its power base of 1853. It had first entered the Know Nothing movement with the idea that the Maine Law issue would be revived once the power of foreign voters had been broken. When the Know Nothing movement itself disintegrated, with its nativist goals effectively suppressed within the Republican party, loyal prohibitionists were left totally stripped of political influence. Moreover, the issue of slavery expansion had provoked a sectional crisis in America that dominated public attention by the late 1850s. Temperance reform seemed destined to fade from public view.

Temperance activists realized that the sectional issue preempted all other public concerns in the political campaigns of 1856. But, like many other Americans, they assumed that conflicts over slavery expansion would somehow be resolved, leaving the field once again open to their prohibition efforts. "In a few weeks the present political tornado will have passed away," wrote one temperance leader during the fall 1856 election campaigns. "For the next two years . . . the Prohibition of the Liquor Traffic will be the commanding issue at the ballot box."[45] By the following summer, however, a revival of the temperance issue still seemed remote, and the expectations of Cincinnati's steadfast temperance organizers were less confident: "as soon as Kansas has bled to death, or her wounds are entirely healed," commented Dr. Joshua Wadsworth, editor of the *Templar's Magazine*, "we suppose temperance will occupy a share of public attention."[46] Even this modest hope proved overly optimistic. Except for a brief increase in interest and activity following the Panic of 1857, temperance agitation practically disappeared from public view. Temperance organizations continued to hold meetings but with little attendance, publicity, or sense of purpose. This was not just the case in Ohio, where prohibition had failed to pass, but throughout the country. State after state either voided or repealed its Maine Law, so that, of the thirteen states which legislated prohibition in the 1850s, only Maine, Massachusetts, and Vermont were still dry at the outbreak of the Civil War.[47]

Why did temperance reform decline so drastically even in states where prohibition campaigns had initially been successful? Much of the explanation lies in the public preoccupation with sectionalism, the effort of the Republican party throughout the North to suppress the liquor question, and the failure of every state that passed prohibition to enforce it effectively.[48] But Cincinnati evidence suggests two other factors as well: a leveling off of the incidence of social disorder, and a lessening of its ethnic associations. European immigration peaked in the early 1850s. Afterward, fewer newcomers entered the city each year, and the percentage of foreign-born in the population declined over the next two decades. As Table 9 indicates, the percentage of the foreign-born within the total number of relief recipients in the city dropped markedly in the latter part of the 1850s. The total number of police arrests in the 1859–60 municipal year was actually lower than the figure for 1853–54 (6,644 versus 6,769). Social disorder remained a pressing problem: the number of felony crimes continued to rise, as did the total number of relief recipients. But the level of disorder that existed in the 1850s became familiar, comprehensible, less alien, and less immediately threatening. As Samuel Cary, explaining the decline of the temperance movement, wrote in 1858: "The moral sense is deteriorated and stupefied [when familiarized with an evil], and fails, of course, to appreciate the evil in all its length and breadth. Scenes of drunkenness, debauchery, crime, poverty, and destitution become familiar, and we come to regard them as a matter of course."[49]

At the same time, loyal temperance activists lapsed into despair over the future of America. For years they had believed resolutely that only prohibition could save the country from chaos, and now it was clear that prohibition would not succeed. "Whither are we drifting as a nation?" asked *The Cru-*

Table 9. Birthplaces of indoor and outdoor relief
recipients in Cincinnati.

	1853–54	1857–58	1859–60	1860–61
United States	20.7%	30.7%	32.4%	34.0%
Germany	25.9	21.1	23.0	22.2
Ireland	47.3	39.0	36.8	36.4
Other	6.1	9.2	7.8	7.4
	100.0%	100.0%	100.0%	100.0%

SOURCE: Cincinnati City Departments, *Annual Reports*, "City Infirmary, Clerk's Report," 1854, 1858, 1860, 1861.

sader in 1858. Defeating the liquor traffic "is not merely vital to our *prosperity*, it involves our very *existence*."[50] The reformers believed they had been defeated by a combination of the "Liquor Power," the "mightiest power in the Republic";[51] corrupt politicians who cared nothing for "honesty, integrity, [or] ability";[52] and "degraded and vicious foreigners,"[53] the "refuse of Europe."[54] The Maine Law had been kept from passage by power-hungry political parties which had vied for the support of the "foreign miscreants"; where the Maine Law had passed, the liquor trade had defeated its operation by suborning juries and bribing courts and legislatures. "If the friends of virtue and good order cannot be induced to break the traces of party and combine against the powers of evil," concluded *The Crusader* in 1857, "we may bid adieu to all that is lovely, excellent, and of good report in our Republic."[55] From the perspective of loyal temperance advocates, America's future looked bleak indeed in the late 1850s.

The outbreak of the Civil War only quickened the decline of the temperance cause and heightened the frustration of its remaining supporters. The reformers realized that wartime was likely to bring increased drinking, as young soldiers left behind the protective influence of their families and communities and experienced the fierce, frightening, and vulgar world of the campground and the battlefield. For temperance advocates this prospect was particularly threatening, since they believed that an intemperate northern army would be far less capable of defending the Union than would an abstinent one. The Grand Worthy Patriarch of the Ohio Templars of Honor enlisted in September, 1861, "for the purpose of wielding an influence in favor of temperance among the men that compose our Northern army."[56] Temperance spokesmen challenged as a dangerous myth the widely held belief that liquor was necessary "to fit . . . [soldiers] to endure the fatigues, privations, and exposure of camp life and military marches."[57] Cary's pamphlet on temperance for soldiers, 30,000 copies of which were distributed by the Sons of Temperance, concluded: "Let the rebel army drain the cup of the devils—it is *their* appropriate drink. They would stab the nation's heart, and they need the 'beverage of hell' to enable them to perpetrate their damning crime."[58] But few listened to the cautions of the temperance reformers. More typical of the wartime mood was the quip of President Lincoln, a former Son of Temperance, that he should find out General Grant's brand of whiskey and send a barrel of it to his less successful generals.[59]

With the attention of the nation elsewhere, and most former supporters in uniform, the temperance organizations reached a nadir of membership, activity, and influence. The Ohio Independent Order of Good Templars (see Chapter 6) declined from 5,054 members in 101 temples in 1861 to 2,392 members in 42 temples in 1862. The national membership of the Sons of Temperance dropped from 94,213 in 1860 to 55,788 in 1862, lower than it had been since 1847. The Cincinnati-based *Templar's Magazine*, national organ of the Templars of Honor, suspended publication at the end of 1862. Editor Wadsworth, in the next to last issue, noted: "Temperance and its associate virtues do not flourish in war times, and none of the organizations having in view the promotion of total abstinence are making any headway. Most of them, indeed, are going backward."[60] It seemed that the temperance reform movement was at its end, dying unnoticed amidst the ravages of war. Few at the time would have thought it possible that a half-century of temperance agitation, culminating in national prohibition, still lay in America's future.

Notes

1. *Templar's Magazine*, Dec., 1857, 381.

2. See, for example, Ray A. Billington, *The Protestant Crusade 1800–1860: A Study of the Origins of American Nativism* (New York, 1938), 118 and *passim*; Oscar Handlin, *Boston's Immigrants: A Study in Acculturation* (New York, 1968), 199–201.

3. *Cincinnati Commercial*, Jan. 5, 1854, Dec. 31, 1853 (hereafter cited as CC); William Baughin, "Nativism in Cincinnati before 1860" (M.A. thesis, University of Cincinnati, 1963), 166, 177; Eugene H. Roseboom, *The Civil War Era, 1850–1873* (vol. 4 of *The History of the State of Ohio*, ed. Carl Wittke, Columbus, Ohio, 1944), 289; Rev. James F. Connelly, *The Visit of Archbishop Gaetano Bedini to the United States of America (June, 1853–Feb., 1854)* (Rome, 1960), quoted in William E. Gienapp, "The Transformation of Cincinnati Politics, 1852–1860" (unpublished seminar paper, Yale University, 1969), 46. Bedini sparked protests in every city he visited, although none were as vehement as Cincinnati's.

4. CC, July 24, 1854; Eugene H. Roseboom, "Salmon P. Chase and the Know Nothings," *Mississippi Valley Historical Review*, 25 (1938): 339.

5. *Western Christian Advocate*, May 17, 1854.

6. Rutherford B. Hayes, *Diary and Letters of Rutherford Birchard Hayes*, ed. Charles R. Williams (Columbus, Ohio, 1922), 1:470, Hayes to S. Birchard, Cincinnati, Oct. 13, 1854; Michael F. Holt, "The Politics of Impatience: The Origins of Know Nothingism," *Journal of American History*, 60 (1973): 313 and *passim*.

7. *Cincinnati Enquirer*, Apr. 1, 1854, quoted in Gienapp, "Transformation," 52; CC, Apr. 5, 1854.

8. *Cincinnati Gazette*, Apr. 1, 1854, quoted in Gienapp, "Transformation," xvii, fn. 124.

9. CC, Mar. 8, 25, 1854. Paul Kleppner has noted that in Pittsburgh Know Nothingism was more anti-Catholic than anti-immigrant ("Lincoln and the Immigrant Vote: A Case of Religious Polarization," *Mid-America* 48 (1966): 188).

10. *Western Christian Advocate*, May 17, 1854; CC, Aug. 14, 1854. Kathleen Neils Conzen notes that in Milwaukee German Democrats attacked antislavery agitation as a smoke-screen for nativists and temperance fanatics. The Democratic paper warned, "As soon as the Germans desert the Democracy and go with the abolitionists, they will elevate to power and prestige a sect which thinks to turn the entire country into a 'Water-Cure'; which wants to command what each citizen may and may not drink . . ." (quoted in *Immigrant Milwaukee, 1836–1860: Accommodation and Community in a Frontier City* (Cambridge, Mass., 1976), 215).

11. CC, Aug. 14, 1854.

12. Ibid., Sept. 30, 1854.

13. Gienapp, "Transformation," 55, 59.

14. Hayes, *Diary*, 1:470, Hayes to S. Birchard, Cincinnati, Oct. 13,

1854; CC, Oct. 10, 16, 1854. In Indiana there was a similar blurring between the slavery issue and issues of temperance, anti-Catholicism, and nativism during the 1854 fall election there. For example, after the election C. B. Davidson of Evansville wrote to his brother (Oct. 14, 1854): "Our elections have just passed off and the dominant [Democratic] party in the state is completely routed. The passage of the Nebraska and Kansas bill has produced a complete revolution in the political parties here. The democratic majority in this state was very large, and their defeat is a great victory. We hope now to have a legislature that will give us a strong prohibitory liquor law. . . . Great fears were entertained that there would be a riot, and indeed there was ground for such fears. The excitement between the natives and foreigners had been very great . . ." (James D. Davidson Collection, Indiana State Library, photocopy of letter in McCormick Agricultural Library).

15. *Cincinnati Enquirer*, Oct. 11, 12, 15, 1854, quoted in Gienapp, "Transformation," 63.

16. Quoted in Baughin, "Nativism," 181–82.

17. CC, Mar. 27, 1855.

18. Ibid., Mar. 29, 1855.

19. Ibid., Mar. 30, 1855. In 1850 there were approximately 2,800 Jews in Cincinnati; in 1860, approximately 7,500 (Stephen G. Mostov, "The Jewish Component in Mid-Nineteenth Century American Cities: Cincinnati, 1840–1875" (paper presented at Fifth Annual Meeting of Social Science History Association, Rochester, N.Y., 1980), 3).

20. William Baughin, "Ballots and Bullets: The Election Day Riots of 1855," *Historical and Philosophical Society of Ohio Bulletin*, 21 (1963): 267–72.

21. CC, Apr. 3, 5, 7, 1855.

22. Ibid., Sept. 30, 1854; Handlin, *Boston's Immigrants*, 202; Roseboom, *Era*, 291.

23. CC, Sept. 30, 1854.

24. Ibid., Sept. 30, 1854; Holt, "Politics," 325–28; Ira M. Leonard and Robert D. Parmet, eds., *American Nativism, 1830–1860* (New York, 1971), 51; Zane Miller, *The Urbanization of Modern America: A Brief History* (New York, 1973), 46–47.

25. In Illinois a split developed in the Know Nothing state council between the "Jonathans" and the "Sams." "The Sams are anti-foreign and anti-Catholic. The Jonathans are anti-slavery, but not against foreigners. They will admit all foreigners who disavow temporal allegiance to the Pope" (*Chicago Democrat*, May 5, 1855, quoted in John P. Senning, "The Know-Nothing Movement in Illinois, 1854–1856," *Journal of the Illinois State Historical Society*, 7 (1914): 19).

26. Hayes, *Diary*, 1:481–82, Hayes to S. Birchard, Cincinnati, Apr. 8, 1855.

27. CC, Mar. 30, 10, 20, 21, 26, 29, 1855.

28. Ibid., Feb. 17, 1855; *Templar's Magazine*, May, 1855.

29. CC, July 6, 1855; *Western Christian Advocate*, Apr. 18, 1855.

30. For a discussion of the temperance/Know Nothing coalition in Chicago and the manner in which it alienated non-Catholic German voters who had at first supported the Know Nothing party, see Richard Wilson Renner, "In a Perfect Ferment: Chicago, the Know Nothings, and the Riot for Lager Beer," *Chicago History*, 5 (1976): 163–70. Renner concludes that the Know Nothings in Chicago "were brought low by a group—the Germans—with whom they had no particular quarrel and over an issue—temperance—which was not even part of their platform" (170).

31. CC, July 14, 1855; Roseboom, "Chase," 343.

32. CC, July 14, 1855; Roseboom, "Chase," 344–45.

33. CC, July 20, Sept. 22, 1855; Roseboom, *Era*, 311; Roseboom, "Chase," 346–47.

34. Edward L. Pierce Papers, Houghton Library, Harvard Library, Salmon P. Chase to Edward L. Pierce, Oct. 20, 1855, quoted in Stephen Maizlish, "The Triumph of Sectionalism: The Transformation of Politics in the Antebellum North, Ohio, 1844–1860" (Ph.D. thesis, University of California, Berkeley, 1979), 431.

35. CC, Oct. 13, 1853, July 20, Aug. 22, 31, Oct. 1, 11, 15, 1855; *Cincinnati Times*, Sept. 3, 1853; *Western Temperance Journal*, June 15, 1841; Gienapp, "Transformation," 75, 78. Chase had been associated with the temperance movement for over two decades (the Ohio state temperance convention *Proceedings* of 1833 lists him as one of two delegates from the Young Men's Temperance Society of Cincinnati), but his temperance credentials did not necessarily attract prohibitionist votes, as Trimble was also a temperance advocate of long standing (see John A. Krout, *The Origins of Prohibition* (New York, 1925), 160–61).

36. *Cincinnati Gazette*, Mar. 27, Jan. 9, 12, 1856.

37. Chase MS. Collection, Library of Congress, Stephen Molitor to Salmon P. Chase, Cincinnati, Mar. 27, 1856.

38. *Cincinnati Gazette*, June 21, Mar. 28, Apr. 11, 1856; Gienapp, "Transformation," 81–82.

39. Ohio Historical Society Library, Samuel F. Cary to Rev. E. W. Jackson, Dec. 12, 1856.

40. Roseboom, "Chase," 349; Eric Foner, *Free Soil, Free Labor, Free Men: The Ideology of the Republican Party before the Civil War* (Oxford, 1970), 242.

41. Roseboom, *Era*, 315–17; *Cincinnati Gazette*, Apr. 29, Nov. 4, 1856.

42. *Cincinnati Gazette*, Nov. 5, 1856; Roseboom, *Era*, 315–17.

43. *Cincinnati Enquirer*, Oct. 17, 1856, quoted in Gienapp, "Transformation," 86; *Cincinnati Gazette*, Nov. 6, 1856.

44. *Cincinnati Gazette*, Nov. 5, 1856.

45. International Order of Good Templars, Ohio Grand Lodge, *Proceedings*, 1856, 7.

46. *Templar's Magazine*, May, 1857, 163.

47. See, for example, ibid., Sept., 1857, 286, Feb., 1858, 63, July,

1858, 208, Jan., 1859, 32–33; *Crusader*, Oct., 1857, 151, Dec., 1857, 223, Jan., 1858, 245, Aug., 1858, 81, Oct., 1858, 144; Donald W. Beattie, "Sons of Temperance: Pioneers in Total Abstinence and 'Constitutional' Prohibition" (Ph.D. thesis, Boston University, 1966), 211.

48. For examples of the temperance issue being "jettisoned" by the state Republican parties of Maine, New York, Indiana, Illinois, Wisconsin, and Iowa (particularly in order to appeal to German voters in the cases of Illinois, Wisconsin, and Iowa), see Foner, *Free Soil*, 241–42, 247. For examples of the decline of state temperance movements, see John A. Krout, "The Maine Law in New York Politics," *New York History*, 17 (1936): 266–71; Frank L. Byrne, "Maine Law versus Lager Beer: A Dilemma of Wisconsin's Young Republican Party," *Wisconsin Magazine of History*, 52 (1958–59): 115–20; Asa E. Martin, "The Temperance Movement in Pennsylvania prior to the Civil War," *Pennsylvania Magazine of History and Biography*, 49 (1925): 228–29.

49. *Crusader*, Nov., 1858, 185; Charles Cist, *Sketches and Statistics of Cincinnati in 1851* (Cincinnati, Ohio, 1851), 47; Cincinnati City Departments, *Annual Reports*, "Annual Report of the Mayor," Mar. 1, 1854, "Aggregate of Police Returns," Apr. 1, 1860; *Ninth Census of the United States, 1870*, 1:231; CC, Dec. 10, 1854; *Historical Statistics of the United States, Colonial Times to 1957* (Washington, D.C., 1960), 57. Between 1850 and 1854 Irish immigration to the United States averaged 161,800 annually; between 1855 and 1859 the average figure dropped to 44,000; the respective figures for German immigration are 130,800 and 64,400.

50. *Crusader*, Oct., 1858, 146.

51. Ibid., Aug., 1858, 80–81.

52. Ibid., Sept., 1858, 118.

53. Ibid., Sept., 1857, 113.

54. Ibid., Aug. 29, 1856.

55. Ibid., Sept., 1857, 113.

56. *Templar's Magazine*, Sept., 1861, 286–87. This attitude toward war was not new to the temperance movement. During the Mexican War the *Ohio Washingtonian Organ* wrote, "Our reform must of course suffer by this great calamity. The army will have the burning poison dealt out to them by the officers of the government. Habits will be formed by many which will be their ultimate ruin. . . . Many of those who fought the battles of the Revolution, and the last war, died drunkards" (May 30, 1846).

57. International Order of Good Templars, Ohio Grand Lodge, *Proceedings*, 1861, 6.

58. Samual F. Cary, *Letter to Volunteers in the Federal Army, Warning against Intemperance* (Cincinnati, Ohio, 1861), 4; Beattie, "Sons," 188.

59. Carl Sandburg, *Abraham Lincoln: The War Years*, 2 (New York, 1939): 119–20.

60. *Templar's Magazine*, Nov., 1862, 355; International Order of Good Templars, Ohio Grand Lodge, *Proceedings*, 1861, 8–9, 1862, 8; Beattie, "Sons," 398.

6

Women and Temperance prior to the Woman's Crusade

On Sunday, December 23, 1873, Boston-based itinerant lecturer Dio Lewis spoke in the town of Hillsboro, Ohio. His topic for the evening was temperance reform. Lewis urged the women of the community to band together and pray in the local saloons in an attempt to close them. The next day, Christmas Eve, a group of Hillsboro women enacted Lewis's plan. The Woman's Crusade had begun.

In the next four months over 32,000 women in more than 300 Ohio communities participated in the Crusade. The movement spread throughout the country to several hundred other communities, and in many the crusades succeeded in closing, at least temporarily, all the local retail liquor outlets. The Woman's Crusade severely disrupted the liquor trade and forced out of business manufacturers and wholesalers as well as retailers. Within the year the Crusade had evolved into the Woman's Christian Temperance Union (WCTU), an organization that was to help shape American history for many decades to come.[1]

The Woman's Crusade was so dramatic and its emergence so sudden that it seemed to have appeared from nowhere. Indeed, most historians of the Crusade and of the WCTU have viewed the Hillsboro incident as the starting point for any analysis of the shift to female dominance of the temperance movement in the last quarter of the nineteenth century. Within this context some historians have looked for specific, immediate causes of the Crusade: the charisma of Dio Lewis; the Panic of 1873; the Ohio constitutional convention of 1873–74; or the enactment of a permissive bill to allow local liquor prohibition in New Zealand and a liquor Licensing Amendment Act in Great Britain. Other historians have searched for the causes of the Crusade in psychological motivations unconnected either to the history of temperance reform or to real problems linked with drinking. The Crusade and the WCTU have been viewed as symbolic reassertions of cultural dominance; indications of moral anxiety generated by Reconstruction era corruption; disguised attacks on male culture and expressions of anti-male feelings; responses to the decline of the importance of the family and the woman's place within it; and opportunities for women to exercise power, to make men and communities do what they wanted, under the protective cover of an altruistic and religious movement.[2]

All these factors may have played a role in the Woman's Crusade, but none of them takes into account the history of the temperance movement prior to 1873. Temperance reform was one of the most popular, long-lived, and influential social movements in American history, and first became a pressing national issue nearly half a century before the Woman's Crusade. Women had been actively involved in the reform since its earliest years, and their particular perspectives and problems had produced as early as the 1850s an approach to the liquor issue distinct from that of men. The Crusade, and the WCTU which developed from it, were inextricably linked to several decades of prior female temperance activity, and can only be fully understood within the context of that earlier activity.

Female participation in temperance agitation in the decades prior to 1873 was not static and monolithic, nor did it evolve gradually and evenly. Rather, a period of turbulent transition at mid-century sharply divides the history of women's temperance activism in this period into two distinct phases. Prior to 1850, women had been willing to remain subordinate to men in the areas of public activity and organizational leadership within the temperance movement because the reform efforts they carried out in their homes, within their domestic roles as mothers, wives, and sisters, were considered by all to be vital to the success of moral suasion. When in the 1850s temperance tactics shifted from the advocacy of moral suasion to that of prohibition, women were left without a meaningful function to perform in the movement, and they quickly began to demand an equal role in traditionally male spheres of action. Their efforts to gain full participation brought to many temperance women a new feminist perspective, causing them to swell the ranks of the emerging women's rights movement.

Although women did secure an expanded role within the temperance movement, their inability to vote still left them largely powerless in the political arena. At the same time, temperance women began to fear for the safety of their own families. The acceptability of drinking among members of the native-born Protestant middle class had declined steadily since the 1830s, so that by mid-century middle-class imbibing was rare and intoxication quite scandalous. During the 1850s, however, temperance reform experienced a reversal of fortunes, and drinking seemed to regain some of the popularity and respectability it had previously lost, while the drink trade itself gained in economic and political power. Women saw this change as immensely threatening to the security of their families. With traditional moral suasion discredited and with political efforts floundering beyond direct female influence, women, as early as the 1850s, adopted more direct, nonpolitical methods of confronting the liquor trade. In communities throughout the country bands of women turned to extralegal militant action and forcibly destroyed the liquor stock of local drinking establishments. The years of the Civil War and Reconstruction only added to the danger of drink, from these women's perspective, and aggravated their frustration at the political emphasis of the temperance movement. Physical assaults on saloons, as well as assaults by nonviolent bands of praying women, continued intermittently throughout the 1860s and early 1870s, culminating in the spectacular phenomenon of the Woman's Crusade in 1873–74.

Women were active in the temperance cause from the time of its foundation as a national movement in the late 1820s. In many early societies female members equaled or outnumbered male members. Yet their organizational role was highly circumscribed: typically they did not hold office, did not vote, and did not speak at meetings where men were present. Nevertheless, women were considered critical to the success of the movement. At the 1833 Ohio state temperance convention the delegates (all male) passed a resolution stating "that it is a matter of high importance to the cause of temperance that the united influence and energies of females should be enlisted actively in its support: *Resolved, therefore,* that a committee of five be appointed to prepare an address to the ladies of this State on that subject. . . ."[3] Female influence within the domestic sphere was the key to the success of the moral suasion efforts that dominated temperance reform activity after 1830. Within her role as the ultimate moral authority of the family, a woman could inculcate strict temperance ideals in her children, refuse to serve alcoholic beverages to guests, abandon their use as ingredients in cooking and in medicines, maintain so attractive a home and fireside that male family members would not be tempted to seek the conviviality of the saloon, and urge sons, husbands, fathers, brothers, and suitors either to adopt or to maintain teetotal pledges.[4]

So long as the temperance movement focused on moral suasion, women could play a central role in the reform yet never engage in activities that society considered inappropriate to their sphere. "In the cause of humanity she may labor," wrote a male temperance leader, "and in the spirit of a moral heroine battle with vice and misery successfully . . . and at the same time never step out of the position in which God has placed her, never assume the control of affairs in which she is the 'dependant' on man. . . ."[5]

Because women's activities were fundamental to moral suasion, their participation in the temperance movement expanded steadily during the 1840s, first in the Washingtonian and Martha Washington societies, and then in the Daughters of Temperance unions (see Chapter Two). The female role in this phase of the temperance movement was meaningful, if subordinate, and prior to 1850 few women showed signs of dissatisfaction with it. Even Virginia Allen, radical female editor of *The Pearl: A Ladies' Weekly Literary Gazette Devoted to the Advocacy of the Various Ladies' Total Abstinence Associations*, who used her columns to condemn the "capitalists" and "rich monopolists" who exploited working women, to espouse full property rights for women, and to argue the case for female suffrage, nevertheless generally expressed satisfaction with the power women wielded in the area of temperance reform: "Yes—however woman may be oppressed—however deprived of political or social rights, her God-given influence upon the destiny of the race may still be exerted. . . . It is for her to say, if she but choose to say it, whether the intoxicating bowl shall be dashed from the lips of mankind. . . ."[6]

During the next few years, however, many temperance women began to demand equal participation in the movement, full membership in men's organizations, and the right to speak in public. Some even advocated the right to vote. In these years a close link developed between women's rights and female temperance activitism. When the women's temperance convention of New York met in May, 1852, women who were or who were soon to be nationally prominent feminists officiated. Elizabeth Cady Stanton presided, and Amelia Bloomer and Susan B. Anthony served as secretaries. Bloomer's journal, *The Lily*, had begun as a temperance paper, its original motto reading "Devoted to Temperance and Literature." By 1852 it had evolved into a feminist journal, and its new masthead read "Devoted to the Interests of Women." Like Stanton, Anthony, and Bloomer, other prominent feminist leaders such as Lucretia Mott and Lucy Stone had been active in the temperance movement before they became involved in agitation for women's rights.[7]

What sparked this sudden change in the attitude of temperance women? Historian Lois Banner has suggested that the emerging women's rights movement, and in particular the 1848 Seneca Falls convention, "seemed to energize many women into asserting themselves in other, more socially acceptable reforms, primarily temperance." They had realized for the first time, in Amelia Bloomer's words, "that there was something wrong in the laws under which they lived."[8] Underlying this realization, in Banner's opinion, was an anti-male animus generated by experiencing or viewing the oppression of women at the hands of drunken husbands. Another historian, Keith Melder, has reached a similar conclusion: "Man the drunkard . . . was seldom accorded the status of a brother; he was a sinner, an enemy, an oppressor, who made a kind of slave of women."[9] Certainly temperance women were acutely aware of the special burden borne by the wives of inebriates. However, the timing and the character of the change in the attitudes of temperance women in the early 1850s suggest that this confluence of feminism and female temperance activism was not so much a reaction to male drinking as it was a response to the uselessness and powerlessness women felt when the temperance movement abandoned moral suasion in favor of prohibitionism.

Concern for women who suffered at the hands of drunkards had been shared by all temperance reformers, male and female, for several decades, and had been a recurrent theme of temperance literature written by both sexes. This concern, however, did not tend to generate anti-male feelings among temperance women, since they shared with their male colleagues a sympathy for the inebriate. By the 1840s temperance reformers generally considered drunkards to be blameless, the victims of the drink trade's evil rapaciousness. "I believe the drunkard is far superior to him who knowingly furnishes him with materials for his own destruction," wrote "Florella" in an 1846 issue of the *Weekly Messenger, Literary Wreath & Factory Girl's Garland*.[10] In the same year Virginia Allen in *The Pearl* advised: "Wife, if thy husband fall [into drunkenness], cast him not aside; reproach him not with bitter words, but by kindness win him back. . . ."[11] Moreover, women were active in temperance reform in large numbers prior to the 1848 Seneca Falls convention. Rarely did women become involved in women's rights and then turn to temperance reform; rather, women who had previously been active in the crusade against drink suddenly began to swell the ranks of the emerging women's rights movement. To understand the increasing assertiveness of temperance women in the 1850s, it is necessary to review the dramatic changes which occurred within the temperance movement at that time.

In the early and mid-1840s temperance reformers everywhere believed they were winning the battle against the drink trade. Contemporary observers continually noted the astonishing decline in the use of alcohol, particularly within the middle class. One of the most crucial aspects of the incipient victory, particularly for female temperance activists, was that it promised to secure a social environment within which children could be imbued successfully with strict teetotal principles. An Indiana temperance leader commented in 1845: "Ask the most violent opposer to temperance if he is willing to go back & witness the scenes of 20 years past & prefer to raise his sons with the men of the habits of that day or the present?" [12] The temperance movement, claimed *The Pearl* in 1846, had "created in the *young mind* of this nation a higher and purer idea of what is *right*, just and true; and to a great extent, made these principles *fashionable* and *popular*." [13]

Temperance progress, however, suddenly began to seem less certain in the late 1840s. Temperance reformers were soon convinced, in fact, that the tide had turned and that, in the words of *The Pearl*, "drunkenness is again in the ascendant." [14] Susan B. Anthony wrote to her mother in 1849 that the "retrograde march of the temperance cause is truly alarming." [15] The principal causes of this changed perception were the massive influx of German and Irish immigrants during those years and the concurrent rise in urban social disorder. Temperance activists argued that only legal suppression of the drink trade could counteract the enslaving nature of alcohol addiction, the growing influence of the cabalistic "Rum Power," the relative inaccessibility of the new immigrants to moral suasion appeals, and the fearful increases in poverty and crime.

Women at first resisted the abandonment of moral suasion; such a change promised to destroy the very foundation of their importance within the temperance movement. "We have more faith in the PLEDGE and MORAL SUASION, than we can have in the passage of laws against rumdrinking, or in the elevation of Temperance men to political offices," *The Pearl* argued. "If Moral Suasion is abandoned by the men, it is the duty of females to take up and carry on the cause. . . ." [16] However, when Maine in 1851 successfully passed the nation's first law to ban entirely the manufacture and sale of alcoholic beverages, all objections were swept aside. The stunning victory of prohibition in Maine reinvigorated the nation's temperance forces, and gave them hope that the precipitous increase of intemperance and disorder they perceived at mid-century could be not only arrested but dramatically reversed. Suddenly the potential power of the state to effect immediate social change seemed to dwarf the questionable accomplishments of three decades of moral suasion.

As the temperance crusade turned away from its previous commitments to oppose drink in the local and personal spheres, and instead undertook statewide Maine Law campaigns consisting of mass political rallies, legislative lobbying, public referendums, and independent temperance electoral slates, the effect was to undermine drastically the role women had taken in the reform. Suddenly moral suasion activities were perceived as useless. At the same time women were prevented from taking any significant part in the new phase of the movement, since propriety forbade them to campaign publicly and the law denied them the right to vote on crucial temperance issues. Amelia Bloomer wrote that the Daughters of Temperance "may toil and strive, and year after year perform their regular round—yet the stream [of poisonous liquor] flows on, in no way obstructed in its course by their labors, their resolutions, or accessions. It must be so, for they have no power to make it otherwise. Men hold the power in their hands to say when the infamous traffic shall cease, and all that women can now do will not affect the matter in the least."[17] Woman, she concluded, must demand political rights, so "that she may not only use this power in obtaining a prohibitory law, but in seeing it enforced when obtained."[18] For some female temperance workers, the question of political power took on a significance it had never had before. Mary Vaughn, the Presiding Sister of the Oswego, New York, Union of the Daughters of Temperance, recalled in late 1851 that "less than a year ago, . . . the idea that woman should go to the polls, was utterly repugnant to me. But when once convinced that she could act in no other way to any extent in the Temperance reform, there came a complete change over my feelings upon that subject."[19]

The desire of temperance women to wield direct power in the fight for prohibition encouraged some to embrace the cause of female suffrage, the most radical feminist demand of the nineteenth century, since it constituted the greatest and most direct challenge to the male monopoly on the public arena. Others thought a more obtainable goal would be a limited franchise, allowing women to vote only on liquor issues. Cincinnati's women's rights journal, the *Genius of Liberty*, asked: "How shall the [prohibitory] law be enacted, and this burning fluid destroyed all over the State? We answer: petition the legislature to empower Woman with the right of voting upon the Temperance question. . . ."[20]

The majority of female temperance activists, although not ready to advocate the extreme position of women's suffrage, were nevertheless quite prepared to fight against what they considered a more galling and restrictive ban: that against public speaking by women. The struggle for a place on the public platform, far more than the issue of voting, created a feminist perspective among temperance women. "The very moment woman rises in public to protest against the blighting traffic in rum," observed the reformer Frederick Douglass, "just so soon is raised the question of woman's rights."[21] Susan B. Anthony had shown little interest in the organized women's rights movement until, as a Rochester Daughters of Temperance delegate to the New York Sons of Temperance convention in early 1852, she was prevented from speaking and was informed by the presiding officer that "the sisters were not invited there to speak but to listen and learn."[22] The same issue disrupted the June, 1852, New York State Temperance Society convention. Anthony and Amelia Bloomer attended as delegates from the state Woman's Temperance Society. A bitter debate took place over whether the women should be seated, with clergymen leading the opposition. When the women were excluded by two votes, the "liberals" organized a separate evening session to allow them to give their addresses.[23]

Soon thereafter the women of Ohio created a separate organization for themselves in order to fight for a state Maine Law. When the first woman's state temperance convention assembled in Columbus in January, 1853, the mood was asser-

tive and unabashedly political. The convention itself had been
planned to coincide in time and place with the 1852–53 legislative session, and the women delegates prepared a memorial
in favor of prohibition to be presented to the lawmakers.
Moreover, in their resolutions they declared their "fixed determination" to use their "influence for the support of the man
for office who is known to be in favor of" prohibition. But, in
an effort to prevent an open break with propriety and with
their male colleagues, the women stopped short of specifying
just what such "influence" might include. Other resolutions
called on women to "use all honorable and laudable means" to
suppress the liquor traffic, and to labor against intemperance
"in such ways as her judgement shall dictate."[24] Through such
ambiguities the women were temporarily able to dodge the
question of how far into the public and political sphere they
felt it was their right to venture.

Cincinnati women at first followed the same cautious
course. As soon as the shift to prohibition had become apparent in 1851, they had tried to gain access to the public forum
indirectly by calling a special "Ladies' Meeting" to endorse the
idea of a Maine Law for Ohio, and afterward had ordered a
circular of their views to be printed and distributed throughout the city and read in churches. But as the prohibition campaign gathered force, such indirect efforts began to seem in-
substantial and ineffective. During the Maine Law campaign
of 1853 the women formed a separate Hamilton County
Ladies Temperance Association, "the object of which is to be
co-laborers with our male friends in the cause of temperance...."[25] The official resolutions they passed were, like
their state counterparts, couched in ambiguous terms that
would not provoke discord between their association and the
male organizations. A typical resolution called on the women
of Ohio "to put forth every proper effort, both in public
and private, to induce all legal voters" to vote for candidates
pledged to prohibition. There was no attempt to clarify what a
"proper" effort would be. However, the speeches the women
made among themselves hinted at more assertive, even militant,
feelings. One speaker stated that "the ladies here knew what
they were doing—they could *smell* the meaning of things. If

moral suasion wouldn't answer, a little *force* wouldn't be out of place. (Cheers) We must look to politics a little more—our hands are tied, but thank God we can *see*. . . ." Another speaker noted that the women assembled could expect taunts of "'cold dinners and buttonless shirts' for the husbands at home," but that the convention was for the highest good of their families. She added that if "the men did not take this matter in hand and abolish the liquor traffic *peaceably*, the ladies would come up to the work and put an end to the evil. Let the liquor sellers take warning of the signs of the times. (Cheers)."[26] It is significant that the rhetoric of temperance women hinted at the use of force and direct confrontation with the liquor trade as soon as the reform movement shifted to a political approach which largely excluded them.

The conflict over female public participation surfaced in Ohio very soon after the Hamilton County meeting, in response to the actions of Samuel Cary at the "World's Temperance Convention" held that September in New York City. The call to convention had invited delegates from all temperance organizations, but at a preliminary national organizational meeting in May a split developed over the right of women to serve as delegates and to speak at the convention. When the pro-feminist position was defeated, a number of the planners seceded and made arrangements for an alternate "Whole World's Temperance Convention," which would admit both women and blacks as full delegates. Both the "Whole World" and "World" gatherings met in New York. The "Whole World" convention met first, and many of its delegates stayed on in the city to attend the "World" meeting and to press the issue of female participation. The feminist group at the second convention was led by the Reverend Antoinette Brown. She succeeded in being recognized as a delegate by convention president Neal Dow, but when she attempted to speak she was drowned out by shouting from the floor.

It was at this point that Cary stepped in with a series of resolutions, intended to create a moderate compromise that would head off a threatened walkout by conservative delegates, primarily southerners and northern clergymen. The resolutions, which passed by a two-thirds majority, stated that "the great and only purpose" of the temperance cause was "to prohibit the manufacture and traffic of intoxicating liquors," and that the movement must resist involvement "with any other question, moral, social, political or religious." Moreover, "the common usages of society have excluded women from the public platform, and whether right or wrong, it is not our province now to determine; but we will conform our action during the present Convention to public usage. . . ." The resolutions, in effect, implicitly recognized the women as delegates but barred them from addressing the convention.[27]

Cary had mixed feelings about the role of women in the temperance movement. "We need her influence and aid in the cause of temperance," he had written, "but not upon the public platform. . . ." Women, he believed, had "an appropriate sphere," the private, domestic sphere of the home.[28] Cary had been the first within the national Sons of Temperance organization to press for the admission of women, but only as nonvoting "visitors." Like many other reform-minded men, he wanted to enlist the aid and influence of women and yet maintain barriers, demarcation lines, which if not crossed would supposedly keep them in their "appropriate" private sphere even while they acted publicly. Thus women could attend Sons of Temperance meetings as "visitors" but could not be voting members; they could sit in conventions as delegates but could not speak in those conventions.[29]

Cary's resolutions had been intended as a compromise, but some press accounts portrayed him as the leader of the anti-feminist delegates. Even so, he did not expect a negative reaction at home; he still believed that Ohio's temperance women "generally . . . [had] no sympathy with those of their sex who mount the stump on any subject."[30] He was shocked, therefore, when the women at their state temperance convention in late September passed a resolution vehemently condemning the convention's action against women, and Cary's part in it: "we regard the tyrannical and cowardly conformation to the '*usages of society*,' in thrusting woman from the platform in the late so-called, but *mis*-called World's Temperance Convention, as a most daring and insulting outrage upon all *woman kind*; and it is with deepest shame and mortification that we learn that our own State of Ohio furnished the delegate to officiate in the writing and presenting of the resolution, and who presided at the session when the desperate act was accomplished."[31] Perhaps Cary's action in opposition to the feminists in New York had stirred the Temperance women of Ohio to abandon caution and to declare openly their support for woman's right to the public platform.

Women gradually won their demands for greater participation. As male temperance reformers began to suffer serious setbacks in the campaign for state prohibition laws, they found that the movement needed all the loyal supporters it could get. By mid-decade it was common for women to address public temperance gatherings. When the old fraternal orders were slow to admit women to full membership, new temperance organizations sprang up at the local level that did not discriminate on the basis of sex.[32]

One such organization, the Independent Order of Good Templars, spread throughout the North in the mid-1850s. The IOGT began as an unauthorized offshoot of a Templars of Honor chapter in Fayetteville, New York, in 1852. A few more lodges appeared and joined together in forming a new fraternal temperance order. The IOGT admitted women on an equal basis with men (some local lodges also admitted blacks), required minimal dues (as low as 1¢ per week), rejected all mutual benefit plans, de-emphasized ritual and regalia, and lowered the minimum age of members to thirteen. By instituting these changes, the order came to resemble a club or society open to any member of the public who wished to join. It fulfilled the need for a more family-oriented source of social contact for teetotalers, and provided young men and women an opportunity to meet and mix with one another in a highly respectable setting.[33]

Early in 1853 an IOGT lodge formed in Seneca Falls, New York. Amelia Bloomer and her husband were charter members, and Bloomer began to promote the order in the pages of *The Lily*, helping it to spread beyond upstate New York. For a few years the order grew dramatically, and by 1857 its membership had climbed to nearly 80,000 (see Table 10). In Ohio the order first appeared in Alliance, after a man there read of

Table 10. Membership, Independent Order of Good
Templars, Ohio and Grand Lodges, 1856–71.

Year	Number of Ohio Lodges	Members in Ohio Lodges	Members in Grand Lodge (national and international)
1856	144		
1857	176	10,000	
1858	70		53,200
1859			
1860	110	5,505	80,166
1861			
1862	61	2,392	
1863	64	2,324	52,484
1864	50	3,000	70,458
1865	55	3,314	75,932
1866		6,384	
1867		13,184	291,180
1868	531	24,836	389,672
1869	476	27,329	377,502
1870	430	20,630	363,205
1871	368	19,865	385,720

SOURCES: Independent Order of Good Templars, *Journal of Proceedings
of the Grand Lodge*, 1865, 1869, 1870, 1871, 1872; William W. Turn-
bull, *The Good Templars: A History of the Rise and Progress of the Independent Order of Good Templars* (n.p., 1901).

the new organization in *The Lily* and sent away for a charter.
After the Bloomers moved to Mt. Pleasant, Ohio, in 1854, the
order developed rapidly, numbering 36 lodges in the state by
November of that year and 176 lodges two years later.[34]

Women in the order held position as officers and as national representatives, and addressed large public gatherings.
Their participation in the Good Templars exemplified the expansion of their role in the temperance movement in the 1850s.
But they still did not have the vote. Passage of prohibition was
the all-important objective, and women were continually reminded of their inability to affect the political outcome directly. When, in state after state, prohibition failed to pass, was

vetoed, rescinded, or ruled unconstitutional, or simply got lost in the antebellum political tug-of-war, women came to feel that not only were they still effectively excluded from political power but that political action itself was an ineffective means for battling the liquor trade.

Women could not, however, turn back with any confidence to the traditional moral suasion methods of the 1830s and '40s. Those tactics had assumed that education and persuasion would steadily eradicate the use of alcoholic beverages. By the 1850s it was clear that moral suasion had not brought steady progress toward an abstinent society. Indeed, the state prohibition battles revealed sharp lines of conflict within America over the drink issue that had not been fully apparent before.

At mid-century the nation was divided between drinkers and abstainers, a division reinforced by the ethnic, religious, and class lines that also divided the two groups. German and Irish immigrants were in the forefront of resistance to prohibition, and effectively used their newly acquired political power to block passage of prohibitory laws, to prevent enforcement of anti-drinking legislation, and to elect members of the drink trade to the governing councils of most large American cities. Political parties, in open deference to immigrant groups, opposed or jettisoned prohibition measures at the first opportunity. The hierarchy of the Catholic church also openly opposed Maine-Law efforts. The centralization of the distilling industry and the growth of brewing and wine making made drink big business; wealthy elites used their power against prohibition not only because they enjoyed the personal use of wine and brandy but because they often had investments to protect. At the other end of the social spectrum, unskilled laborers (who were also frequently foreign-born) resisted efforts to outlaw saloons, the recreational centers of their neighborhoods. By the 1850s large cities numbered their drinking establishments in the thousands, and even a small town might have half a dozen or more.

Rather than receding, the use of alcohol seemed an increasingly well-established part of American community life. For temperance women this changed social climate was a direct threat to the safety of their families. Mothers, responsible for the moral protection of their children, might nurture correct values only to see them undermined by the lures of the local saloon. In the immaturity and impetuosity of youth, a son might succumb to the ever-present temptation and break his pledge; a single misstep could well lead to utter ruin. This danger was magnified by the presence of gambling and prostitution in some saloons. Maternal fears seemed confirmed, moreover, by reports of increased drinking among middle-class youths. For the first time in many years temperance writers began regularly to cite shocking examples of inebriation among respectable young men. One Cincinnati journalist wrote with dismay in 1857 of the drinking expressions of the day: "Who has not heard one 'fast' young man say to another 'Won't you smile?' when he meant 'won't you drink?'" The mischievousness of the phrase, he added, would "convey to the shrewd student of 1900" deep insight into "the social characteristics of our 'Young America.'. . ."[35] *The Crusader* spoke with horror of students who would "close up their college term with a spree that would disgrace a band of savages."[36] A student at Ohio's Miami University recorded in his journal in 1858 that a commencement address had been canceled owing to the drunken state of the graduating senior who was to have delivered it.[37]

Lager beer especially found favor with young adults. Nationally, the annual adult per capita consumption of beer more than doubled in the 1850s, from 2.7 to 6.4 gallons for every person age fifteen and older. Well-appointed German beer gardens attracted large numbers of native-born patrons. In 1856 the Cincinnati Chamber of Commerce noted that lager beer had become "a fashionable drink."[38] *The Crusader* reported in 1858 that it had "for several years been astonished and alarmed at the rapid increase in the consumption of this Dutch swill [lager beer]. Our native-born citizens who are not particularly fond of stinking 'kraut' are learning to imbibe very freely the juice of rotten barley."[39] A few years later the Chamber of Commerce noted "the taste which has been acquired for 'Lager,' as a beverage, not only among the native German population, but all classes. Beer gardens, where this beverage is swallowed by old and young and in incredible quantities, have become institutions of great magnitude in this and all the large cities of the Union. . . ."[40]

Thus, as the decade progressed, women saw the danger of alcohol come closer to home, while at the same time they stood helpless as male voters and male-dominated political parties brought about the collapse of political temperance reform. Rather than accept the deteriorating situation, many turned to direct action. Increasingly in the 1850s women resorted to confrontation and extralegal force in order to attack the liquor trade directly. A woman's temperance novel published in 1858 dramatized the female outlook: "The ladies of the knitting committee had decided to make a more extensive effort for the suppression of the baneful traffic, that was gaining ground with such a fearful rapidity, luring the young and gifted ones into its terrible vortex. Parents . . . had their worst fears excited and alarmed for the safety of the treasured ones of their household, for temptations were to be met at almost every turn—not a ward in the growing city but could number its various drinking establishments."[41] The "more extensive effort" the fictional knitting committee undertook involved entering a local saloon as a group, sitting down, and knitting. The regular customers refused to enter and the saloon keeper soon promised to abandon his business.

In real life the actions women took were frequently a good deal more spectacular. Between 1853 and 1859 women in dozens of communities formed into bands and physically destroyed the liquor stock of local saloons. In a political system that gave them no legal redress for the encroachments of the liquor trade on the stability of the family, women adopted vigilante justice. In the words of the *Templar's Magazine*, "the ladies have taken the rumsellers into their own hands and enforced laws of their own making."[42] A participant in one such raid in Kewanee, Illinois, described and defended the action: several saloon keepers had "persisted in keeping in our midst their infernal dens of licentiousness, drunkenness and crime, which were fast drawing into their fatal snares our young men and women." When one retailer, after being stabbed by a customer, abandoned the business and publicly destroyed his

Hauck Brewery workers, Cincinnati, n.d. (courtesy Cincinnati Historical Society)

"Lady Crusaders." (from Shaw, *History*)

"The Saloonist's Pledge." (from Shaw, *History*)

NOTICE TO THE LADIES OF HILLSBOROUGH.

WHEREAS, Many of you, among whom are:

Mesdames Wm Scott, Wm Trimble, Sams, W O Collins, J M Boyd, A Evans, Reece Griffith, Jonah Langley, Wm Hoyt, O. M. Miller, Wash Doggett, W P Bernard, Jas H Thompson, Jos Ellifritz, John A Smith, Stacey Foraker, Wm Barry, Emily Dill, Moses Willitt, E G Smith, James J Brown, James Brown, Richard Evans, T S Cowden, W J McSurely, G B Gardner, Jennie Stockton, J J McDowell, Eli Stafford, Philip Janes, James Patterson, Samuel Clayton, Asa Haynes, Jonathan Van Pelt, J N Hiestand, Van Dokkum, John Jolly, George Barrere, Marshall Nelson, Saml Amen, E Carson, J L Boardman, Geo Glascock, Lewis Ambrose, Dan Murphy, Thos Miller, Hugh Swearingen, E Grand-Girard, John Perkins, H Foraker, George Stevens, J Y Crothers, T A Walker, Jake Sayler, J S Ervin, W H Glenn, W Bowers, P Harsha, Robt Nevin, F F Kibler, J F & J R Doggett, Allen J Cooper, J F Nelson, Ben Conard, A G Matthews, C M O'Hara, J K Pickering, Hardin Rhodes, Henry Doggett, Burch Foraker, Lewis McKibben, Josi Stevenson, Sanford W Creed, J J Seibert, Jos Glascock, J S Black, Thos Barry, Samuel Hibbon, H S Fullerton, Thos Rogers, Vanwinkle, John West, Mary Fenner, H S Scarborough, Mather, Wm Brown, T G Hoggard, W G Richards, J C Norton, J Merkle, C B Miller, O J Eekley, E L Ferris, N B Gardner.

Misses Maria Stewart, Rachael Conard, Sallie Stevenson, Maggie Bowles, Clara Rhodes, Annie Wilson, Grace Gardner, Jennie Harris, Emma Grand-Girard, Mollie Van Winkle, Emily Grand-Girard, Libbey Kirby, Ella Dill, Laura Rockhold, Eddy, Alice Spees, Kate Trimble, Alice Boardman and sister.

Who are aided by the following named gentlemen:

Messrs. E L Ferris, H S Fullerton, Samuel Amen, Asa Haynes, J J Brown, J S Black, W C Barry, E Carson, Jos Glascock, Wm Scott, Taos Barry, S E Hibben & Son, T C Lytle, R S Evans, L McKibben, R Griffiths, J L Boardman, John Cowgill, Lewis Ambrose, H Scarborough Wm Ambrose, Wash Doggett, H Swearingen, Rev E Grandgirard, Rev W McSurely, Rev T S Cowden, Rev J H Ely, Rev S D Claytan, Rev N B Gardner, J J McDowell, John Mathews J K Pickering George Stevens, John L Evans, Jona Vanpelt, J M Hiestand, John Young col'd E Davis, col'd, J Y Crothers, T A Walker, W M Browning, H C Glascock, J M Barrere T S Patton, J Sayler, A G Mathews, B J Harris, W H Trimble, M T Nelson Jas S Ervin, Hardin Roads, R A Linn W H Glenn, J C Gregg, H S Doggett, E G Smith, Dr Spees, Warren Johnson, Is'c Bennett, W Bowers, J L West, Jas Brown, S Wilson, Ch s Barry P Harsha, Rob Nevin M R Orr, N T Ayres, F F Kibler, J F and J R Doggett, A T Cooper, J F Nelson, T Rogers, T Hoggard, B Conard, W G Richards, Eli Stafford, J R Ervin, Dr Quinn, J Langley, J W Patterson, J Merkle. Eddy Glascock, C B Miller, D ... ... Ricard, J C Norton.

And who, although not directly participating in your daily proceedings, are, nevertheless, counseling and advising you in your unlawful proceedings by subscriptions of money, and encouragement in the commission of daily trespasses upon my property since the 24th day of December last, by reason of which my legitimate business has been obstructed, my feelings outraged, and my profession and occupation sought to be rendered odious, by reason of which I have suffered great pecuniary damage and injury. Therefore, you and each of you, together with your husbands, (or such as may have them) and the persons who are thus aiding you with their money, encouragement and advice in your unlawful proceedings, are hereby notified that I can not, nor will not, longer submit to your daily trespasses on my property and injury to my business.

While I am willing to excuse your action in the past, I can not submit to such outrages in the future Cherishing no unkind hostility toward any one, but entertaining the highest regard for the ladies of Hillsborough, distinguished heretofore, as they have been, for their courtesy refinement and Christian virtues, I feel extremely reluctant to have to appeal to the law for protection against their riotous and unlawful acts.

You are therefore hereby further notified that if such action and trespasses are repeated I shall apply to the laws of the State for redress and damages for the injuries occasioned by reason of the practices of which I complain.

All others aiding or encouraging you by means of money or otherwise are also notified that I shall hold them responsible for such advice and encouragement.

Yours respectfully.

W. H. H. DUNN.

"Notice to the Ladies of Hillsborough" (Hillsboro, Ohio) published by W. H. H. Dunn during the Woman's Crusade, 1875.

stock, about fifteen women "comprising some of the most respectable and intelligent in town" approached another saloon
and asked its keeper to close down as well. When he refused,
the women "brandished their hatchets" and said "they should
do it for him. . . ." While they began their work in his cellar,
the owner fetched a shotgun, aimed it at the women, and ordered them out. As they left the cellar, a group of "gentlemen
who had been attracted by the cry of the ladies" disarmed the
owner, the women returned to finish the destruction, and then
demolished the town's other two remaining saloons "amid the
cheers and plaudits of the assembled multitude." The women,
the report concluded, "regret the necessity which led to these
acts of violence, but we appeal to the virtuous and the good
everywhere, whether they will not excuse and justify" such
action.[43]

The Kewanee attack was typical in many respects. The
women there were "some of the most respectable and intelligent in town"; contemporary accounts of other saloon assaults described the participants as, for example, among the
community's "most respectable ladies," or as women "of high
respectability."[44] A saloon keeper in Winchester, Indiana, had
to bring in a lawyer from another community to sue for damages after his place of business was wrecked, because all the
local lawyers' wives were defendants. Like the men of Kewanee who disarmed the saloon keeper, males in other communities sometimes helped protect the women while they carried
out their assaults. The thirty Otsego, Michigan, women who
took axes to the town's liquor supply in 1854 were "backed up
by some fifty men."[45] In Farmington, Illinois, a band of a few
dozen women was "protected by about 300 men and boys,"
according to the 1856 newspaper account.[46] A participant in
the Rockport, Massachusetts, raid testified in a subsequent
trial: "All the men appeared to be affirming except the rum
sellers. . . . The select men ministers deacons policemen were
present[;] none of them forbade what was done but all was
peace and harmony. They appeared to be happy and the shouts
came up from the gentlemen[.] The justices of the peace were
there."[47] Boys of fourteen and fifteen helped roll the casks out.
Over 700 citizens gathered in the town square after the raid,

and several men made speeches praising the women for their "glorious deed."[48] Male supporters arrived on the scene after the attacks were underway; there is no indication that men participated in the initiation or the planning of the raids. The *Akron Beacon*, for example, noted that in Cuyahoga Falls, Ohio, the women "prudently kept their own counsels, their husbands even not having the plan and time of assault confided to them."[49] Yet the women, acting independently from men, nonetheless won widespread male support.

Not only did male bystanders often protect the women during their attacks, but men also readily defended after the fact these attacks on legally protected private property. The Cincinnati Sons of Temperance held an entertainment in 1855 in honor of the women who had destroyed liquor in Mt. Pleasant, Ohio. Samuel Cary wrote later: "We believe in the right of resolution—you may call it mob-law if you please. Our creator has never required us to submit forever to wrong and outrage."[50] The *Canton* (Illinois) *Register* wrote: "Although we do not believe in riotous and illegal proceedings, yet we rejoice that the citizens of Farmington [Illinois] have shown a determination to have their town freed from the influence of intoxicating drinks, and we hope they will persevere in that determination."[51] The *Urbana* (Illinois) *Union* echoed the *Register's* stance: "Although we deplore a mob spirit, yet we are bound to respect them [the women] for their fearless action when law fails to accomplish its nominal object—the protection of the weak from the strong and malignant."[52] When nine Marion, Illinois, women were brought to trial for saloon destruction in 1854, one of their lawyers, Abraham Lincoln, claimed the Boston Tea Party as a moral precedent for their action.[53]

Not only were the women defended in court and in print, but they enjoyed widespread community support as well. An observer in Otsego, Michigan, concluded that although the women there "will be brought before the Court . . . there can be nothing done to them, as they have the sympathy of the great majority of the people of the county. . . ."[54] The editor of the *Templar's Magazine* noted that he had "yet to learn of a single instance" where the women had been punished for destroying liquor. "And why should they be? They were only exercising a heaven-born right—that of self-protection—removing out of the way that which was destroying their husbands, sons and brothers—destroying their own happiness and placing their lives in jeopardy."[55] He observed that "these ladies have the sympathy and countenance of the better portion of the community in their work."[56] Men on three separate juries refused to convict the principal defendent from the Rockport, Massachusetts, raid, despite the judge's instructions at the third trial that the defendant's own testimony showed she was guilty of at least criminal trespass.[57] And in Winchester, Indiana, the self-named "Lady's Temperance Army" met after their trial and formally thanked their jury for the impulse it had given to temperance reform by finding them not guilty.[58]

The female vigilantes of the 1850s won male support for their actions because, however indecorous, illegal, and violent saloon destruction may have been, men saw it as essentially domestic in nature. The women were considered to be protecting their homes and families in a manner that suggested almost instinctual maternal behavior. At the same time temperance men recognized that the attacks were an effective form of propaganda, a sort of public morality play which juxtaposed the saloons to the bands of moral, abstinent, and compassionate mothers and wives and thereby brought into sharp focus the disparity, the incompatibility, of saloon life and proper middle-class domestic life.[59] This dramatization of the saloon problem undoubtedly had a greater emotional impact on the community than did the men's speeches and pamphlets.

The growing willingness of temperance women in the late 1850s to organize separately from men and to use methods of direct confrontation with liquor sellers suggests that something like the Woman's Crusade might have developed much earlier than it did, had the war not intervened. With the attention of the nation focused on the war, the temperance issue seemed, for the moment, less urgent in the public mind. Moreover, as males entered the army and left their homes to fight, local problems with drinking receded except in areas where soldiers were stationed. But even though the war delayed the emergence of some form of unified militant action by women against saloons, it also intensified their grievances. As a result, the stage was set for an even more dramatic outburst of opposition to the liquor traffic after the war.

The primary causes of the female attacks on saloons in the 1850s had been the isolation of women from meaningful participation in the temperance movement, the floundering of prohibition in a male-dominated political environment, and the increasing danger the drink trade posed to middle-class youth. During the Civil War and Reconstruction years these original motivations for direct female action against the liquor trade were intensified rather than alleviated. The war itself greatly accelerated the spread of drinking among young middle-class males. They were exposed to a lifestyle in the army camps—drinking, smoking, gambling, swearing, consorting with prostitutes—that had been undreamed of at home. One soldier wrote to his wife that "many a poor fellow has been turned to the road to Ruin here in the Army and I have almost been lost[;] thank God I saw my danger in time. . . . I have turned *teetotaler* again and am determined to die one."[60] Another asked his sister for more news from home about the Good Templar lodge, noted that others were breaking their pledges, but added that "thoughts of home and friends have enabled me thus far to resist the temptation."[61]

The effect of the war on drinking habits lingered on after peace had been restored. The *Western Christian Advocate*, the Ohio Valley's Methodist journal, remarked in 1866: "Our young men have become loose in temperance principles, by the practice of the camp and the field; and the present generation is deplorably cursed in consequence."[62] Mother Stewart, later one of the leaders of the Woman's Crusade, recalled: "Many of our young soldiers returned with the appetite [for liquor] acquired in the army, fastened upon them. And so the curse, more fearful than southern slavery, has ever since been steadily gaining upon us."[63] The change in American drinking patterns, however, was not reflected in a simple increase in overall comsumption, which remained stable in the decade after the war. Indeed, the annual adult per capita intake of hard liquor actually dropped by 20 percent. This decline was compensated for, however, by a 60 percent increase in wine consumption and a 74 percent jump in beer drinking, to over ten gallons in 1875 for every man or woman aged fifteen and older. The *Western Christian Advocate*, commenting on this growing popularity of light alcoholic beverages, noted that in "social circles wine is, with lamentable frequency, proffered to guests. At tables, both private and public, malt and other liquors are a constant beverage. With many, and even Christians, total abstinence is regarded as among the puritanic follies of a past age. . . . This state of things began before the war . . . but it has been vastly augmented by the war." [64] For many young veterans a glass of beer among friends in a pleasant beer garden must have seemed tame indeed compared to their war experiences. But for their mothers the trend away from total abstinence made the need for effective temperance reform more vital than ever.

The anxiety of women for the safety of their families in the 1850s had been compounded by anger and frustration over their exclusion from political temperance efforts and their disillusionment after the failure of prohibition. In the postwar years events not only heightened their domestic fears but also served to increase their distrust of politically oriented temperance reform.

During the war, with many men in uniform, women had taken on most of the work necessary to keep the national temperance organizations running. Once the war ended, however, male members returned to the organizations and expected to resume control. Even in the International Order of Good Templars, with its professed equality for women, men dominated the upper echelons and made the important decisions. [65] As men took back the reins of the temperance movement, they pushed it further than ever into the political realm. At the Good Templars' annual conventions, a growing block of delegates advocated formation of a separate prohibition political party. The 1868 meeting endorsed the idea, and a year later a resolution urged the convention to take steps toward forming such a party. Six prominent Good Templars issued a call to convention and in September, 1869, some 500 delegates formed the National Prohibition party. [66] The early forays of the Prohibition party into state and national politics were utter failures, discouraging to even its most enthusiastic supporters. John Black, candidate for president in 1872, won a mere 5,607 votes nationwide that year. The Prohibition party effort seemed ludicrous and, to temperance women, dangerous, since it concentrated time, money, and effort in an arena that was very distant from the threat they saw close to home.

Moreover, events of the 1872 presidential campaign demonstrated that the two major parties were unlikely to support the goal of prohibition in the near future. The Republican national convention passed a platform resolution, authored by a German-born delegate, disapproving of prohibitory laws. The Democratic endorsement of "Liberal Republican" candidate Horace Greeley was a disaster for the party for many reasons, not the least of which was Greeley's past association with temperance reform. The United States Brewers' Association, which in 1867 had resolved to "sustain no candidate, or whatever party, in any election, who is in any way disposed toward the total abstinence cause," [67] labeled Greeley "a pliant tool in the hands of the temperance party," and resolved that "sooner than pass our votes for any of these apostles of bigotry and intolerance, we will waive all political predilections. . . ." [68] The 1872 campaign clearly indicated that the opponents of prohibition were prepared to act forcefully and openly to prevent the major political parties from considering an endorsement of prohibition.

To make matters worse for the women of Ohio, a constitutional convention in 1873 began to consider eliminating the 1851 constitutional ban on liquor licensing. A return to licensing would have served to increase the aura of legitimacy and respectability around the liquor trade. Moreover, there was a political effort afoot to repeal the 1870 Adair law, which permitted damage suits against liquor dealers in any case where an individual was injured in person, property, or means of support in consequence of intoxication or by someone intoxicated, whether or not the original sale of liquor had been legal. The law had become a tool for temperance activists and a litigational nightmare for the liquor trade, which very much wanted to be rid of it. Through all of this, women once again felt helpless and frustrated as they watched males make political decisions that affected the security of their families.[69]

During and after the war women kept up their vigilante attacks on saloons. Moreover, they developed a new and potentially more attractive method of confrontation, one that avoided the legal and ethical issues raised by saloon destruction. Starting in the late 1850s, female bands discovered that they could invade a saloon and, by praying, frequently prevail upon the saloon keeper to destroy his stock himself, or at least promise to go out of business. The praying technique, a strikingly effective combination of psychological, social, and economic pressure, was popularized by Dio Lewis, later the mentor of the Woman's Crusade. According to Lewis, his mother had devised the strategy, and he first convinced women to put it into action in Dixon, Illinois, where praying bands in 1858 closed all thirty-nine of the town's saloons in one week. Thereafter, praying became as popular a method as axe-swinging for shutting down local liquor establishments, and women tried one or the other of the techniques in numerous communities throughout the late 1860s and early 1870s.

The most interesting occurrence during this period, from a historical perspective, was a physical assault in Greenfield, Ohio, in July, 1865. The women had decided to approach all the saloon keepers in the town with the following ultimatum: "That the ladies of Greenfield are determined to suppress the liquor traffic in their midst. We demand your liquors, and give you fifteen minutes to comply with our request, or abide by the consequences."[70] At their first stop the demand was flatly refused. As they crossed the street to the next saloon, one of the women, whose son had been killed by a stray bullet from a saloon brawl ten months earlier, cried out: "'Here is the place where my boy was killed,'" and, according to a newspaper account, "the cry thrilled through the women's hearts, and fired them to deeds worthy of masculine arms."[71] The women forgot their formal statement, drew out the axes, hatchets, and mallets they had brought, and wrecked that saloon and five others. What makes the Greenfield incident particularly intriguing historically is that the trial for the damage suit

brought by the bar owners took place a year and a half later in
the county seat, Hillsboro. The "first ladies" of Hillsboro met
the defendants when they arrived in town, the *Advocate* reported, "and escorted them to private homes, for generous entertainment during their stay . . . [and] also took seats with
them during the trial, and in every possible way gave dem-
onstration of the morality of the case."[72] Seven years later
Hillsboro was the "birthplace" of the Woman's Crusade, and
Greenfield was one of the first communities to which the
movement spread.

The Crusade's direct links to the Greenfield raid and Hillsboro trial of the 1860s, and to Dio Lewis's prayer bands of the
1850s, make explicit and concrete the already evident conclusion that the Crusade was not the beginning but rather the
climax of a social movement, and that it must be considered
within the context of the decades of female activity that preceded it. By 1873 women across the country were demonstra-
bly ready to fight the saloons for what they saw as the safety of
their families; only a catalyst was needed to bring about an ex-
plosion of concerted attacks. Observers at the time felt that
such an outburst was coming. After a saloon destruction in
Perrysville, Ohio, in 1869, a participant wrote: "The people in
this part of Ohio honestly think that the next war in this country will be between women and whisky; and though there may
not be much blood shed, you may rest assured rum will flow
freely in the gutter. As the women here have taken the matter
in hand once before, we claim to have fought the Bunker Hill
of the new revolution."[73]

The Woman's Crusade of 1873–74 was the beginning of
a new period of development, organization, and expansion for
the temperance movement, one that led directly to the formation of the WCTU and indirectly to the victory of national
prohibition nearly a half-century later. But the Crusade cannot
be adequately understood if it is viewed simply as a starting
point, a sudden outbreak of assertiveness and enthusiasm
among American women that bore no relationship to the half-
century of temperance reform that preceded it. It was during
the turbulent decade of the 1850s that women first found their

own voice, developed their own perspective, and exercised their own power in the battle against the drink trade. In so doing, they changed the course of temperance reform. They also gained significantly greater access to the public platform through their demands within the temperance movement, and at the same time gave a strong impetus to the developing women's rights effort.

Moreover, the saloon destruction of the 1850s and 1860s suggests that the threat alcohol posed to the family became in those decades an extremely important element in the consciousness of middle-class American women. The militant female vigilantism of that period has until now remained an entirely forgotten historical development, and yet it was a truly remarkable phenomenon: respectable women deliberately armed themselves and openly engaged in illegal acts of massive vandalism. The grass-roots temperance activities of women prior to 1873 are rich and revealing sources of information on sex roles, domestic attitudes, and family life. The issues of drink and temperance reform deserve a place of prominence in any historical discussion of the mid-nineteenth-century American woman.

Notes

1. The story of the Woman's Crusade is told in many contemporary sources. See, for example, Annie Wittenmyer, *History of the Woman's Temperance Crusade* (Philadelphia, 1878); J. E. Stebbins and I. A. H. Brown, *Fifty Years History of the Temperance Cause* (Hartford, Conn., 1876); W. H. Daniels, *The Temperance Reform and Its Great Reformers* (Cincinnati, Ohio, 1878); E. D. Stewart, *Memories of the Crusade: A Thrilling Account of the Great Uprising of the Women of Ohio in 1873, against the Liquor Crime* (Columbus, Ohio, 1889); Matilda Gilruth Carpenter, *The Crusade; Its Origins and Development at Washington Court House and Its Results* (Columbus, Ohio, 1893); *New Reporter*, Sept. 1, 1876. For statistics on the Woman's Crusade, see Jack S. Blocker, Jr., "Why Women Marched: The Temperance Crusade of 1873–1874" (paper presented at annual meeting of the American Historical Association, New York, 1979), 4–5.

2. See, for example, Norman Clark, *Deliver Us from Evil: An Interpretation of American Prohibition* (New York, 1976), 70–71, 73; Joseph R. Gusfield, *Symbolic Crusade: Status Politics and the American Temperance Movement* (Urbana, Ill., 1963), 6–7, 72–74; Blocker, "Why Women

Marched," 1, 4; Ruth Bordin, "'A Baptism of Power and Liberty': The Woman's Crusade of 1873–74," *Ohio History*, 87 (1978):393–404, and *Woman and Temperance: The Quest for Power and Liberty, 1873–1900* (Philadelphia, 1981), 32–33; Susan Dye Lee, "Evangelical Domesticity: The Woman's Temperance Crusade of 1873–74" (paper presented at conference "Women in New Worlds: Historical Perspectives on the United Methodist Tradition," Cincinnati, Ohio, 1980), 2–3; Randall C. Jimerson, "The Temperance and Prohibition Movement in America, 1830–1933," in *Guide to the Microfilm Edition of Temperance and Prohibition Papers*, ed. Randall C. Jimerson, Francis X. Blouin, and Charles A. Isetts (Ann Arbor, Mich., 1977), 10; Donald W. Beattie, "Sons of Temperance: Pioneers in Total Abstinence and 'Constitutional' Prohibition" (Ph.D. thesis, Boston University, 1966), 215; Samuel Unger, "A History of the National WCTU" (Ph.D. thesis, Ohio State University, 1933), 3; Norton Mezvinsky, "The White-Ribbon Reform, 1874–1920" (Ph.D. thesis, University of Wisconsin, 1959); Ellen DuBois, "The Radicalism of the Woman Suffrage Movement: Notes toward the Reconstruction of Nineteenth-Century Feminism," *Feminist Studies*, (1975): 68–69; Daniel Scott Smith, "Family Limitation, Sexual Control, and Domestic Feminism in Victorian America," in Mary S. Hartman and Lois Banner, eds., *Clio's Consciousness Raised: New Perspectives on the History of Women* (New York, 1974), 120.

3. Ohio State Temperance Convention, *Proceedings*, 1833, 5; Redford (Mich.) Temperance Society, *Minutes*, 1832–1848 (Joint Ohio Historical Society–Michigan Historical Collections, Woman's Christian Temperance Union microfilm edition, Mid-Nineteenth Century Temperance Movement series, roll 1, frames 22–68); Paul R. Meyer, Jr., "The Transformation of American Temperance: The Popularization and Radicalization of a Reform Movement, 1813–1860" (Ph.D. thesis, University of Iowa, 1976), 89; William Graham Davis, "Attacking 'the Matchless Evil': Temperance and Prohibition in Mississippi, 1817–1908" (Ph.D. thesis, Mississippi State University, 1975), 22–23; Robert Louis Hampel, "Influence and Respectability: Temperance and Prohibition in Massachusetts, 1813–1852" (Ph.D. thesis, Cornell University, 1980), 68; C. C. Pearson and J. Edwin Hendricks, *Liquor and Anti-Liquor in Virginia, 1619–1919* (Durham, N.C., 1967), 62; Joan Bland, *Hibernian Crusade* (Washington, D.C., 1951), 15; Daniel D. Pratt, Indiana State Library, address delivered in Logansport, Ind., Oct. 10, 1836; McCreath Family Papers, 1836–92, Pennsylvania State Archives, Young Men's and Young Ladies' Total Abstinence Society of Harrisburg (Pa.), Fourth Annual Report of the Board of Managers, 1841; Charles D. Parr Papers, University of Georgia Libraries, letters, 1850. Mary Ryan has pointed out that women's organizations such as maternal associations and female moral reform societies frequently predated female participation in temperance reform at the community level, and that the experience of women in those organizations influenced the role they subsequently played in the temperance movement (*Cradle of the Middle Class: The Family in Oneida County, New York, 1790–1865* (Cambridge, Mass., 1981), 140.

4. Essex Institute Library, West Bradford (Mass.) Female Temperance Society, Records, 1829–34, Secretary's Reports for 1830 and 1831; *Indiana Temperance Advocate*, Nov., 1837, 38; Waterloo Historical Society, Waterloo (N.Y.) Female Temperance Society, Records, 1841–42, Dec. 29, 1841; *The Pearl: A Ladies' Weekly Literary Gazette Devoted to the Advocacy of the Various Ladies' Total Abstinence Associations*, June 6, 1846, 4.

5. Lorenzo D. Johnson, *Martha Washingtonianism, or a History of the Ladies' Temperance Benevolent Societies* (New York, 1843), 41–42.

6. *Pearl*, Oct. 3, 1846, 140; see also June 13, 52; Oct. 10, 148; Nov. 7, 180, all 1846.

7. *Lily*, May, 1852; Elizabeth Cady Stanton, Susan B. Anthony, and Matilda J. Gage, eds., *History of Woman Suffrage*, 3 vols., 2d ed. (Rochester, N.Y., 1889), 1:480–85; Ida Husted Harper, *The Life and Work of Susan B. Anthony*, 2 vols. (Indianapolis, 1898), 1:53–69; Eleanor Flexner, *Century of Struggle: The Woman's Rights Movement in the United States* (Cambridge, Mass., 1959), 85, 185; Keith Melder, *Beginnings of Sisterhood: The American Woman's Rights Movement, 1800–1850* (New York, 1977), 145; Blanche Glassman Hersh, *The Slavery of Sex: Feminist-Abolitionists in America* (Urbana, Ill., 1978), 108, 167.

8. Lois W. Banner, *Elizabeth Cady Stanton: A Radical for Woman's Rights* (Boston, 1980), 53–54.

9. Melder, *Sisterhood*, 55; see also Philip S. Foner, ed., *Frederick Douglass on Women's Rights* (Westport, Conn., 1976), 17; Flexner, *Century*, 185; Hersh, *Slavery of Sex*, 48, 167.

10. July 11, 1846, Exeter, N.H., quoted in Philip Foner, ed., *The Factory Girls* (Chicago, 1977), 287–88.

11. *Pearl*, June 6, 1846, 4; see also Young Men's and Young Ladies' . . . Harrisburg, 1841, 2–3; Illinois Historical Society, Sangamon County (Ill.) Temperance Union, *Proceedings*, 1846–50, May 22, 1847; Daniels, *Temperance Reform*, 101, 107. It was this tradition of sympathy for drunkards that made Elizabeth Cady Stanton's 1852 espousal of divorce from drunkards so unacceptable to other temperance women. In Lois Banner's words, "Criticism of the speech was overwhelming. . . . A woman with an alcoholic husband must reform him; she had no right to end the relationship" (*Stanton*, 62–63).

12. Calvin Fletcher, *The Diary of Calvin Fletcher*, ed. Gayle Thornbrough and Dorothy L. Riker, 7 vols., 3 (Indianapolis, 1974): 159, address delivered to the temperance society at Noblesville, Ind., June 20, 1845.

13. *Pearl*, Sept. 26, 1846, 132.

14. Ibid., May 15, 1847, 397.

15. Susan Brownell Anthony Papers, Schlesinger Library, Harvard University, Anthony to her mother, Feb. 7, 1849.

16. *Pearl*, Mar. 6, 1847, 316.

17. *Lily*, Nov., 1851.

18. Ibid., Jan., 1852.

19. Ibid., Oct., 1851.

20. *Genius of Liberty*, Jan. 12, 1853, 29; Davis, "Attacking," 23; Du-Bois, "Radicalism," 63–71.

21. Foner, ed., *Douglass*, 62.

22. Harper, *Anthony*, 1:64–65. Before the shift to prohibitionism, Anthony's conception of woman's role in the temperance movement was quite limited. As revealed in her 1849 address as Presiding Sister of the Canajoharie, N.Y., Daughters of Temperance, Anthony saw a field of effort for women that extended from "our own home circle" only as far as "public and private parties," where she believed the use of brandy and wine should be discountenanced (see Harper, *Anthony*, 1:53–55, and Anthony Papers, Anthony to her mother, Mar. 7, 1849).

23. *Lily*, July, 1852; Stanton, *History*, 1:485–88.

24. *Genius of Liberty*, Feb. 15, 1853, 38–39; Dec. 15, 1852, 24.

25. *Cincinnati Times*, Sept. 2, 1853; *Cincinnati Commercial*, Sept. 8, 1851 (hereafter cited as CC).

26. CC, Sept. 2, 1853.

27. *Whole World's Temperance Convention Held at Metropolitan Hall in the City of New York, September, 1853* (New York, 1853); *Ohio Organ of the Temperance Reform* (hereafter cited as *Organ*, May 27, June 3, Sept. 9, 23, 1853; *Cincinnati Times*, Sept. 5, 6, 9, 10, 12, 1853.

28. *Organ*, May 27, 1853.

29. Ibid., Sept. 16, 1853; Beattie, "Sons," 167.

30. *Organ*, June 3, Sept. 10, 23, 1853.

31. Ibid., Sept. 30, 1853.

32. CC, Feb. 14, Mar. 7, 1855. Indiana temperance leader Calvin Fletcher's diary entry for Jan. 24, 1854, suggests that many men in local temperance organizations supported the expansion of the role of women in the movement; at a meeting where he was to address the temperance women of Indianapolis, Fletcher noted: "Dr. Thompson wanted the ladies to occupy the chair. Indeed, many gentlemen seemed to wish it" (Fletcher, *Diary*, 5:166).

33. Isaac Newton Peirce, *The History of the Independent Order of Good Templars* (Philadelphia, c. 1869), 31–42, 74, 80, 169–70 (the name of the organization was later changed to the International Order of Good Templars); *Templar's Magazine*, Dec., 1856, 381–82; *Temperance Journal* (Indianapolis), Mar. 29, 1866.

34. *Lily*, July 15, 1853, Feb. 15, 1854; Peirce, *History*, 59, 67, 105, 152, 213, 330; Beattie, "Sons," 398.

35. William Turner Coggeshall, "Slang, or American Talk and the Lessons It Suggests" (Cincinnati Historical Society Library).

36. *Crusader*, July, 1858, 50.

37. Donald K. Gorrell, "Presbyterians in the Ohio Temperance Movement of the 1850's," *Ohio State Archeological and Historical Quarterly*, 60 (1951): 296; see also Stewart, *Memories*, 18.

38. Cincinnati Chamber of Commerce, *Annual Report*, 1856, 12, quoted in William L. Downard, "The Cincinnati Brewing Industry,

1811–1933: A Social and Economic History" (Ph.D. thesis, Miami University, 1969), 42–43.

39. *Crusader*, Apr., 1858, 336; Eugene H. Roseboom, *The Civil War Era, 1850–1873* (vol. 4 of *The History of the State of Ohio*, ed. Carl Wittke, Columbus, Ohio, 1944), 226; B. P. Aydelott, *The Church's Duties in the Temperance Cause* (Cincinnati, Ohio, 1865), 15. The national adult (age fifteen and over) per capita consumption of beer rose from 2.7 to 6.4 gallons, and the increase in beer drinking accounted for two-thirds of a 17 percent increase over the decade in the adult per capita consumption of absolute alcohol (see W. J. Rorabaugh, "Estimated U.S. Alcoholic Beverage Consumption, 1790–1860," *Journal of Studies on Alcohol*, 37 (1976:361).

40. Quoted in Downard, "Brewing," 42–43.

41. Henrietta Rose, *Nora Wilmot: A Tale of Temperance and Woman's Rights* (Columbus, Ohio, 1858), 194, 206–7.

42. *Templar's Magazine*, June, 1858, 191.

43. *Lily*, May 15, 1856. For other references see *Ohio Organ of the Temperance Reform*, Apr. 8, 1853: CC, Jan. 31, 1855; Roseboom, *Era*, 225, 228; Peirce, *History*, 289; *Crusader*, Apr., 1858, Feb., 1859; Arthur C. Cole, *The Era of the Civil War: 1848–1870* (vol. 3 of *The Centennial History of Illinois*, Springfield, Ill., 1919), 211; Jacob Piatt Dunn, *Indiana and Indianans: A History of Aboriginal and Territorial Indiana and the Century of Statehood*, 2 vols., 2 (Chicago, 1919): 1043; Stanton, *History*, 1:475; Meyer, "Transformation," 182–83; J. C. Furnas, *The Life and Times of the Late Demon Rum* (New York, 1965), 236–37.

44. *Lily*, May 15, 1856, letter from Kewanee, Ill., Mar. 27, 1856; Dunn, *Indiana*, 2:1043.

45. *Lily*, May 15, 1856; *American Temperance Union Journal*, Jan., 1855, 12–13, reprinted from the *New York Tribune*, correspondence column, Otsego, Mich., Dec. 15, 1854.

46. *Canton* (Ill.) *Register*, Mar. 20, 1856.

47. Sandy Bay, Mass., Historical Society, Hatchet Gang Papers, transcript of Chief Justice Shaw's trial notes, 1858, testimony of Mary E. Hale.

48. Hatchet Gang, transcript of report from "L" in *Gloucester Telegraph and News*, July 12, 1856; transcript of entry in Ebenezer Pool Manuscripts, 4:379; transcript notes of oral interview with Mrs. Lowe, June, 1933 (age 92), eyewitness of raid.

49. Quoted in *Crusader*, Apr. 1858, 344; see also Hatchet Gang, trial notes, testimony of Mr. Perkins.

50. *Crusader*, Oct., 1858, 147; CC, Feb. 15, 1855.

51. *Canton Register*, Mar. 20, 1856.

52. *Urbana Union*, Mar. 27, 1856; see also *Glouster Telegraph and News*, July 9, 1856.

53. Carl Sandburg, *Abraham Lincoln: The Prairie Years*, 2 (New York, 1926): 63. Lincoln had been active in the Sangamon County, Ill., Temperance Union in the 1840s (see Sangamon, *Proceedings*, Aug. 31, 1846, June 28, 1847). See also Abraham Lincoln, *The Collected Works of Abra-*

ham Lincoln, ed. Roy P. Basler, 9 vols. (New Brunswick, N.J., 1953–55), 2:271–79.

54. *American Temperance Union Journal*, Jan., 1855, 12–13.

55. *Templar's Magazine*, Jan., 1859, 33.

56. Ibid., June, 1858, 191.

57. Hatchet Gang, typescript of legal proceedings.

58. *Temperance Union*, Aug. 15, 1854.

59. The raids were, in part, an extreme extension of earlier tactics. Bands of women in the 1840s visited local liquor dealers in an attempt to persuade them politely to abandon their businesses, and also undertook legal actions against them (see Nathan Jenks Papers, Indiana Historical Society Library, Mary Hawkins to Mrs. Nathan Jenks, Mar. 23, 1845; *Pearl*, June 27, 1846, 29, Aug. 29, 1846, 101). Also perhaps underlying the attacks was a history of "maternal martyrdom," a method of child socialization described by Mary Ryan that had sometimes been used by mothers in a semi-public context; for example, the Utica, N.Y., Female Moral Reform Society reported in 1842 an instance of a mother following her son into a brothel in order to shame him into repentance (see Ryan, *Cradle*, chs. 3 and 4).

60. Luman Jones Papers, Indiana Historical Society Library, Jones to Elizabeth Jones, Aug. 6, 1863.

61. M. C. Severin Collection, Indiana State Library, F. N. Kellogg to his sister, Nov. 20, 1862; Richard H. Coolidge, *Statistical Report on the Sickness and Mortality in the Army of the United States, 1855–1860* (Washington, D.C., 1860), 97, quoted in James H. Cassedy, "An Early American Hangover: The Medical Profession and Intemperance, 1800–1860," *Bulletin of the History of Medicine*, 50 (1976): 406; Roseboom, *Era*, 227; Samuel F. Cary, *Letter to Volunteers in the Federal Army, Warning against Intemperance* (Cincinnati, Ohio, 1861), 1; Pearson, *Virginia*, 152–53.

62. *Western Christian Advocate*, Jan. 10, 1866.

63. Stewart, *Memories*, 27; see also Wittenmyer, *History*, 498.

64. *Western Christian Advocate*, Nov. 8, 1865; Rorabaugh, "Consumption," 361.

65. Beattie, "Sons," 170; Peirce, *History*, 503; Elizabeth Cooper Matheson Papers, 1861–73, Michigan State University Archives and Historical Collections, diary, Dec. 20, 1862, April 19, 1863.

66. Ernest H. Cherrington, *The Evolution of Prohibition in the United States of America* (Westerville, Ohio, 1920), 164–66; James Ross Turner, "The American Prohibition Movement, 1865–1897" (Ph.D. thesis, University of Wisconsin, 1972), 8–9, 22–29.

67. Turner, "Prohibition," 21, 41; John G. Woolley and William E. Johnson, *Temperance Progress in the Century* (London, 1903), 155.

68. Woolley, *Century*, 154.

69. Roseboom, *Era*, 229, 473, 480; *Western Christian Advocate*, Mar. 20, Apr. 10, 1872; Frances E. Willard, *Women and Temperance: or, The Work and the Workers of the Woman's CTU* (Hartford, Conn., 1883), 94;

Report of the Temperance Fair Held in Greenwood Hall, Cincinnati, Ohio, April 5–14, 1875 (Cincinnati, Ohio, 1875), 7.

70. Henry Howe, *Historical Collections of Ohio in Two Volumes* (Cincinnati, Ohio, 1902), 1:923; *Union Signal*, Dec. 20, 1883; J. H. Beadle, *The Women's War on Whisky: Its History, Theory, and Prospects* (Cincinnati, Ohio, 1874), v–vi (introduction by Dio Lewis); Mary Earhart, *Frances Willard: From Prayers to Politics* (Evanston, Ill., 1944), 140; Earle Leslie Vail, "The Decline of the Temperance Movement and the Growth of Intemperance during the Decade, 1856–1866" (M.A. thesis, University of Pittsburgh, 1934), 55–56. Vail notes two attacks that occurred during the war; both were in communities that had soldiers stationed nearby.

71. *Western Christian Advocate*, Jan. 30, 1867.

72. Ibid.; Howe, *Historical Collections*, 1:924.

73. Letter to *New York Tribune*, reprinted in *Woman's Advocate*, Mar., 1869, 167, quoted in Earhart, *Willard*, 140.

7

The Woman's Crusade and the WCTU, 1873–74

The attacks by women on saloons in the years preceding the Woman's Crusade were localized events. Undoubtedly many of the women who participated in an attack knew that other women elsewhere had taken similar action, but the attacks never achieved any interrelated momentum. Each new assault was precipitated primarily by local conditions, perhaps by an incident that particularly incensed the community's citizens, by an act of unusually dynamic leadership from some local temperance reformer, or by a lecture from Dio Lewis, who gave his talk on how to organize a saloon praying band some 300 times prior to December, 1873.[1] The Crusade achieved its spectacular intensity because a cluster of southwestern Ohio communities developed prayer bands all at once, attracted significant newspaper attention, proselytized their successes, so that instances of praying crusades suddenly began to snowball. Thereafter, the principal catalyst for local crusades in the more than 400 communities that experienced them in 1874 became simply the awareness of the existence, the methods, and the successes of a multitude of other crusades.

Dio Lewis's lectures stimulated the formation of prayer bands in four communities in December, 1873: Fredonia and Jamestown, New York, and Hillsboro and Washington Court House, Ohio. The two Ohio towns, within twenty-five miles of one another, began their campaigns one day apart, Hillsboro on the 23rd and Washington Court House on the 24th. By chance, a visiting Methodist minister, the Reverend I. P. Patch, was in Washington Court House at the time, and the actions of the women there deeply impressed him. According to a local crusader, "It seemed to him that God's time of great deliverance had come, and the impulse to be an instrument in spreading the glad tidings took hold of him. Thenceforth . . . he went everywhere preaching the new method for the suppression of the liquor traffic."[2] During the winter Patch was responsible for starting crusades in four other counties in the region. His first success came in the town of Wilmington just at the beginning of the new year, and by January 14 the women there had closed all the local saloons. The movement also spread quickly to Greenfield. Greenfield women had been tried in Hillsboro in 1867 for saloon destruction and had been supported by Hillsboro's women (see Chapter Six). Undoubtedly, the temperance women of the two communities were still in contact. This clear link between the Woman's Crusade and the earlier saloon attacks re-emphasizes the continuity in the actions of temperance women over a period of many years.

With several crusades in progress simultaneously, the participants began to feel that they were leading something of more than local importance. They began to forward reports of their successes to the Cincinnati daily newspapers. Crusaders sent telegrams of support to one another, and delegations from the different towns exchanged visits. By mid-January crusades were underway in several other nearby communities. This flurry of temperance activity attracted the interest of the *Cincinnati Commercial,* so that in mid-January a staff reporter traveled to the crusade towns and began sending back colorful eyewitness accounts from the towns. The *Commercial* circulated as an exchange paper throughout the Ohio Valley, and its reports of the movement were widely reprinted by other papers.

Soon the women's temperance leagues, as they began to call themselves, were being flooded with requests for information and advice. By February 11, women were campaigning in about twenty-five towns in Ohio and Indiana. National attention focused on the phenomenon, and newspapers devoted many columns to detailed descriptions of the Hillsboro and Washington courthouse experiences, and to the progress being made in other towns. The Crusade began to gain recruits, building excitement, intensity, and momentum as it grew.[3]

At first the Crusade flourished primarily in communities with populations of less than 5,000, where the women generally had two dozen or fewer saloons to contend with. Reports frequently described the women active in the movement as "respectable," and a recent study of the Hillsboro crusaders concludes that their husbands were prosperous, of native-born parentage, and in professional, white-collar, proprietary, or skilled labor occupations.[4] Most of the women involved in the crusades were married, and of those who were not, many were the daughters of married crusaders. After Ohio, with its 144 known crusade communities, the states most affected were Illinois (46), Michigan (39), and Indiana (38); these were also the states that had experienced the most numerous saloon attacks prior to 1874. But the Crusade did, in fact, sweep the country, from Maine to California, with only the deep South left untouched.[5]

Crusade tactics were best suited to smaller communities where the psychological, social, and economic pressure they exerted could have a strong effect. For example, the women of Washington Court House, faced with a particularly strong-willed German beer garden proprietor named Charlie Beck, set up a "tabernacle," a small wood frame enclosure with chairs and a stove, next door to Beck's. They shone powerful locomotive lamps at the front of his premises, and from early morning to late night for several weeks they kept up a vigil which included not only praying and singing but speaking to and taking down the names of all customers. The following day they would read the names publicly. Such concentrated effort and focused community pressure would have been impractical and ineffective in a large metropolitan area.[6]

Eventually, however, the enthusiasm of the Crusade did spread to the large cities: praying bands appeared in Springfield, Columbus, Dayton, Cleveland, and Cincinnati in Ohio, as well as in Chicago, Pittsburgh, Philadelphia, Boston, and many other major cities. In Cincinnati Methodist Episcopal ministers took the first organizational step. On March 2 they called for a meeting of all interested clergy "in order to inquire what God would have us do on this subject."[7] The next day several dozen clergymen met, endorsed the Crusade effort, and scheduled a mass meeting for the 5th. There, according to the reporter from the *Cincinnati Gazette*, speakers of both sexes "called upon the women of Cincinnati to organize and push forward the work begun by their sisters throughout the state."[8] Three hundred women held their own meeting the next day; "they were not from the wealthy and aristocratic classes of society," wrote the *Gazette* reporter, "nor did they represent the opposite extreme. They were well-to-do, intelligent, thoughtful ladies, many of whom had been prominent in charitable and Christian enterprises."[9] One of those present was Abby Fisher Leavitt, who soon emerged as the leader of the Crusade in Cincinnati and eventually became one of the national leaders of the WCTU.

Abby Leavitt was thirty-eight at the time of the Crusade, and married to the Reverend Samuel K. Leavitt of Cincinnati's First Baptist Church. She was the state secretary of the Baptist Women's Foreign Missionary Society of Ohio and also worked actively in the Sunday-school. Born in Bangor, Maine, she had lived there until the age of nineteen. In 1854, three years after Maine had passed the nation's first prohibitory law, she moved to the South, where she taught school until the war. From 1861 until her marriage in 1866 she was the principal of an Evansville, Indiana, grammar school. The Leavitts moved to Keokuk, Iowa, in 1870 and then to Cincinnati two years later. Her twelve years as a school teacher and a principal and her organizational work in the missionary society undoubtedly helped Leavitt develop her talents for organizing and public speaking. As a crusade leader she was strong-willed, tenacious, tireless, and fearless, always ready to lead her praying bands into the most hostile of crowds or to engage in arguments with the city's most powerful men. She also had a wry sense of humor which she could use with telling effect against her opponents or simply to entertain; her speeches and reports were usually interspersed with laughter from her audience. A firm believer in the importance of communication in an organization, she established in Cincinnati the first WCTU newspaper, and later pressed for and helped organize the first national organ. Leavitt's leadership talents were so remarkable that at the first national convention of the WCTU she was the only woman besides Annie Wittenmyer seriously considered for president. Even though she lacked the national reputation Wittenmyer had gained for benevolent work during the war, the two women tied on the first ballot. Leavitt withdrew, giving the election to Wittenmyer; a year later she became national treasurer, a post she held for many years.[10]

Despite Abby Leavitt's strong leadership, the prevailing mood in the early days of the Cincinnati crusade was one of caution. The *Western Christian Advocate* reported that "the general sentiment among the more prominent ladies engaged in the movement is, that an immediate advance should not be made on the saloons, but that some time should be spent in prayer and religious preparation."[11] The women had good cause to feel some trepidation about undertaking a crusade in Cincinnati. Instead of one or two dozen saloons to deal with, they faced well over 3,000. Many of these were in German neighborhoods, where community opinion would hardly work in favor of the Crusade.

Even outside the German neighborhoods, their efforts were unlikely to be welcome. The *Gazette* reported:

> Social drinking among Americans, also, was quite prevalent. The wealthy and aristocratic families in the city and suburbs had their cellars stocked with choice wines and liquors, which figured conspicuously in the hospitalities of the house. Prominent business men, lawyers, physicians, and politicians took their occasional or regular dram, as they had done for years. Young men, with plenty of money, consumed vast quantities of choice drinks at the high-toned places; while in the common beer saloons gathered thousands of laboring men and mechanics. . .[12]

Moreover, liquor consumed within the city accounted for only a small part of the importance of alcoholic beverages to Cincinnati's economy. The distilling and brewing industries had a capital investment in the city of over $33 million, and altogether, according to one contemporary estimate, the liquor trade provided employment for 30,000–40,000 inhabitants.

The *Gazette's* reporter described the drink trade's influence: "The money made by the breweries and distilleries built scores of massive business blocks and elegant private residences. Banks and business men were largely dependent on whiskey money for the conduct of their trade. Many of the wealthiest men in the city were whiskey dealers, and their rank in society high."[13] According to Abby Leavitt, twenty-three of the forty-eight members of the City Council were in the liquor trade. She recalled that "merchants did not like to have their wives engage in temperance work for fear of bad results to their businesses. . ."[14] The *Cincinnati Enquirer* concluded that in smaller communities "the melodious devotion of the ladies may cause a fifty-dollar interest to succumb or hide itself, but fifty millions of dollars will conquer all the hymns the well-meaning women can sing and all the prayers they can pray."[15] Even before the effort in the city began, the damage to the wholesale liquor trade done by crusaders in the surrounding area had stirred up much hostile public opinion. "The Whisky Crusade is affecting the business of Cincinnati materially," stated the *Enquirer.* "Next to pork, whisky is our main dependence. Another 'panic' appears on the horizon."[16] The women knew they had no hope of closing even a small portion of Cincinnati's drink establishments, and it is no wonder that in such circumstances they took time to gather their forces and proceeded carefully.

For three weeks the women visited the saloons in twos and threes, attempting in vain to persuade individual saloon owners to abandon their trade. On March 26 they finally began full-scale prayer band visitations. Two days later the mayor issued a proclamation "warning all persons against assembling so as to obstruct the streets. . . ."[17] Almost always the news of the women's approach preceded them, and saloons were locked upon their arrival. In order to obey the nonobstruction law, they would stay in double file stretched out along the sidewalk, stop to pray and sing, and then move on from saloon to saloon until, having gathered a large crowd, they would stop in one of the open squares or market places and hold a public prayer meeting.

Leavitt led the bands into hostile neighborhoods where the crowds were often abusive. The *Advocate* described one day when the women were "insulted, jeered, and hooted at, the crowd even going so far as to pull the ribbons of their bonnets, and spit in their faces. The ladies were badly frightened, and cried on the way home; but before separating, they resolved to go out again the next day."[18] They kept up the marches all of April and half of May. The mood of the crowds, particularly in German neighborhoods, worsened. On May 15, when the prayer band started services in front of the offices of the Foss, Schneider & Brenner brewery, according to the *Advocate*, men leaned out of the windows, beat copper cans with clubs, and threw eggs and beer down on the women. A very abusive crowd surrounded them, yelling angrily. The mayor arrived on the scene and tried to persuade the women to turn back, only to be told by that day's leader, the wife of a Methodist minister, that she "would, if necessary, sacrifice her own life to the cause." The crowd pushed, insulted, and threatened the mayor for his efforts.

The next day the mayor issued another proclamation that forbade the prayer group to go out again; he referred to an old ordinance prohibiting groups of three or more from occupying the sidewalk, and he also cited a danger to public order posed by the marches. The women stated later that they were not informed of the new proclamation before they went out on the 16th, but they certainly knew that trouble might result from a march that day. The special policeman assigned to them, who had had to draw his pistol three times the previous day in an effort to control the crowd, "begged the ladies," according to the *Advocate*, "to remain in the Church, as he feared bloodshed would be the result if they ventured out."[19] Nevertheless, a group of forty-three went out under Abby Leavitt's direction. At the first stop they were all arrested. In court, the judge dismissed the case, but with a warning that in the future the law would be enforced. The Cincinnati women abandoned the prayer band marches and the city's crusade came to an abrupt end.[20]

At about that time the Crusade was fading out everywhere, its emotional intensity and enthusiasm impossible to maintain. Moreover, the drink trade had learned how to counterattack through laws on trespass, obstruction, or public nuisance, and in many places the women were under court injunctions to desist. A number of local spring elections had turned on the saloon issue, and in many the vote had gone against the women. As soon as the crusading stopped, saloons reopened everywhere, and within a few months there was often little evidence within the communities to show that the crusades had ever taken place.

The damage to the liquor industry was dramatic but temporary. The temperance movement claimed that the federal tax revenue on liquor in the Cincinnati district had dropped $3 million in the first half of 1874. The United States Brewers' Association blamed the Crusade for the first decline ever in the annual production of beer, and admitted: "Very severe is the injury which the brewers have sustained in the so-called temperance states."[21] In Ohio, 68 of 296 breweries closed. Nationally, over a thousand breweries went out of business between 1873 and 1875 (although some failures may have been due to the depression of 1873). Ironically, the long-range effect of the Crusade may have been to strengthen the drink industry. Even though the number of breweries dropped by 27 percent, the production of beer was back to within 3 percent of its 1873 total by 1875. The effect of the Crusade was to drive out of business the smaller, more marginal operations and to encourage a trend toward consolidation and centralization in the industry that made it more efficient, powerful, and economically stable.[22]

What, then, had the Crusade accomplished? What had its participants hoped to accomplish? Despite the different circumstances crusaders faced in small and large communities, the answers to these questions are the same for both Cincinnati and the movement as a whole. More than anything else, the Crusade was a public theater of propaganda, aimed at stripping social drinking of its growing respectability within the middle class. It also forged a spiritual (and later organizational) link between women throughout the country who had been fighting isolated skirmishes against the drink trade in defense of their families since the 1850s. The Crusade had many other facets as well. It was an expression of deep religious feeling, very much in the tradition of evangelical revivalism. The movement also focused the dissatisfaction women felt with the way men had run the temperance reform, and enabled them to take over the movement in large part. Finally, the Crusade in a sense updated the ethnocultural antagonisms that had emerged in the 1850s in relation to liquor: no longer was the issue simply that of trying to convince immigrants to accept native-born middle-class Protestant culture, but now it was rather that of fighting a rear-guard action to keep their children from adopting some of the cultural standards of the immigrants. In all these areas of basic concern the Crusade was, at least temporarily, more successful than it had been in its ostensible goal of destroying the drink trade in America.

Mother Stewart, leader of the Springfield, Ohio, crusade and later prominent in the work of the national WCTU, recalled that after the Crusade had died out, "repeated questions . . . came to us from such as were not able to see the effect in the awakening of the people, nor to take in the broad meaning of the great uprising," as to whether it had been a failure. Stewart quoted a list of "Benefits of the Crusade," written by the secretary of the Ohio YMCA, which began: "1. It called attention to the evils of intemperance. 2. It aroused public sentiment against it. 3. It made saloons odious in the eyes of young men." [23] Obviously saloons did not become odious to all young men, but the crusaders were interested principally in safeguarding the sobriety of middle-class men and particularly members of their own families.

The dominant theme of the Crusade was the danger the women felt the drink trade posed domestically, especially for their sons. According to the minutes of the first national WCTU convention, a delegate from Ohio reminded the women that "'many as intelligent, as high-minded, as pure in purpose as they [the delegates present], have had sons whom intemperance has destroyed.'" Another delegate from Wisconsin added, "'All the sons of this land are liable to become drunkards, the high in life as well as the low.'" A third, touching on a circumstance that undoubtedly added to the anxiety of many a mother, asked: " 'How many mothers are here in our land to-day who have sons away from home!' " She concluded, " 'In this noble work of temperance, we feel that God has called us to meet a sin which is fast undermining and destroying our nation.' "[24]

The crusaders in Adrian, Michigan, in their articles of association, began: "Intemperance has become a great evil in our city. It is increasing with alarming rapidity. It is invading our homes. The tempter seeks even after our children."[25] Abby Leavitt recalled a time in Cincinnati when, as the woman's prayer band approached "an elegant sample room, . . . one lady in the band remarked—'I don't know why *I* am here. I have no one in my family who drinks.' But just as we came to the saloon she caught sight of one of her sons in there. . . . The mother who did not dream that *her* sons were tipplers looked pale as death. She was one of the first to offer prayer in that place, and ever since has been active in the temperance work."[26] The leader in Washington Court House wrote simply that the Crusade was "a war to the death . . . between the Home and the Liquor Traffic."[27]

Sometimes the danger women foresaw for their families in the saloons encompassed more than simply intemperance. When the bands of women visited the saloons, recalled a crusader, they saw for the first time the places where "those they loved best were being landed, through the allurements of the brilliantly lighted drug store, the fascinating billiard table, or the enticing beer gardens, with their syren [*sic*] attractions."[28] Although the idea of a son drinking was a dreadful thought in itself, given the long-standing middle-class belief that any imbibing could lead to alcoholism and ruin, references to sin and siren attractions suggest that the danger of drink was compounded with another element in the minds of the women. They were responding not only to the breakdown of total abstinence but to a saloon lifestyle that included such idle pastimes as billiards, bowling, gambling, and, most dangerous of all, familiarity with prostitutes.

After the Civil War there was a steadily growing link between saloons and prostitution, and therefore between saloons and venereal disease. "Nine-tenths of all the licentiousness which curses society," the *Advocate* claimed, "is perpetrated under the inflamatory influence of ardent spirits. . . . It is notorious that the inmates of the dens of shame are habitual drinkers, and nine-tenths of their patrons . . . [are] under the influence of stimulants."[29] By the turn of the century this danger had become an explicit focus of the temperance movement, but it was a genuine concern much earlier, as was surely present in the Woman's Crusade, even if it could only be hinted at.[30]

Understanding the Crusade as, at heart, a defense of the family helps to explain why its tactics were adopted even in large cities like Cincinnati where they had no chance of success. The street prayer bands were like public morality plays that juxtaposed the saloons to the bands of moral, abstinent, pious, and compassionate mothers and wives and thereby brought into sharp focus the disparity, the incompatibility, of saloon life and proper native-born middle-class domestic life. Certainly many sons must have felt ashamed as they thought of their mothers kneeling in prayer on the floor of the saloons they secretly frequented. The crusaders also shamed clergymen, educators, and town leaders into speaking out forcefully against the drink traffic. The Crusade, in short, was a form of dramatized propaganda for middle-class morality, an attempt to make the saloon once again unrespectable. Here lay the "broad meaning" of the Crusade, as Mother Stewart had observed: calling attention to intemperance, arousing public sentiment against it, and making the saloons "odious in the eyes of young men."[31]

Just when the crusades were getting well underway, and long before the first efforts were made in Cincinnati, the *Gazette* indicated that it understood this basic purpose of the movement: "It raises up a public sentiment, zeal, enthusiasm, and influence which unite the community in the cause, and which will make drinking disreputable. In this it seems to us will be its great and permanent effects."[32] In the smaller communities the women had attempted to shame those reputable citizens who frequented saloons by taking their names down and reading them in public. The Cincinnati women used a more generalized variant of this tactic. The first saloon they visited in the city was the fashionable Custom House, next door to the Merchant's Exchange. "The time chosen for the visit," recounted the *Gazette* reporter, "was about half past eleven o'clock—just the hour when the business men on 'Change were wont to step in next door to 'take something.' The band of women descended upon the place so suddenly that some of the honorable merchants who were inside had no chance to escape, and were compelled to sit for half an hour and listen to the praying and singing."[33]

If the Crusade is viewed as a war of propaganda, it is easier to understand why the Cincinnati women seemed to deliberately provoke hostile crowd reactions. The more they were ill-treated, the greater became the onus of rowdiness and disreputability on their opponents. In this sense, their mass arrest was not their final defeat but their ultimate victory. The *Times* recognized immediately that the Crusade's opponents had "blundered badly" by making the arrests.[34] When the mayor arrived at the station house, Leavitt recalled, he looked like "the man who drew the elephant in a lottery, and then didn't know what to do with it."[35] The arrests produced a wave of indignation throughout the city, and a demand for stricter enforcement of the liquor and Sunday laws. Annie Wittenmyer, in her history of the Crusade, summed up the result of the arrests: "Nearly all the pulpits of Cincinnati thundered against the liquor traffic, a strong public sentiment was created . . . and it is no longer respectable to sell or drink intoxicating liquors in Cincinnati."[36] By becoming martyrs, the crusaders achieved one of their primary goals, that of making the liquor dealers and their allies appear morally reprehensible and socially disreputable.

Of course, not everyone in the city was outraged by the arrests. The *Catholic Telegraph* wrote: "This degradation of religion and womanhood had been permitted to go too long unchecked. Among those whose civil rights these persecuting fanatics were continually trampling under foot, there had grown up a fierce determination to retaliate."[37] On the day after the arrests the mayor was interviewed by a reporter from the Democratic party's newspaper, the *Enquirer*, which had a pro-Catholic stance and had been hostile to the Crusade. The reporter, making no effort to conceal his own opinions, concluded: "The influence of the Evangelical churches, Mr. Mayor, seems to have had a great deal to do with [the Crusade]. For the past few years it almost looks as though the Evangelicals were making efforts to have the laws of the city remodeled according to their special theological codes, and this temperance movement would seem to be their final and forlorn-hope effort in that direction."[38]

The Crusade brought into sharp relief the ethnocultural division that existed over drink, as it had in the 1850s. The temperance reformers were generally native-born Protestants, usually of evangelical faiths. Their most vociferous opponents were Catholics and immigrants. However, few crusaders saw the conflict in anti-Catholic terms; they rarely mentioned the Catholic church. Even the Irish and their many saloons were generally ignored. For the crusaders, the enemy was the German saloon keeper and brewer.

Crusade literature is filled with hostile or ridiculing references to Germans, not just in the large cities but in practically every crusade community. Washington Court House was situated in Fayette County, which in 1870 had only 135 German-born residents, less than 1 percent of the population. But Charlie Beck's beer garden became the focus of the local crusade. The *Commercial* reporter described Beck's establishment: "It was after the pattern of a country school house, in the same enclosure with Beck's residence, with well arranged grounds, and in the center of a fine suburban neighborhood."[39] Beck's beer garden was just the sort of saloon that seemed most dangerous to the women crusaders, since its clientele came from the town's respectable middle class. Accounts of the legendary struggle with Beck invariably lampooned his thick German accent; in one report Beck was said to have cried out to the first band that visited him: "'Go vay, vimmins, go home; shtay at home, and tend to your papies. . . .'"[40] Such renderings of accent not only ridiculed but emphasized the foreignness of the speaker; it was a technique the crusaders used in almost all of their many anecdotes about Germans.

The crusaders considered proprietors like Beck as their principal enemies not only because of the growing acceptability of beer drinking and of clean and attractive beer gardens in their communities, but also because Germans were often the most resistant to the Crusade appeals, the most articulate in the defense of their rights and liberties, and the most canny in the use of the law to protect their businesses. Beck himself hired a lawyer, won a court injunction against the women, and had their "tabernacle" removed by the sheriff. In Ashland, Ohio, "the saloonists," according to Annie Wittenmyer, "were under the leadership of one of their number, a man of influence in the German church, who kept the most respectable place in town; a place where the young men congregated, and where many of the older ones found it pleasant to linger."[41] The German-dominated U.S. Brewers' Association had become the most effective lobbying group for the drink trade in the political sphere, and exercised such an influence that temperance reformers believed their power had to arise from bribery and corruption. A German Lutheran minister in Cincinnati protested that "if the *brewers* are Germans, the *distillers* are Americans. If the saloons are kept by Germans, the largest wholesale liquor establishments are in the hands of Americans."[42] But for most crusaders, the evil influence of the drink trade was epitomized by the German saloons and breweries that formed such a visible part of it.

The conflict with Germans was predictably intense in Cincinnati during the crusade there. "One-third of the population of the city were Germans," Wittenmyer wrote, "accustomed to beer-drinking, which tended to make the traffic respectable. . . . Many of them were ignorant bigots and infidels, who were ready, on any pretext, to cry out against the Bible and Puritanism. . . ."[43] Even before the prayer band marches began, when the crusade women were making visitations in groups of two and three, the *Advocate* reported that they were experiencing much "rudeness and insult . . . the German women being worse than their husbands and sons in hooting and yelling."[44] The hostile crowds that followed the prayer bands were predominantly German. Nevertheless, the crusaders continued to work in German neighborhoods and to pass out temperance tracts and pamphlets written in German. Occasionally they even won a German convert to the principle of temperance.[45] Such victories, however rare, might have

given the women hope that some day their total abstinence beliefs would triumph over the German cultural traditions that
approved social drinking. But for the moment at least the
crusaders felt they were fighting defensively, trying to regain
the ground they had lost in their own native-born middle class
in that conflict of cultural values.

The Crusade attacked not only a decline in teetotalism but
also a decline in religiosity. Like the Washingtonian movement
and the 1858 upswing in temperance activism, the Crusade
took place within a context of religious revivalism that followed a period of economic depression. The religious content
of the Crusade reflected not only the anxieties induced by the
depression but also a feeling that religion in general had lost
ground during and after the Civil War. At times the revivalism
inherent in the movement became quite explicit. Abby Leavitt
recalled a Good Friday prayer meeting on the Cincinnati es-
planade at which the street band had been surrounded by a
large crowd of "roughs." "We began to sing 'Rock of Ages';
next 'Jesus the Water of Life will give,' and then a dear Quaker
lady began to exhort those roughs to give their hearts to God.
We forgot all about temperance, and held a real gospel meeting, which made a profound impression on the crowd." [46]
The whole idea of the movement, she concluded, was "soul-
saving." [47]

Religion was a constant reference point for the women
during the Crusade; many participants recalled that they had
decided to join the movement after seeking guidance in prayer.
In the smaller towns and cities, when the last saloon hold-out
surrendered, typically the women would sing the Doxology,
the church bells would begin to ring, and large crowds would
gather in the streets for communal rejoicing, giving the event a
strong flavor of millennial expectation. Mother Thompson,
leader of the Hillsboro crusade, said that it seemed to the
women of her district "that the millennium was coming." [48]
Evangelical fervor added intensity and emotional power to the
Crusade effort, although, in the characteristic fashion of revivals, its intensity could not be sustained for long. An awareness of rapidly fading spiritual fervor probably contributed to
the sudden collapse of all the crusading efforts.

Unlike the Washingtonian temperance revival, however, the Woman's Crusade left an organization intact. The WCTU became the most tangible permanent accomplishment of the movement. Although many American women had felt anger, frustration, and anxiety about the drink trade's influence in their communities in the decades since the first saloon attacks of the 1850s, they had generally not been able to share these feelings with women in other communities. The Crusade brought spiritual and then organizational linking of women throughout the country who shared these emotions. The movement brought them together, made them aware of their mutually held perspective, and gave them the collective strength to break away from male-dominated, politically oriented temperance organizations and to form their own separate movement.

Almost as soon as the Crusade was well underway in Ohio, participants took steps to set up a statewide organization. A convention in Columbus on February 24, 1874, established "The Woman's Temperance Association of Ohio." Two months later a largely different group of leaders called for a convention of the state's women's temperance leagues, to convene in Cincinnati at the same time that the constitutional convention there was considering the repeal of the anti-licensing clause of the state constitution. Both of the women's conventions set up executive committees, and by June the two groups had merged and organized a third convention in Springfield. There the Woman's Christian Temperance Union of Ohio came into being. Over the summer other states established similar organizations, and in November Cleveland hosted the first meeting of the national Woman's Christian Temperance Union.[49]

Although the transition from spontaneous mass movement to structured national organization was relatively smooth and trouble-free, the women did encounter one problem. Almost immediately they had to consider whether they should continue to eschew political action, or attempt to use their new-found collective power to exert significant influence in the political sphere for the first time. At the February convention in Columbus men as well as women were delegates (the call to convention issued by Dio Lewis had suggested that delegations be divided evenly by sex). The women protested a scheduled evening address by the Reverend John Russel of Michigan, Prohibition party vice-presidential candidate in 1872, and asked that his speech be canceled and replaced with a prayer meeting at the legislature. Russel refused to withdraw, and the issue caused considerable friction among the delegates. A few days after the convention Russel addressed the Mt. Vernon crusaders while the Prohibition party held its convention in that town. Claiming that one hundred years of their praying would not create a temperate society, Russel urged the women to admit that only prohibition could achieve any permanent results. "The remark was not very well received by the women," the *Advocate* reported, since they "had in ten days shut up twenty-five out of the thirty saloons in the town."[50] A distrust of politics was one of the underlying themes of the Crusade, and the women were understandably hostile to this male attempt to subordinate their thriving movement to the faltering efforts of the Prohibition party.

The prohibition issue raised its head once again at the April convention in Cincinnati but with less divisive effect, since only about one-tenth of the delegates were men. The resolutions committee voted against an endorsement of prohibition fifty-eight to six, but a male member of the committee introduced a minority report on the floor of the convention in an attempt to override this decision. Woman after woman rose to speak against endorsing prohibition, one asking rhetorically if they were at a man's or a woman's convention. The minority report was overwhelmingly defeated.

Then the women faced a more perplexing dilemma on the license issue. The main purpose of the convention had been to take action against the effort to reinstitute liquor licensing in the new state constitution. Some of the state's male temperance reformers were in favor of renewed licensing, feeling that it might give them some legal leverage over the drink trade. Women, however, were united in opposition to licensing. According to one Crusade leader, licensing put the state in the position of saying: "This man has paid me a certain amount of money. In consideration of this, I have guaranteed to him that your sons and your daughters shall be his legitimate prey, and I will protect him in destroying your homes."[51] The convention passed a memorial to the constitutional convention calling for a continued ban on licensing. But the constitutional convention chose to submit the license issue separately to the voters, just as had been done in 1851, in order not to place the rest of the proposed constitution in jeopardy. Suddenly the women were faced with the necessity of organizing politically in order to prevent the political sanctioning of the drink trade.

The Springfield meeting in June agonized over this paradoxical situation. The question first arose indirectly: a resolution was introduced to "oppose the giant evil of intemperance by personal, social, and political influence, by the press, by the pulpit, by speech, and by prayer." A motion was made to strike the word "political," and a vigorous debate ensued. Finally the delegates worked out a convoluted compromise wording that left the original motion intact but preceded it with the phrase "That we each in our appropriate sphere, and by all proper means, not as partisans, but as Christian citizens, will increasingly oppose . . ." etc.[52]

By specifically excluding partisan political action, the amendment made it clear that no endorsement of the Prohibition party was intended. However, some women were left with the uneasy feeling that the organization was in danger of becoming politically oriented. A woman from Wilmington, the *Advocate* reported, "made a feeling and beautiful exhortation to the ladies to cling to the spiritual part of the Temperance work, and not engage in the political field."[53] Abby Leavitt, in an effort to calm these fears, introduced a resolution that had earlier been passed at an executive committee meeting, stating "that while we acknowledge that a result of the Woman's Movement will be to create temperance laws, we do believe the more exclusively it is confined to prayer work, regarding woman's part as spiritual and of Divine origin . . . the greater will be our success."[54] The motion passed unanimously, and the women returned to their communities reassured, but still in doubt as to precisely how the WCTU was to create temperance laws while confining itself to prayer work.

Abby Leavitt soon indicated that her definition of prayer work was broadly conceived. During the anti-license campaign that summer she organized a canvassing of all Hamilton County, and persuaded the local WCTU organization to distribute thousands of free copies of her WCTU journal, the *New Temperance Era*. In addition, according to Frances Willard, WCTU president after 1879, Leavitt "spoke in halls, churches, tents, and groves against license." [55]

Leavitt was not alone in her efforts; women throughout Ohio used their freshly developed writing, organizing, and speaking skills, and their network of local WCTU chapters, to help defeat the license clause in Ohio. At the national level of the WCTU the question of political involvement was not resolved until 1879, when the organization finally endorsed prohibition and when social and political activist Frances Willard triumphed in her leadership struggle with Annie Wittenmyer. Willard's election as president of the WCTU was not the first step in a shift toward political action. Rather, it reflected the fact that rank-and-file members throughout the country had already discovered they could not escape political involvement. As Ohio women had learned in 1874, once temperance women were organized and had the potential for political power, they could hardly refrain from using it when the safety of their families seemed at stake. It was this inevitability of political involvement that led to the election of Willard and also to the WCTU's endorsement of female suffrage as a necessary tool to secure, in Willard's phrase, "Home Protection." [56]

Thus, when temperance women did enter the political sphere, it was not a capitulation to the male-dominated wing of the temperance movement. Instead they turned to politics with their own objectives, on their own terms, and with their own distinct perspective on temperance reform shaped over the previous quarter of a century. Indeed, for several decades to come, women dominated the American temperance movement, providing its most dynamic and creative leadership and its most extensive and effective organization. Temperance reform entered a new period of development and expansion, one that culminated in 1920 with the victory of national prohibition.

Notes

1. J. H. Beadle, *The Women's War on Whiskey: Its History, Theory, and Prospects* (Cincinnati, Ohio, 1874), v–vi (introduction by Dio Lewis).

2. Matilda Gilruth Carpenter, *The Crusade; Its Origins and Development at Washington Court House and Its Results* (Columbus, Ohio, 1893), 62, 29.

3. Carpenter, *Crusade*, 50–64; Beadle, *Women's War*, 18; E. D. Stewart, *Memories of the Crusade; a Thrilling Account of the Great Uprising of the Women of Ohio in 1873, against the Liquor Crime* (Columbus, Ohio, 1889), 146; Henry Howe, *Historical Collection of Ohio in Two Volumes* (Cincinnati, Ohio, 1902), 1:924; *Western Christian Advocate* (hereafter cited as *Advocate*), Feb. 11, 1874; *New Reporter*, Sept. 1, 1876; Charles Isetts, "The Women's Christian Temperance Crusade of Southern Ohio" (M.A. thesis, Miami University, 1971), 26, 58, 65.

4. Charles A. Isetts, "A Social Profile of the Women's Temperance Crusade: Hillsboro, Ohio," in Jack S. Blocker, ed., *Alcoholism, Reform and Society: The Liquor Issue in Social Context* (Westport, Conn., 1979); *Advocate*, Feb. 11, 1874.

5. Susan Dye Lee, Northwestern University, unpublished manuscript on the Woman's Crusade.

6. Carpenter, *Crusade*, 73–84; W. H. Daniels, *The Temperance Reform and Its Great Reformers* (Cincinnati, Ohio, 1878), 257–58; *New Reporter*, Sept. 1, 1896. For other examples of name-taking, see Annie Wittenmyer, *History of the Woman's Temperance Crusade* (Philadelphia, 1878), 52, 193, 212, 265, 296, 308, 448.

7. *Advocate*, Mar. 11, 1874; Isetts, "Women's . . . Southern Ohio," 71–72; Stewart, *Memories*, 372–79.

8. Jane E. Stebbins and T. A. H. Brown, *Fifty Years' History of the Temperance Cause* (Hartford, Conn., 1876), 452; *Advocate*, Mar. 11, 1874.

9. Stebbins, *Fifty Years*, 453.

10. *Advocate*, Mar. 11, 1874; Frances E. Willard, *Women and Temperance: or, The Work and the Workers of the Woman's CTU* (Hartford, Conn., 1883), 88–94; *Cincinnati Enquirer*, May 17, 1874; Ohio WCTU, *Minutes* (manuscript minute book, Ohio WCTU offices, Columbus, Ohio, hereafter cited as manuscript minutes), Apr., 1874, 13; May, 1875, 108; National WCTU, *Minutes of the First Convention of the National Woman's Christian Temperance Union Held in Cleveland, Ohio, Nov.* [18, 19, and 20,] *1874* (Chicago, 1889), 12, 34; *Minutes of the Second Convention of the National Woman's Christian Temperance Union Held in Cincinnati, Ohio, Nov. 17, 18, and 19, 1875* (Chicago, 1889), 71.

11. *Advocate*, Mar. 11, 1874.

12. Stebbins, *Fifty Years*, 451; Daniels, *Temperance Reform*, 269.

13. Stebbins, *Fifty Years*, 450–51; *Enquirer*, Mar. 18, 1874; National WCTU, *Minutes, Nov., 1875*, 44.

14. Daniels, *Temperance Reform*, 269–70; Wittenmyer, *History*, 240.

15. *Enquirer*, Mar. 14, 1874.

16. Ibid., Mar. 13, 1874.

17. *Advocate*, Apr. 1, 1874; Stebbins, *Fifty Years*, 453–59.

18. *Advocate*, Apr. 1, 1874.

19. Ibid., May 20, 1874; Wittenmyer, *History*, 237–42.

20. *Enquirer*, May 17, 1874; *Advocate*, May 27, 1874.

21. *Advocate*, June 16, 1874; Wittenmyer, *History*, 235–36. Abby Leavitt wrote that about the time of the Cincinnati arrests the Crusade had begun "to change its form from active crusading into steady, organized work . . ." (Wittenmyer, *History*, 242).

22. Stanley Baron, *Brewed in America: A History of Beer and Ale in the United States* (Boston, 1962), 226; *Advocate*, June 16, 1875.

23. Stewart, *Memories*, 431.

24. National WCTU, *Minutes, Nov., 1874*, 15–16. For similar references, see Wittenmyer, *History*, 31, 216, 251–52, 366, 433, 546, 583; Daniels, *Temperance Reform*, 251–52; Carpenter, *Crusade*, 35–36.

25. Adrian (Mich.) Ladies' Temperance Union, *Minutes*, 1874 (Joint Ohio Historical Society–Michigan Historical Collections—Woman's Christian Union microfilm edition, Mid-Nineteenth Century series, roll 1, frame 320).

26. Daniels, *Temperance Reform*, 269–70.

27. Carpenter, *Crusade*, 20.

28. *New Reporter*, Sept. 1, 1876.

29. *Advocate*, Feb. 15, 1871; see also Wittenmyer, *History*, 444, 448, 538.

30. David J. Pivar, *Purity Crusade: Sexual Morality and Social Control, 1868–1900* (Westport, Conn., 1973), 6; Norman Clark, *Deliver Us from Evil: An Interpretation of American Prohibition* (New York, 1976), 58–67.

31. Stewart, *Memories*, 431.

32. *Cincinnati Gazette*, Feb. 9, 1874.

33. Stebbins, *Fifty Years*, 456; Wittenmyer, *History*, 229.

34. *Cincinnati Times*, May 18, 1874.

35. Wittenmyer, *History*, 241.

36. Ibid., 243; *Advocate*, June 3, 1874. One indication of the success the Ohio crusaders had in generating public opposition to the drink trade lies in the dramatic increase in prosecutions for liquor offenses in the state from 0.8 per 10,000 population in 1873 to 2.1 per 10,000 in 1874. Although the rate dipped to 1.4 in 1875, that was still nearly double the 1873 figure, suggesting that community intolerance toward liquor offenses remained high. The rate declined gradually in subsequent years (Eric H. Monkkonen, *The Dangerous Class: Crime and Poverty in Columbus, Ohio, 1860–1885* (Cambridge, Mass., 1975), 31).

37. *Catholic Telegraph*, May 21, 1874; see also Feb. 19, Mar. 12, 1874.

38. *Enquirer*, May 17, 1874.

39. Carpenter, *Crusade*, 64–65; see also Wittenmyer, *History*, 86, 110, 138, 153–54, 190–93, 199, 211, 221, 228, 295, 324, 384, 772.

40. Daniels, *Temperance Reform*, 257–58.

41. Wittenmyer, *History*, 175; Carpenter, *Crusade*, 84–91.

42. *Advocate*, May 27, 1874; Stewart, *Memories*, 27; Wittenmyer, *History*, 28.

43. Wittenmyer, *History*, 228; Stebbins, *Fifty Years*, 450.

44. *Advocate*, Mar. 12, 1874.

45. Ibid., Mar. 18, Apr. 22, 1874; Wittenmyer, *History*, 248–50.

46. Daniels, *Temperance Reform*, 270–72; Eugene H. Roseboom, *The Civil War Era, 1850–1873* (vol. 4 of *The History of the State of Ohio*, ed. Carl Wittke, Columbus, Ohio, 1944), 218.

47. Daniels, *Temperance Reform*, 269–70.

48. National WCTU, *Minutes, Nov., 1874*, 19; Lee, unpublished manuscript; *Advocate*, Apr. 8, 1874; Daniels, *Temperance Reform*, 273.

49. For an example of the evolution from prayer band to WCTU chapter at the local level, see Walnut Hills (Ohio) Women's Temperance Organization, manuscript minutes, entries from Mar. 9 to Oct. 30, 1874 (MS, Cincinnati Historical Society).

50. *Advocate*, Mar. 4, 1874; manuscript "Call to Convention," signed by Dio Lewis (MS, Cincinnati Historical Society).

51. Carpenter, *Crusade*, 168, 163–70; Ohio WCTU, manuscript minutes, Apr., 1874, 3–18; *Advocate*, Apr. 29, 1874.

52. Ohio WCTU, manuscript minutes, June, 1874, 44–45.

53. *Advocate*, June 24, 1874.

54. Ohio WCTU, manuscript minutes, June, 1874, 46.

55. Willard, *Women and Temperance*, 94; Ohio WCTU manuscript minutes, "Quarterly Report," Aug., 1874, 67; "Second Annual Convention," May, 1875, 96.

56. *Report of the Temperance Fair Held in Greenwood Hall, Cincinnati, Ohio, April 5–15, 1875* (Cincinnati, Ohio, 1875), 7, Clark, *Deliver*, 75.

Afterword

Temperance reform in mid-nineteenth-century America developed within a complex matrix of social influences. Its history was shaped by changes in drinking habits, migration and immigration rates, residential and work environments, religious attitudes, family structure, occupational and trade patterns, political alignments, gender roles, reform and associational impulses, religious and ethnic relationships, poverty and crime rates. In turn, many of these areas were affected by the course of temperance agitation. The development of organized temperance reform was highly disjunctive. The movement's concerns, objectives, tactics, and membership all changed markedly from one phase of the reform to another. This diversity and intricacy within the history of the crusade against drink can tell us much. To understand the changes that occurred within the temperance movement is to understand more about the concurrent dynamics of all of American society.

But it is also important to seek elements of unity and coherence in this rich and variegated history. The very ambiguity and amorphousness of "drink" as an issue, and the constant mutability of the temperance cause, enabled temperance reform to adapt to the times and to achieve influence and popularity in a number of guises over a lengthy period. At the same time, much of its power lay in its ability to embody the fundamental concerns of a society undergoing rapid change.

By signifying order and control, temperance reform at times appealed to those who sought to control others: the elite founders of the movement, for example, or the xenophobes of the 1850s and later. More often it represented the aspirations of groups seeking social influence, independence, and freedom from exploitation. For reformers advocating the liberation of slaves or women, the temperance cause was a natural ally: it liberated its adherents from dependence, degradation, and exploitation, and gave them control of their own destinies. For workers and shopkeepers struggling in an emerging capitalist economy, and for women seeking protection for themselves and their families in a society that allowed them little power, temperance activism was a form of group assertion and solidarity.

These qualities of temperance reform are also evident in the experiences of other cultures. Temperance groups were closely allied with organized socialism throughout Europe, with nationalist movements in Ireland, Iceland, Yugoslavia, and India, and with feminist struggles in Australia and New Zealand.[1] In other words, temperance reform has most frequently been linked with historical movements usually classified as liberal, progressive, leftist, or radical. Temperance reformers argued that society as a whole bore the responsibility for the condition of all its members; that sense of social interdependence and mutual responsibility lay at the heart of the temperance movement's progressive and humanistic bent.

The decline of temperance activism in the United States and throughout the world in recent decades reflects both a lessening of the cultural significance attached to drinking and a belated recognition of alcohol's enduring popularity and social utility as a recreational drug. That recognition, however, should not lead to a condemnation of the temperance movement. Rather, it should serve as a reminder that our society condones alcohol because it is popular and culturally entrenched, not because it is harmless. Two prominent researchers on the effects of alcohol have written:

> If, like LSD, this drug [alcohol] had only recently been discovered or, like marijuana, rediscovered, government agencies and legislators would likely be busy banning its production, distribution, and consumption. We make no claim that LSD and marijuana are harmless, but we must point to the enormous toll in terms of health, happiness, economics, and traffic hazards represented by excessive use or abuse of alcohol. Only the lengthy acquaintanceship of man and alcohol and the integra-

tion of alcohol into social and cultural customs prevent this substance from being placed on some dangerous drug list.[2]

Alcohol's relatively easy accessibility in American society today contrasts markedly with the strict prohibitions imposed on other, less destructive drugs. The right of the individual to use potentially dangerous substances versus the right of society to protect itself from the effects of that use has been and will continue to be a debate of vital public importance. It is not necessary to claim that the temperance movement was in some sense "right" in order to recognize that it confronted difficult, complex issues, dealt with genuine social problems, and reflected both a concern for human welfare and a vision of a better society for all.

Notes

1. For a fuller discussion of these points, see Jed Dannenbaum, "Anti-Alcohol Mass Movements: The Cross-Cultural Perspective" (paper delivered at American Historical Association annual meeting, Los Angeles, Dec., 1981).

2. John A. Ewing and Beatrice A. Rouse, "Drinks, Drinkers, and Drinking," in Ewing and Rouse, eds., *Drinking: Alcohol in American Society—Issues and Current Research* (Chicago, 1978), 16.

Appendix

The statistical method used to arrive at Table 8 is an extension to a four-way grid of the procedure used to produce a two-way grid described in W. Phillips Shively's article, "'Ecological' Inference: The Use of Aggregate Data to Study Individuals," *American Political Science Review*, 63 (1969): 1183–96.

Assuming that we wish to complete a grid as follows:

	R_1	R_2	R_3	R_4	$= 100\%$
S_1	$P_{11}R_1$	$P_{21}R_2$	$P_{31}R_3$	$P_{41}R_4$	
S_2	$P_{12}R_1$	$P_{22}R_2$	$P_{32}R_3$	$P_{42}R_4$	
S_3	$P_{13}R_1$	$P_{23}R_2$	$P_{33}R_3$	$P_{43}R_4$	
S_4	$P_{14}R_1$	$P_{24}R_2$	$P_{34}R_3$	$P_{44}R_4$	

100%   100%   100%   100%   100%

where $R_1 \ldots R_4$ represents portions of the vote in one election, and $S_1 \ldots S_4$ represent portions of the vote in a second election, and the Ps are the transitional probabilities, we can say that:

$$S_1 = P_{11}R_1 + P_{21}R_2 + P_{31}R_3 + P_{41}R_4$$

and that:

$$R_4 = (100 - (R_1 + R_2 + R_3))$$

Therefore:

$$
\begin{aligned}
S_1 &= P_{11}R_1 + P_{21}R_2 + P_{31}R_3 + P_{41}(100 - R_1 - R_2 - R_3) \\
&= P_{11}R_1 + P_{21}R_2 + P_{31}R_3 + 100P_{41} - P_{41}R_1 - P_{41}R_2 - P_{41}R_3 \\
&= 100P_{41} + (P_{11} - P_{41})R_1 + (P_{21} - P_{41})R_2 + (P_{31} - P_{41})R_3
\end{aligned}
$$

Our multiple regression equation is:

$$S_1 = a + b_1R_1 + b_2R_2 + b_3R_3$$

Therefore:

$$P_{41} = a/100; \quad P_{11} = b_1 + a/100; \quad P_{21} = b_2 + a/100; \quad \text{and} \quad P_{31} = b_3 + a/100$$

Thus, by regressing S_1 on R_1, R_2, and R_3, we can complete the first line of the grid, using the coefficients of R_1, R_2, and R_3 as the values for the first three squares and the intercept as the value for the fourth square.

To make a second, indirect estimate, we first regress R_1 on S_1, S_2, and S_3. This gives us P' values (see Shively, pp. 1192–93), as follows: $P'_{11}R_1$, $P'_{12}R_1$, $P'_{13}R_1$, and $P'_{14}R_1$.

To convert, for example, $P'_{11}R_1$ to a second estimate of $R_{11}R_1$, we can use the equation:

$$P = \frac{P' \times S_1}{R_1}$$

Thus, we can complete the entire grid with both direct and indirect estimates of the values.

Index

Adair law, 202
Adrian, Michigan, 221
Akron *Beacon,* 198
Alcohol: and other beverages, 2; varieties of, 3; linked to social problems, 70, 77–79
Alcohol consumption: between 1810 and 1830, 3; compared to present, 3; decline in, 54; in German culture, 126; in 1850s, 194–95. *See also* Drinking
Allen, J. J., 144
Allen, Virginia, 11, 183, 185
American party, 170–71. *See also* Know Nothings
American Protestant Association, 166
American Reform ticket, 161
Amerian Temperance Society: organization of, 17; and temperance movement, 17–21, 38; membership of, 19–20, 41; mentioned, 55, 77
American Temperance Union, 23
American Tract Society, 17
American Wine Growers Association, 135, 136, 147
Anthony, Susan B., 18, 39, 184, 186, 188
Anti-Catholicism: in politics, 114, 117–19, 121; in temperance press, 122, 123; and nativism, 157–60, 161; and 1853 riot, 158
Anti-Convention Free School ticket, 119

Anti-license campaigns, 93–95, 229–30
Artisans: and teetotalism, 22; and Washingtonian movement, 34–35; and Sons of Temperance, 56
Ashland, Ohio, 225

Baltimore, Maryland, 33
Banner, Lois, 184
Baptist Women's Foreign Missionary Society, 214
Barnett, Redmond, 3
Beck, Charlie, 213, 224–25
Bedini, Archbishop Gaetano, 158
Beecher, Lyman, 19, 42, 86
Beer, 195–96, 201
Black, John, 202
Bloomer, Amelia, 39, 184, 187, 188, 192–93
Bloomer, Anthony, 188, 192–93
Brown, Rev. Antoinette, 190

Canton (Illinois) *Register,* 198
Carey, Matthew, 18
Cary, Samuel Fenton: and Washingtonian movement, 36, 38, 41; and temperance movement, 38, 44–45, 128–29, 173, 190–91; early career of, 43–44; and Sons of Temperance, 45–46, 53–54; and politics, 85–87, 97, 131–32, 139–40, 170; and German radicals, 122, 123–24; on alcohol, 78, 136–37; on "Rum Power," 84; and Maine Law, 143–44; and nativism, 148; and

Note on the Author

Jed Dannenbaum was born in Warren, Ohio. He received his B.A. (1968) and M.A. (1969) degrees from the University of Wisconsin at Madison and his Ph.D. (1978) from the University of California at Davis. He is presently an independent movie producer in Atlanta, Georgia. He has published several articles on the subject of the temperance reform; *Drink and Disorder* is his first book.